Bernard Denvir
is the author of a four-volume documentary
history of taste in art, architecture and design in Britain,
as well as of books on Chardin, Impressionism, Post-
Impressionism and Fauvism. A contributor to many
journals and magazines, he was head of the Department of
Art History at Ravensbourne College of Art and Design, a
member of the Council for National Academic Awards,
and for several years President of the British section of
the International Association of Art Critics. His other books
include *The Chronicle of Impressionism* and, in the World
of Art, *Toulouse-Lautrec* and *The Thames and Hudson
Encyclopaedia of Impressionism* (ed.).

WORLD OF ART

This famous series
provides the widest available
range of illustrated books on art in all its aspects.
If you would like to receive a complete list
of titles in print please write to:
THAMES AND HUDSON
30 Bloomsbury Street, London WC1B 3QP
In the United States please write to:
THAMES AND HUDSON INC.
500 Fifth Avenue, New York, New York 10110

Printed in Singapore

LA PRESSE

AVANT LE SALON

L'Exposition des Révoltés

En toute
sition du b
importaut
ne saura
tre laque
la prem
la seco
gourev
là dig

Ce n'
artistes se so
s'affranchir de la tute
il y a quinze ans environ un
tentative a été faite
au boulevard des
ciés pour exposer
vendre directemen
expositions intéres
public avait déjà
l'Exposition de la
beaux-arts, quand le
rection des beaux-ar
liquidation de la soci

Aujourd'hui, l'assoc
artistes ne rencontre
thies de la part de l'ad
annoncé, officiellemen
à la direction des expos
à partir de l'année proc

Je sais que bien des
terreur arriver cette ép
tistes abandonnés à eux-mêmes auront
à s'occuper de l'organisation de l
exposition annuelle, rédiger
glement, formeront le
ou refuseront les
exposées, d
ou tout au m
nistration la
les plus méri

La Société anonyme des artis
tres a tranché de la façon la pl
ces questions difficiles; elle a suppr
le jury d'admission, supprimé les récom-
penses. L'absence de toute règle est-elle
un bien? C'est l'avenir seul qui nous
éclairera et répondra à cette question.

LES CONTEMPORAINS

10 Centimes — Jeudi

FÉLICIEN CHAMPSAUR

JOURNAL HEBDOMADAIRE

Administrateur M. DUTERTRE, 5, Faubourg Montmartre, Paris — L'AN 6fr

EDOUARD MANET

L'IMPRESSIONNISTE

N° 4. — l'Expo-
Prix: 15 centimes.

28 Avril 1877

JOURNAL D'ART

Paraissant tous les Jeudis

En vente : 15, rue du Croissant, 15
ET DANS TOUS LES KIOSQUES

Administ

LES ROUGON-MACQUART

HISTOIRE NATURELLE ET SOCIALE D'UNE FAMILLE SOUS LE SECOND EMPIRE

L'ŒUVRE

PAR

ÉMILE ZOLA

TRENTE ET UNIÈME MILLE

PARIS
G. CHARPENTIER ET Cie, ÉDITEURS
13, RUE DE GRENELLE, 13

1886

JUST OPEN!

EXHIBITION

OF THE

GREAT PAINTING

OF THE CELEBRATED FRENCH ARTIST

E. MANET,

"THE EXECUTION OF THE EMPEROR MAXIMILIAN"

ADMISSION, . . 25 CENTS.

Open daily, Sundays excepted, from 10 A M to 9 P M at
737 BROADWAY, cor. 8th St., under DANIELL & SON'S

ÉMILE ZOLA

ÉD. MANET

ÉTUDE BIOGRAPHIQUE ET CRITIQUE
ACCOMPAGNÉE D'UN PORTRAIT D'ÉD. MANET PAR BRACQUEMOND
ET D'UNE EAU-FORTE D'ÉD. MANET
D'APRÈS OLYMPIA

PARIS
E. DENTU, ÉDITEUR
LIBRAIRIE DE LA SOCIÉTÉ DES GENS DE LETTRES
Palais-Royal, 17 et 19, Galerie d'Orléans

1867

L'OPINION NATIONALE

Le Gaulois

The Impressionists At First Hand

Edited by Bernard Denvir

195 illustrations
17 in color

THAMES AND HUDSON

© 1987 Thames and Hudson Ltd, London

First published in the United States of America in
1987 by Thames and Hudson Inc., 500 Fifth Avenue,
New York, New York 10110
Reprinted 1995

Library of Congress Catalog Card Number 86-51261
ISBN 0-500-20209-5

Printed and bound in Singapore

Contents

MONET *Corner of a Studio* 1861

Introduction

One of the problems about history is that it involves the imposition on the past of the ideas of the present. Apparent in every branch of the subject, this tyranny of hindsight is especially evident where art is concerned. To coax into some comprehensible pattern the constantly changing manifestations of painting and sculpture, the mutability of taste, brutal categories have to be forced on recalcitrant phenomena. People, whether artists, critics or mere spectators, have to be denuded of their real personalities, with all their various interests, their contradictions of character, their inconsistencies, and their awareness of the recurrent problem of matching action with intent, to be transformed into lay-figures, playing the role assigned to them in the art historian's drama.

This of course is largely inevitable. Our minds hunger for certainties, for the people of the past to be frozen for ever in the attitudes we think proper to them. This is strikingly true of our reactions to that revolution in art and general visual sensibility which took place in Europe in the latter half of the nineteenth century. For the most part, all we can do is to quiz the portraits of the participants. None of the Impressionists wrote as extensively and as illuminatingly as Van Gogh or Gauguin. However, the considerable correspondence of Camille Pissarro reveals one of the most charming and intelligent personalities in the history of art; and there is, scattered around, far more material by and about those involved in what we roughly call 'Impressionism' than most people realize. The purpose of this book is to bring some of it together in an accessible form.

Artists such as Manet, Renoir, Monet, Degas, Pissarro and the rest were individually various: bachelors, family men, well-off, anarchists, reactionaries, anti-Semites, atheists, devout Christians, generous, envious; most of the antitheses in humanity existed amongst and between them. Above all else they did not realize that they were old-fashioned, that they were living in the past; and this is a truth which we often fail fully to comprehend. They never heard the voice of the auctioneer in Sotheby's sale rooms a century later; they had no inkling of the tens and hundreds of thousands of people visiting the monster exhibitions of their works in Paris, New York, London and Tokyo. Degas had to worry about a new lease for his flat; Renoir about whether his steam tricycle would get him safely

7

from Saint-Cloud to Paris, Monet about whether or not he should chop down his cypresses. They thought and talked a lot about the art to which they were all passionately devoted; their comments are often of immense value in fostering an appreciation of their work, which was sometimes more complex in its motivation, sometimes more simple than we are apt to think.

But people are not just themselves. They exist partly as others see and judge them, so in addition to their own writings this book also contains opinions by their contemporaries. Here again a certain degree of revisionism is necessary. Compulsively attractive though the 'goodies and baddies' concept of history is, it is hardly ever completely justified by facts, and though it suits our sense of drama to see the Impressionists as lonely rebels, harassed by obtuse critics, ground down by mercenary dealers, this was not the case. It is true that Max Nordau could attribute to the degeneracy of their 'flickering eyeballs' their revolutionary techniques; that the painter of *Derby Day* expressed his opinion that 'this craze will pass away as everything foolish and false does sooner or later', and that in London some twenty years later the art critic of *The Times* was thundering on about the impossibility of anybody ever seeing beauty in *Le déjeuner sur l'herbe* (though he did confess admiration for Degas and for Manet's portraits). But many critics, even apart from those who were firm protagonists of the new movement, were not hostile to it, and though not enthusiastic, were often just and fair. There were art dealers too who, often to their own immediate loss, were prepared to gamble on the future by offering the Impressionists support and intelligent encouragement.

The Impressionists were people of their own time in a more deliberate way, perhaps, than any previous group of artists had been, reflecting the society in which they lived deliberately, and depicting it as a matter of conscious aesthetic policy rather than as part of that inescapable reflex which links all artists with their own age. It is right to describe them, as so many of their contemporaries did, as 'realists', and, like their literary counterparts such as Zola or the Goncourts, they addressed themselves to recording a new urban proletariat which in Paris, perhaps more than in any other European city, had come to dominate the visual aspects of daily life. Shopgirls, clerks, prostitutes, milliners, barmaids, civil servants, the people who frequented the bars and cafés of the boulevards and the nightclubs of Montmartre, who spent their weekends boating on the Seine, or dancing in the *cafés-chantants* of Argenteuil and Petit Gennevilliers; these were their preferred subjects, not the courtiers of Boucher, the mythologized models of David, the bankers and diplomats of Ingres, or the peasants of Millet and Courbet. It was in some ways a rootless society, composed very largely of people who were, at best, only one generation removed from the countryside or the provinces, as indeed most of the Impressionists themselves were; it was a society seen against the background of a new Paris, created by the political acumen of Napoleon III, and the creative genius of Baron Haussmann, and regarded alternatively as 'the modern Babylon' or '*la ville lumière*'; a Paris which had been converted from an irregular huddle of medieval alleys, seventeenth-century palaces, and eighteenth-century faubourgs, into an ordered array of great boulevards, organized social demarcations, and ostentatious symbols of self-indulgence. The Opéra had succeeded Notre-Dame as the centre of the first great urban achievement of the Industrial Revolution. It is only in endeavouring to savour something of the actual quality of their own lives that we can appreciate the extent to which the Impressionists concerned themselves with that 'painting of modern life' which Baudelaire, in his essay on Constantin Guys, had seen as one of the prime functions of living art.

The Genesis of a Name

Since the time of Delacroix a new attitude had become apparent amongst the younger generation of French painters, which involved an approach to both subject matter and technique different from that which was favoured by official art. They tended to emphasize on the one hand a greater concern with modern life and ordinary people, and on the other a greater freedom of handling combined with an attempt to paint what they actually saw, rather than what their minds and artistic precedents told them. These painters were not numerous and they mostly lived and worked in Paris, where they came into contact with each other, mainly in one or other of those cafés which played such an important part in the cultural life of the time. They came from very different social backgrounds: Renoir's father was a poor tailor from Limoges; Monet's a grocer in Le Havre; Pissarro's a store-keeper in the Danish West Indies; Degas' a banker in Paris; Berthe Morisot's a judge; Sisley's a rich Englishman living in Paris. They had all trained in different ways; some through the official system of the Ecole des Beaux-Arts; some in the studios of teacher-artists such as Lecoq de Boisbaudran, or in academies such as the Académie Suisse, others by private tuition. Their individual styles, too, were far from similar. Manet, on whom they looked as a kind of leader, a position he was not always ready to acknowledge, was essentially a traditionalist; so too was Degas; Renoir's incandescent figures still seemed to depend on Rubens and Delacroix rather than on any unbridled passion for innovation. Only of Monet, Pissarro, Cézanne and Sisley could it be said that they shared a new vision, a new stylistic syntax.

Bound together by the loosest of ties, dependent as much on social affinities as on shared aesthetic beliefs, but all of them resolved to avoid 'tame' painting, these artists were unlikely to be welcomed by the official Salon, and, despite the support of dealers such as Durand-Ruel, could expect little from commercial galleries. In 1873, therefore, Monet proposed the idea of a group exhibition, organized at their own expense. The idea was vigorously promoted by Pissarro, who, true to his political convictions, suggested a co-operative, whose constitution should be based on that of a bakers' organization which he had known in Pontoise. This particular proposal was rejected, but it was agreed that everyone who participated in the group exhibition should contribute one tenth of the proceeds he might make from sales, to cover expenses. The exhibits were to be classified by size, and the hanging positions determined by lot. Nadar, the well-known photographer, lent them, free of rent, the studio which he had just vacated on the second floor of a building in the rue Danou, which leads off the boulevard des Capucines. Renoir was mainly responsible for the hanging of the 165 pictures on show, which were the work of twenty-nine painters, of whom Cézanne, Degas, Guillaumin, Monet, Berthe Morisot, Pissarro, Sisley, Renoir, Astruc, Boudin, Bracquemond, and Rouart are the only ones to have achieved subsequent fame.

The exhibition opened on 15 April 1874, the public being admitted from ten to six, and for two hours in the evening. The title which this rather heterogeneous group of artists had hit on for themselves was *La Société anonyme* [a word which in the context does not mean 'anonymous' but 'incorporated'] *des artistes, peintres, sculpteurs etc.* It was soon to be supplanted by another more popular term. Ten days after the opening there appeared in the columns of *Charivari* an article by Louis Leroy, whose main claim to fame is that he wrote it: it was entitled 'Exhibition of the Impressionists'. A new word had appeared in the history of art. The word 'impressions' had already been bandied about by critics with reference to the work of artists such as Corot, Jongkind and Rousseau, and Manet had said in 1867 that his intention had been 'to convey an impression', but such uses had been generalized and less specific than Leroy's insistent hammering home of the word.

Leroy's article was, like many reviews of the exhibition, hostile. It assumed the form of a dialogue taking place on a visit to the exhibition between the writer and M. Joseph Vincent, an imaginary landscape painter, 'recipient of medals and decorations under several administrations'. The key word first appears in the discussion of Pissarro's *Ploughed Field*, about which Vincent says:

'Those furrows! That frost! They are just scrapings from a palette arranged on a muddy canvas. The work has no head nor tail, no top nor bottom, no front nor back.'
'Maybe, – but the impression is there.'
'Well, it's a funny impression! And this?'
'*An Orchard* by M. Sisley. I'd like to point out the small tree on the right. It's sparkling, but the impression!'
'Oh, stop going on about your impressions.'

A few paragraphs later Leroy returns to the same theme.

A catastrophe seemed to me to be imminent, and it was reserved for M. Monet to contribute the last straw.
'Ah, there he is, there he is!' he shouted in front of No. 98. 'I recognize him: papa Vincent's favourite! What *does* it depict; have a look at the catalogue.'
'*Impression, Sunrise.*'

'*Impression*; I was certain of it. I was just thinking that as I was impressed, there had to be some impression in it. And what freedom! What ease of handling! A preliminary drawing for a wallpaper pattern is more highly finished than this seascape.'

The article ends with M. Vincent doing a war-dance in front of the Monets singing 'Ho-ho! I am impression on the war-path.'

There were to be seven more group exhibitions of the *Société anonyme*, all using that group title. But to the general public, even perhaps to themselves, they were now 'The Impressionists'. The *jeu d'esprit* of an obscure journalist had created a movement in art, and given to a group of painters with different backgrounds, and often different aims, a coherence and an ideological unity which they are likely to retain for ever.

This book is not meant to be a continuous narrative; it is not a history of Impressionism. Rather it is an attempt to re-create the actuality of the lives and attitudes of a group of artists who by being categorized under a stylistic label have lost something of their human dimension.

PHOTOGRAPH OF NADAR'S STUDIO,
35 BD. DES CAPUCINES

CATALOGUE OF THE FIRST
IMPRESSIONIST EXHIBITION 1874

SOCIÉTÉ ANONYME
DES ARTISTES PEINTRES, SCULPTEURS, GRAVEURS, ETC.

PREMIÈRE

EXPOSITION
1874
35, Boulevard des Capucines, 35

CATALOGUE

Prix : 50 centimes
L'Exposition est ouverte du 15 avril au 15 mai 1874,
de 10 heures du matin à 6 h. du soir et de 8 h. à 10 heures du soir.
PRIX D'ENTRÉE : 1 FRANC

PARIS
IMPRIMERIE ALCAN-LÉVY
61, RUE DE LAFAYETTE
—
1874

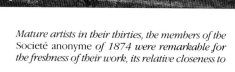

The first exhibition

Mature artists in their thirties, the members of the
Societé anonyme of 1874 were remarkable for
the freshness of their work, its relative closeness to

MONET *The Luncheon* 1868

MORISOT *Hide and Seek* 1873

MONET *Impression, Sunrise* 1872

everyday life, and its freedom from the academic
constraints of 'finish', rather than for any uniformity of style.

RENOIR *Ballet Dancer* 1874

CÉZANNE *La Maison du Pendu* 1872-3

RENOIR *Les Grands Boulevards* 1875

PHOTOGRAPH OF THE BOULEVARD DES CAPUCINES, *c.* 1890

The boulevards of Paris

This was a new townscape, and the Impressionists introduced it into art with the aid of new viewpoints suggested by photography.

MONET *Boulevard des Capucines* 1873-4

Monet as a young man   1855-58

Monet's career, which ranged from early hardship, through persevering industry, to eventual success, represented a pattern which we have come to think of as typical of all avant garde artists. In 1900, at the age of sixty, shortly after he had completed his universally praised series of Poplars *and* Haystacks *he gave a lengthy interview to* Le Temps *(27 November).*

I was born in Paris in 1840 in the reign of 'good' Louis-Philippe, in an environment entirely dedicated to commerce, in which everybody professed a contemptuous disdain for art. But my youth was passed in Le Havre, where my father had settled in 1845, and during this period I more or less lived the life of a vagabond. By nature I was undisciplined; never, even as a child, would I submit to rules. It was at home that I learned the little I know. School seemed like a prison, and I could never bear to stay there, even for four hours a day, especially when the sunshine beckoned and the sea was smooth.

Until I was fourteen or fifteen, I led this uncontrolled life, to the despair of my poor father. In the intervals of this life, however, I had picked up the rudiments of arithmetic and a smattering of spelling. This was the limit of my studies, but they were not too burdensome, for I intermingled with them various distractions, drawing bunches of flowers in the margins of my exercise books. On the blue paper covers I designed fantastic ornaments on which I drew, in the most irreverent fashion, caricatures or profiles of my teachers.

I soon became very skilful at this game, and by the time I was fifteen I was known all over Le Havre as a caricaturist. My reputation was so well established that I was sought after from all sides, and asked for caricature portraits. The abundance of commissions and the paucity of pocket-money inspired me with a bold resolve, which

scandalized my family. I began to charge for my portraits, demanding, according to the appearance of each client, ten or twenty francs. The scheme worked marvellously. Within a month the number of sitters had doubled. I was now able to charge everybody twenty francs without reducing the number of my commissions. If I had kept on along these lines, I would be a millionaire by now.

I was soon an important person in the town. In the front window of the only framemaker who was able to make a living in Le Havre, my caricatures were proudly on show. And when I saw loungers in front of them, and heard them pointing out who the subjects were, I nearly choked with vanity and self-satisfaction.

Still there was a shadow hanging over all this glory. Often in the same window I saw, hanging above my own works, seascapes which I, like most of my fellow-citizens, found abominable. Inwardly I was very upset at having to endure the contact between these works and my own, and never ceased to abuse the fool who, thinking he was an artist, had enough self-complacency actually to sign them. His name was Boudin. In my eyes, accustomed as I was to the traditional-

Mentors

Boudin on the Normandy coast, Courbet and Diaz at Fontainebleau and elsewhere, were among the standard-bearers of Realism in the 1850s and 1860s.

COURBET *The Artist on the Shore at Palavas-les-Flots* 1854

BOUDIN *Jetty and Wharf at Trouville* 1863

DIAZ *Jean de Paris Hill, Fontainebleau* 1867

17

ist seascapes of Gudin, to arbitrary colours, false tones and arbitrary compositions displayed by fashionable artists, the sincere little compositions of Boudin, with the truthfulness in his little figures, his ships so accurately rigged, his skies and water so exact, drawn and painted directly from nature, had nothing artistic about them, and their very truthfulness struck me as more than suspicious. His painting consequently inspired me with an intense aversion, and, without knowing the man, I hated him. The framemaker would often say to me, 'You should get to know M. Boudin. He studied art at the Ecole des Beaux-Arts in Paris. He could give you some good advice.'

But I resisted the idea, in my ridiculous pride. What on earth could such a silly man teach me?

Still the fatal day came when chance brought me, despite myself, face to face with Boudin. He was in the back of the shop, and I went in without realizing he was there. Without asking me, the framemaker seized the opportunity and introduced us. 'Here, M. Boudin, is the young man who has such a gift for caricature.' Boudin immediately came over to me, and in his gentle voice congratulated me, saying 'I always look at your caricatures with great pleasure; they are amusing, clever, bright. You have talent. One can see that at a glance. But I hope that you are not going to stop there. It's all very well for a beginning, but soon you will have had enough of caricature. Study; learn to see and to paint; draw, paint landscapes. The sea and the sky are so beautiful – animals, people, trees just as nature has made them, with their personalities, their real way of being in the air, in the light: just as they are.'

But the advice of Boudin slipped off me like water off a duck's back. I liked the man himself. He was earnest, sincere. This I felt, but I could not abide his painting, and when he offered to take me sketching out of doors I always found a polite reason for refusing. Then summer came; my time was my own,

and I could make no excuse. Tired of resisting, I gave in at last, and Boudin with untiring kindness undertook my education. My eyes were finally opened, and I really understood nature. I learned, at the same time, to love it. I analysed its forms with my pencil; I studied its colours. Six months later, despite the protests of my mother, who was worried by the company I kept, and thought me lost in the company of a man of such low repute as Boudin, I announced to my father that I wished to become a painter, and was going to Paris to learn to do so.

'You shall not have a sou from me!'
'I shall do without.'

Indeed I could do without, I had already made my little pile, thanks to my caricatures, for on some days I had done as many as seven or eight. At twenty francs each, my earnings were quite large, and I had entrusted most of it to one of my aunts, just keeping a little pocket-money. At sixteen, one feels rich with two thousand francs. I set out immediately for Paris.

It took me a little time at first to decide on a line of action. I called on some artists, to whom I had letters of introduction, and received excellent advice from them. I also received, I might add, some very bad advice. Troyon wanted me to enter the studio of Couture. Needless to say I emphatically refused. I even admit that for a while it cooled my admiration for Troyon. I began to see less and less of him, and eventually came only to associate with artists who were involved in experimenting. At this juncture I met Pissarro, who was not then thinking of being a revolutionary and was working away in the style of Corot. It was an excellent example to follow, but during the whole of my stay in Paris, which lasted four years, and during the time I frequently visited Le Havre, I was governed by the advice of Boudin, though I tended to see nature more broadly than he.

I reached my twentieth year. The hour of conscription was about to strike. But its approach did not alarm me, nor did it my family. They had not forgiven my leaving home, but had not done much about it because they thought they would catch me when I was conscripted, because then I would sow my wild oats, come home, and settle down to a business career. If I refused they would stop my allowance.

They made a mistake. The seven years' military service which appalled so many were full of attraction for me . . . . In Algeria I spent two really marvellous years. I was constantly seeing new things, and in my free time I was always attempting to record what I saw. You can't imagine how much I increased my knowledge and how greatly my powers of observation improved. I did not realize it at first. The impressions of light and colour which I received there were not to be analysed and worked out till later, but they contained the germ of my future researches.

Renoir's Youth   1855-58

In 1879 (19 June), an article about Auguste Renoir by his brother Edmond appeared in the magazine La Vie Moderne, *which had mounted a one-man exhibition to capitalize on the great success obtained at the Salon of that year with* Portrait of Madame Charpentier and her Children. *It was Madame Charpentier who had been responsible for founding the magazine, and Edmond had assumed responsibility for arranging exhibitions in its offices. His article is revealing about his brother's early days.*

At the age of fifteen my brother was obliged to learn a trade which would ensure him a livelihood. From the way in which he had been scribbling on the walls with charcoal it was decided that he had enough taste to enter an artistic profession. Our parents therefore apprenticed him to a porcelain painter. He had fallen on his feet, which is not a frequent thing to happen. The young apprentice took to his profession, and at the end of the day, carrying a portfolio larger than himself, he would go to free drawing classes. This went on for two or three years.

He progressed rapidly; after a few months of apprenticeship he was given jobs usually reserved for trained workers, which provided a cause for a lot of chaffing; they called him 'M. Rubens' for instance. Nevertheless amongst the workers there was a worthy fellow whose passion it was to do oil-paintings at home. Happy, perhaps, at the idea of having a pupil, he suggested to the young man that they should share their canvases and paint. After some time my brother decided to paint a picture by himself.

The apprentice set himself to the task, and one Sunday the first master of the painter who was to produce *Lise* and *Le Moulin de la Galette* decided to pay us a visit. I can remember the occasion as clearly as if it were yesterday. I was still a kid, but I realized that important things were afoot. The easel on which stood the famous painting was placed in the middle of the drawing room in our modest home in the rue d'Argenteuil. Everybody was excited and impatient. I had been dressed in my best clothes, and told to be a good boy. It was a very solemn occasion. 'The Master' arrived. At a signal I drew up a chair for him in front of the easel; he sat down, and started to inspect the 'masterpiece'. It was, and I can still see it, an *Eve*; behind her the serpent entwined itself around an oak tree, its open jaws darting forward as if to hypnotize her.

The examination lasted at least quarter of an hour, and then, without any other comment, the good old man turned to our parents, and uttered these simple words: 'You should let your son become a proper painter. In our trade he may at the most earn 12 or 15 francs. I predict a brilliant future for him in the world of art. See what you can do.'

That evening our dinner in the rue d'Argenteuil was a sad affair. The joy which this success had brought vanished before the terrible prospect of his having to give up a profession which would secure him a living, for art which might lead straight to destitution. Eventually we became reconciled to the prospect, and the Ecole des Beaux-Arts acquired another student. Auguste entered Gleyre's studio, passing the courses in anatomy and sketching, etc., just like everyone else.

But how did a pupil of Gleyre turn into what he is now? This is how it happened. In those days the students, much more so than now, used to go in groups to the forest of Fontainebleau. They did not have studios there as they do today; that would have been an unthinkable luxury. The inns and lodging houses of Chailly, Barbizon and Marlotte gave them all – big or little – accommodation, and they used to go there to work with their possessions in a bag slung over their shoulders. It was there that my brother met Courbet, who was the idol of young painters, and Diaz, who then had their admiration to an even higher degree. It was Diaz who gave him what was perhaps the best lesson he ever had in his life; it was Diaz who said to him: 'Never must a painter who has any respect for himself touch his brush, unless he has his model in front of him.'

This axiom was to stay indelibly imprinted on his memory. He realized that human models were too expensive, and that he could procure models of a different kind under ideal conditions, the whole forest being his to study at leisure. He stayed there in the summer; he stayed there in the winter; and for several years. It was in the open air that he became an open-air painter. The four cold walls of a studio did not weigh on him; the uniform grey or brown colour of walls did not depress him; having no experience of the constraints to which painters so often submit themselves, he allowed himself to be carried away by his subject, and above all by the surroundings in which he found himself.

Monet in Paris 1859

On 3 June 1859 the nineteen-year-old Claude Monet wrote to Boudin in Le Havre – they had first met in the previous year – to give some of his impressions of the paintings on show at the Exposition Universelle then in progress.

Forgive me for not having done what you asked me to, but work and this overwhelming city have made me forget the duties of friendship; but better late than never, and so here we are.

I have been to Troyon's twice, and he is very much looking forward to seeing you. But, would you believe it, having been to his place twice, I forgot to ask him when he was going to the country, as you had requested me to? But I don't think that he will be going in the near future, as he has several paintings he is currently working on.

Come as soon as possible. The Exhibition is nearly at an end, and in a fortnight's time will be over. They are even saying that some of the exhibition halls will be closed sooner than that. But that is only a rumour, and despite it do hurry up. I have seen M. Gautier several times, and he is looking forward to seeing you. As to the Exhibition, I have been back there on several occasions. I shall tell you what I think about some of the paintings. I may be wrong, but it might interest you to hear my reactions.

Yvon has put in a second work; it is, in my view, better done than the other, but it is not very good. It has an ugly, dark colour; the figures are common, and all wear the same expression. Of the Troyons on view one or two are enormous; the *Returning to the Farm* is marvellous, with a magnificent stormy sky. There is a great deal of movement in the clouds, which are being driven by the wind; the cows and the dogs are all very beautiful. There is also the *Departure for the Market*; it sets out to depict the effect of mist at dawn. It is superb, above all else full of light. A *View at Suresnes* is of a stupefying extent. You feel yourself actually in the middle of the countryside; there are herds of animals; cows in a variety of different poses; but it all has movement and confusion. There are many paintings by him there, and it is he who this year has had the greatest successes. In some of his paintings I find a bit too much black in the shadows. When you get here you will be able to tell me if I am right. A particularly beautiful painting, which I had forgotten, is of a dog with a partridge in its jaws. It is magnificent, you can almost touch the fur. The head is especially carefully painted.

There are also some dogs by a Belgian named Joseph Stevens, which give a very natural impression, but he scamps the finer points.

Rousseau's great work *The Dogs* is too large, and a bit confused. The detail is better than the whole.

In short there are some very fine things. Théodore Rousseau has done some very good landscapes, and there are some portraits by Pils which are very fine both in their execution and in their fidelity to appearances.

M. Morel Fatio has done some marine paintings which don't make sense; that's awful . . . . Théodore Frère has a mass of Oriental pictures, which are magnificent; in all these paintings there is a grandeur, a warm light, and finally they are very beautiful both in their detail and their sense of movement.

Delacroix has done better things than those which he is exhibiting this year. They are no more than indications, sketches, but as ever full of life and movement.

Daubigny, there's a dashing sort of chap, who does very well, and who understands nature. That view of Villerville of which I have spoken to you is really something marvellous. It would be most unfortunate if you did not see it. To describe the details to you is very difficult for me, and time is pressing.

The Corots are absolutely magnificent. There isn't a single marine painting which is even passable.

Isabey has produced a horrible creation. The details are quite nice, and there are some very fine little figures. But the sea painters are absolutely useless, and that is a direction which will take you far.

You have arranged for me to see M. Monginot [*a friend of Manet's*]. At exactly the same time as I received your introduction I had another for him. I have been there and nobody could have received me better. He is a charming fellow, and quite young. He showed me a small seascape of yours. He has done some very fine things, and he has put his studio at my disposal; I shall take advantage of it from time to time.

Since I last wrote to you things have altered, and I shall explain in my next letter which will be more prompt than this one, how I am fixed up here. I think you will approve of me.

Hurry up! There's only little more than a week left to see the Exhibition. At present I am at 35 rue Rodier.

An art school   c. 1859

Most of the Impressionists studied in the ateliers of various artists such as Couture, Gleyre and Le Coq de Boisbaudran. In fact, of course, they did not work in the artist's actual studio, but in a separate building. Emile Zola's account of one such school in L'Oeuvre *(1886) must portray a typical establishment of the kind with which he was familiar during the period when first he came to Paris, and may be based on the* Académie Suisse *in the Quai des Orfèvres, used by Manet and others as students.*

The studio was situated in the narrowest part of the rue du Four, at the far end of a decrepit, tumbledown building. Claude had to cross two evil-smelling courtyards to reach a third, across which ran a sort of big closed shed, a huge outhouse of board and plaster which had once served as a packing-case maker's workshop. From outside, through the four large windows, nothing could be seen but the bare whitewashed ceiling.

Having pushed open the door, Claude remained motionless on the threshold. The place stretched out before him, with its four long tables ranged lengthwise to the windows – broad, double tables they were, with crowds of students on either side. They were littered with moist sponges, paint saucers, iron candlesticks, water bowls, and wooden boxes in which each student kept his brushes, his compasses and his colours. In one corner the stove, neglected since the previous winter, stood rusting by the side of a pile of coke that had not been cleared away, while at the other end a large iron cistern with a tap was flanked by two towels. Amidst the spartan untidiness of this shed, the eye was particularly caught by the walls which were topped with shelves displaying a litter of plaster casts, ranged in haphazard fashion, sometimes hidden behind forests of T-squares, bevels, and piles of drawing boards, tied together with webbing straps.

Gradually over the years such portions of the partitions as had remained unoccupied had become covered with inscriptions and drawings, a constantly rising scum of scrawls traced there as on the margin of an ever-open book. There were caricatures of the students themselves, witticisms so coarse that they would have embarrassed a gendarme, epigrammatic sentences, addition sums, addresses and so on. Above all else, written in large letters, appeared the inscription 'On 7 June. Gorfu declared that he didn't care a damn about Rome.'[1] . . .

Since the previous evening the whole studio, some sixty students, had been shut up there; those who had nothing to exhibit at the competition – the 'blacks', as they were called, – remaining to help those who had to show their work the next day, and who, being behindhand, had to knock off the work of a week in a few hours. By midnight they had stuffed themselves with brawn, saveloys and other cheap food washed down with quarts of *vin ordinaire*. Towards one o'clock they had secured the company of some 'ladies', and without the work abating the feast had turned into a Roman orgy, combined with a smoking marathon. On the damp, stained floor there remained a great litter of greasy paper and broken bottles, while the atmosphere reeked of burnt tallow, cheap scent, highly seasoned sausages and wine.

In Gleyre's studio   c. 1863

The Swiss-born painter Charles Gleyre (1808-74) inherited the studio of the famous Delaroche, and became one of the most famous teachers of his time. Among the six hundred and more pupils he trained were Monet, Sisley, Renoir and Bazille. Some fifty years later, Monet recounted to Marcel Pays how quickly they became disillusioned with the master's teaching (Excelsior, *20 January 1921.*)

---

1 Admission to the French School at Rome, and its various prizes.

At Gleyre's studio I found Renoir, Sisley and Bazille. As we were drawing from a model, who incidentally was superb, Gleyre criticized my work.

'It's not bad,' he said, 'but the breast is too heavy, the shoulder too powerful, and the foot too large.'

'I can only draw what I see,' I replied timidly.

'Praxiteles borrowed the best elements from a hundred imperfect models to create a masterpiece,' retorted Gleyre drily. 'One must always think of classical antiquity.'

That evening I took Sisley, Renoir and Bazille on one side, and said to them, 'Let's clear out of here. The place is unhealthy. There is an absolute lack of sincerity.'

We left after two weeks of lessons of this kind of proficiency. We were well rid of it, because I don't think that any of the most promising pupils in the studio ever made good.

Gleyre + monet did not get along

The Salon des Refusés   1863

New influences were at work. The hanging committee at the 1864 Salon, the all-important annual show of new painting, rejected so much that was of interest that Napoleon III, as part of a series of reforms which included changes in the organization and teaching of the Ecole des Beaux-Arts, instituted a Salon des Refusés for all those whose work had been turned down. And so, for one year only, the existence of an 'alternative' art was recognized by the authorities. Edouard Manet, eight years older than Monet, made his mark at this Salon with Le déjeuner sur l'herbe *(originally titled* Le bain*). This revolutionary work is by no means an open-air painting, but an amalgam of sketches from nature, studio poses and reminiscences of older art. Some reviewers were appalled in equal measure by technique and subject matter.*

In a pamphlet Le Jury et les Exposants – Salon des Refusés, *published shortly after the opening of the exhibition, Louis Etienne wrote:*
A nonchalant *bréda* [a prostitute, so-called because they haunted the rue Bréda, significantly in the Batignolles district where Manet was then living and working], who is completely naked, impudently lounges between two dandies dressed up to the nines. They give the impression of two students on holiday who are behaving outrageously, to try and give the impression of being real men. I have sought in vain for an explanation of this vulgar enigma. It is either a young man's idea of a joke, or a festering sore, unworthy of comment.

In L'Artist *for 15 August 1863 Jules Castagnary commented:*
A great deal of fuss has been made over this young man. But let's be serious. The bathing scene, the *Majo* and the *Espada* are good sketches, I agree. There's a certain life in the colour, a certain directness in the touch that are in no way vulgar. But then what? Is this drawing? Is this painting? M. Manet means to be hard and strong; he is merely hard, strange to say, he is more soft than hard.

In La Presse *on 27 April 1863, Paul Saint-Victor:*
Imagine Goya gone native in the pampas of Mexico daubing his canvases with crushed cochineal, and you have Manet, the most recent of the 'realists'. His pictures in the Boulevard des Italiens are like pages from a coloured comic.

Even so 'progressive' a critic as Théophile Burger, the friend of Baudelaire, wrote in L'Indépendance Belge *on 11 June:*
Le bain *is in questionable taste. The nude woman lacks beauty of form, unhappily, and the gentleman sprawled beside her is as unprepossessing as could well be imagined. I fail to see what could have induced

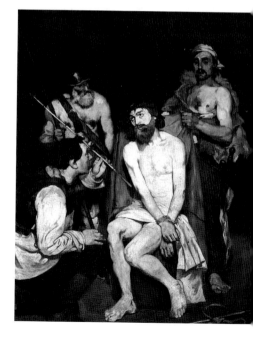

a distinguished and intelligent artist to adopt such an absurd composition. Yet there are qualities of colour and light in the landscape, and indeed some very fine passages of modelling in the torso of the woman.

The influential English critic Philip Hamerton (1834-94), reviewing the Salon des Refusés *in* The Fine Arts Quarterly *for October, commented:*
I ought not to omit a remarkable picture of the realist school, a translation of a thought of Giorgione into modern French. Giorgione had conceived the happy idea of a *fête champêtre* in which, although the gentlemen were dressed, the ladies were not, but the doubtful morality of the picture is pardoned for the sake of the fine colour . . . . Now some wretched Frenchman has translated this into modern French realism, on a much larger scale, and with the horrible, modern French costume instead of the graceful Venetian one. Yes, there they are, under the trees, the principal lady entirely undressed . . . another female in a chemise coming out of a little stream that runs hard by, and two Frenchmen in wide-awakes sitting on the very green grass with a stupid look of bliss. There are other pictures of the same class, which lead to the inference that the nude, whenever painted by vulgar men, is inevitably indecent.

Some three years later Zola took up the whole question of Le Déjeuner *in* Mes Haines.
Le déjeuner sur l'herbe is Edouard Manet's largest picture, in which he has realized the dream of all painters – to pose life-size

MANET *Le déjeuner sur l'herbe* 1863

MANET *Lola de Valence* 1862-7

MANET *Christ Mocked* 1865

figures in a landscape. One knows how skilfully he has overcome this problem. There is some foliage, a few tree trunks, and in the background a stream in which a woman in a chemise is bathing. In the foreground two young men are seated facing a second woman, who has just come out of the water, and who is drying her naked body in the open air.

This nude woman has shocked the public, who can see nothing but her in the picture. Good heavens! How indecent! A woman, without a stitch of clothing, sitting between two fully clothed men; such a thing has never been seen before! But this is completely untrue; in the Musée du Louvre there are more than fifty pictures in which clothed people mix with the nude. But nobody goes to the Louvre to be shocked.

There is the additional fact, too, that the public has decided not to judge *Le déjeuner sur l'herbe* as a true work of art. The only thing which it has really observed is that some people are eating, seated on the grass after bathing. It was considered that the artist's choice of subject was obscene and ostentatious, whereas all the artist had tried to do was to obtain an effect of strong contrasts and bold masses. Artists, especially Manet, who is an analytical painter, do not have this preoccupation with subject matter which, more than anything else, worries the public. For example, the nude woman in *Le déjeuner sur l'herbe* is there only to give the artist an opportunity of painting flesh.

What you have to look for in the picture is not just a picnic on the grass, but the whole landscape with its bold and subtle passages, its broadly painted, solid foreground, its light and delicate background, and that firm flesh modelled in broad areas of light, those supple and strong pigments, and, particularly, that delicate splash of white among the green leaves in the background; in fact to look at the whole of this vast, airy composition, at this attention to nature, rendered with such accurate simplicity.

PHOTOGRAPH OF STATE PURCHASES IN 1865

MANET *Olympia* 1865

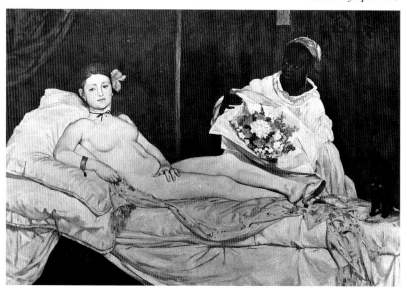

The 1865 Salon

'M. Courbet is left behind, by the whole length of the famous black cat,' remarks Le Journal amusant. The great colourist has chosen the moment when the lady is about to take a much-needed bath.' The caricaturist blames Manet's harsh shadows on the cabinetmaker's ebony shavings. Schutzenberger's academic Rape of Europa (top of page, left) makes a telling contrast.

PROMENADE AU SALON DE 1865, — par BERTALL (suite)

MANETTE, ou LA FEMME DE L'ÉBÉNISTE, par MANET.
Que c'est commé un bouquet de fleurs.
(Air connu.)

Ce tableau de M. Manet est le bouquet de l'Exposition. — M. Courbet est distancé de toute la longueur du célèbre chat noir. — Le moment choisi par le grand coloriste est celui où cette dame va prendre un bain qui nous semble impérieusement réclamé.

BERTALL *Manette, or the Cabinetmaker's Wife*
1865

ÉMILE ZOLA

ÉD. MANET

ÉTUDE BIOGRAPHIQUE ET CRITIQUE
ACCOMPAGNÉE D'UN PORTRAIT D'ÉD. MANET PAR BRACQUEMOND
ET D'UNE EAU-FORTE D'ÉD. MANET
D'APRÈS OLYMPIA

PARIS
E. DENTU, ÉDITEUR
LIBRAIRE DE LA SOCIÉTÉ DES GENS DE LETTRES
Palais-Royal, 17 et 19, Galerie d'Orléans

1867

FRONTISPIECE AND TITLE PAGE OF *EDOUARD MANET*
BY ZOLA (1867)

Monet on the morality of observation 1861

As the Impressionists started to evolve, there was, almost inevitably, a tendency to create codes of practice, impose dogmas, and evolve rules. This becomes very clear in a letter which Monet wrote to his contemporary Frédéric Bazille from Honfleur on 16 July 1861.

I keep asking myself what you could possibly be doing stuck in Paris in such beautiful weather. Here, my dear friend, it is marvellous, and I am always discovering lovely things. I feel crazy, because I'm trying to do everything. My head is spinning! It's very difficult to get everything right in all its aspects. I'm coming to the conclusion that we must all be content with partial success. Well, dear friend, I want to struggle, destroy and start again. It seems to me that when I look at nature I see it all finished in picture-form, completely set down, but afterwards when you actually come to do it, and you're working on it, the whole thing is quite different. All this proves that it is *essential* to think *only* about nature; it is by dint of observation and by reflection that you make discoveries. So we continue to work hard. Are you making progress? I'm sure you are. But I'm also absolutely certain that you're not working hard enough. You can't do real work when you're in the company of playboys like Villa. It's much better to be alone – and, better yet, *completely* alone. You'll find that there are some things you can't work out, and that your picture is terrible, nothing but a crude mess. Have you done your large figure from nature? Some amazing things have happened to me whilst I have been in Paris and Sainte-Adresse during the winter. Do you ever go to the country? Do come and stay with me; I'm expecting you right away, and if not, by 1 August.

Manet's Spanish Connection 1866

The French interest in Spanish art dated back to the Napoleonic period, and had been powerfully reinforced by the creation of the Galerie Espagnole *which Louis-Philippe set up in the Louvre between 1838 and 1848. Manet had always been interested in Spanish art, and works such as* The Spanish Guitar Player *of 1860,* Spanish Dancers *of 1862 and* Mlle V. in the costume of an Espada *had attracted favourable comment. Despite the scandals associated with* Le déjeuner sur l'herbe *in 1863, he had two works accepted at the Salon of 1864, which were highly praised by Baudelaire and others. Two years later, he made his first visit to Spain, and from Madrid he wrote to his friend Henri de Fantin-Latour.*

What a pity you are not here; what pleasure you would have got from seeing Velázquez, who alone is worth the whole journey. The painters of all the other schools who surround him in the museum here, and who are well-represented, all seem second-rate in comparison. He didn't surprise me, he ravished me. The full-length portrait in the Louvre is not by him; only the authenticity of the Infanta is certain. There is an enormous picture here filled with small figures like those in *The Cavaliers* in the Louvre, but the figures of the men and women in this one are perhaps better, and all of them free of retouching. The background, a landscape, is by a pupil of Velázquez.

The most astonishing work in this splendid collection, and perhaps the most astonishing piece of painting which has ever been done, is the one entitled in the catalogue *Portrait of a celebrated actor in the time of Philip IV*. The background fades into nothingness; the old boy, all in black and so full of life, seems to be surrounded by air. And *The Spinners* – what a work; and the lovely portrait of Alonzo Cano; and *Las Meninas*, another extraordinary picture! The philosophers; what astonishing works!

And all the dwarfs too! One in particular, seated frontally, with his hands on his hips; a painting for a true connoisseur. And those magnificent portraits; one would have to include the lot; they are all masterpieces. The well known portrait of Charles V by Titian, which certainly deserves to be appreciated, and which anywhere else would have seemed good to me, here looks wooden in comparison with the works of Velázquez.

And Goya too! Surely the most extraordinary painter since the Master (whom he imitated too much, and in the most servile way). But in spite of this he has great verve. There are two equestrian portraits by him in the same museum, painted in the manner of Velázquez, but they are in fact very much inferior in quality. What I have seen of him up to now does not please me enormously. One of these days I must visit a splendid collection belonging to the Duke of Osuña.

I feel very put out. The weather is very bad this morning, and I'm afraid that the bullfight I was going to tonight will be put off. Tomorrow I shall go to Toledo, where I will see El Greco, and Goya, who, I'm told is well represented there.

FANTIN-LATOUR *Edouard Manet* 1867

Zola, the Impressionists and 'L'Oeuvre'   c. 1866

Ernest Alfred Vizetelly, one of the most enterprising British literary figures of the late nineteenth and early twentieth centuries, was responsible for making Zola's works familiar to English readers. In 1902 his translation of L'Oeuvre *was published by* Chatto & Windus *as* His Masterpiece, *and he prefaced it with an introduction based on his own knowledge of the participants gleaned many years earlier.*

It was at the time of the Salon of 1866 that M. Zola, who criticized that exhibition in the *Evénement* newspaper, first came to the front as an art critic, slashing out to right and left with all the vigour of a born combatant,

and championing M. Manet – whom he did not as yet know personally – with a fervour born of the strongest convictions. He had come to the conclusion that the derided painter was being treated with injustice, and that opinion sufficed to throw him into the fray; even as, in more recent years, the belief that Captain Dreyfus was innocent impelled him in like manner to plead that unfortunate officer's cause. When M. Zola championed Manet and his disciples, he was only twenty-six years old, yet he did not hesitate to pit himself against men who were considered the most eminent painters and critics of France; and, although, as in the Dreyfus case, the only immediate effect of his campaign was to bring him hatred and contumely, time which always has its revenges, has long since shown how right he was in forecasting the triumph of M. Manet and his principal methods.

In those days M. Zola's most intimate friend – a companion of his boyhood and youth – was Paul Cézanne, a painter who developed talent as an Impressionist; and the lives of Cézanne and Manet, as well as that of a certain rather dissolute engraver, who sat for the latter's famous painting *Le Bon Bock*, suggested to M. Zola the novel which he called *L'Oeuvre*, published in 1886. Claude Lantier, the chief character in the book, is, of course, neither Manet nor Cézanne, but from the careers of these two painters M. Zola has borrowed many little touches and incidents. The poverty which falls to Claude's lot is taken from the life of Cézanne, for Manet, the son of a judge, was almost wealthy. Moreover Manet married very happily, and in no wise led the pitiful existence which in the novel is ascribed to Claude Lantier and his helpmate, Christine. The original of the latter was the poor woman who, for many years shared the life of the engraver to whom I have alluded.

Whilst, however, Claude Lantier, the hero of *L'Oeuvre*, is unlike Manet in many respects, there is a close analogy between the artistic theories and practices of the real painter and the imaginary one. Several of Claude's pictures are Manet's, slightly modified. For instance, the former's painting 'In the Open Air' is almost a replica of the latter's *Déjeuner sur l'herbe* shown at the Salon of the Rejected in 1863. Again, many of the sayings put into Claude's mouth in the novel are really sayings of Manet. And Claude's fate at the end of the book is virtually that of a moody young fellow who long assisted Manet in his studio, preparing his palette, cleaning his brushes and so forth. This lad, whom Manet painted in *L'enfant aux cerises*, had artistic aspirations of his own, and being unable to satisfy them, ended by hanging himself.

I had just a slight acquaintance with Manet, whose studio I visited early in my youth, and though the exigencies of life led me long ago to cast aside all artistic ambitions of my own, I have been for more than thirty years on friendly terms with members of the French art world. Thus it would be comparatively easy for me to identify a large number of the figures and incidents figuring in *His Masterpiece*; but I doubt whether such identification would have any particular interest for English readers. I will just mention that Mahoudeau, the sculptor, is, in a measure Solari, another friend of M. Zola's boyhood and youth; that Fagerolles in his main features is Gervex, and that Bongrand is a combination of Courbet, Cabanel and Gustave Flaubert. For instance, his so-called 'Village Wedding' is suggested by Courbet's *Funeral at Ornans*; his friendship for Claude is Cabanel's friendship for Manet; whilst some of his mannerisms, such as the dislike for the praise accorded to certain of his works, are simply those of Flaubert, who (like Balzac in the case of *Eugénie Grandet*) almost invariably lost his temper if one ventured to extol *Madame Bovary* in his presence.

Zola addresses Cézanne   1866

Emile Zola and Paul Cézanne had been schoolfellows in Aix-en-Provence. In 1861, at the age of twenty-two, Cézanne had followed Zola to Paris, where he studied assiduously at the Académie Suisse, and became acquainted with Monet and another contemporary, Camille Pissarro. In 1866 Zola left his job in the publishing house of Hachette to write for the daily paper L'Evénement. Firmly resolved on a stance of aggression in his criticism, he wrote a series of vigorous onslaughts on the Salon and official art, championing with more passion than percipience the works of the painters who were to be the Impressionists. When these pieces were published in book form at the end of the year, he prefaced them with a letter to Cézanne.

I feel the deepest pleasure, dear friend, in a *tête-à-tête* with you. You can't imagine how much I have suffered from this squabble I have had with the masses, with the anonymous herd. I have been feeling so misunderstood. I can feel the hatred around me to such an extent that discouragement often makes me drop my pen. Today however I can indulge in the pleasure of having one of those dialogues with you in which we have so frequently indulged over the past ten years. It is for you alone that I am writing these pages. I know that you will read them with your heart, and that tomorrow you will feel affection for me.

Pretend for a moment that we are alone together in some remote place, far from the hurly-burly of life, and that we are talking like old friends, who know each other's very soul, and understand each other just by a glance.

For ten years we have been talking about art and literature. We have lived together – do you remember? – and often dawn caught us still talking, searching the past, questioning the present, trying to discover truth, and to create for ourselves an infallible and comprehensive religion. We shuffled stacks of terrible ideas, we examined and rejected all ideologies, and after much arduous labour came to the conclusion that outside one's own personal life there exist only lies and stupidity.

How happy are those who cherish such memories! I see your role in my life as being like that of the pale young man of whom de Musset speaks. You are my entire youth; I find you involved in all my joys, all my sufferings. In brotherhood our minds have grown side by side. Today we have faith in ourselves because we have explored and know our hearts and bodies.

We used to live in our own shadow, isolated, unsociable, preoccupied with our own thoughts. We felt lost in the midst of a complacent and superficial crowd. In everything we did we sought the individual; every day, in every painting or poem, we wanted to discover the real person. We cultivated the great masters, the geniuses each of whom had created a world of his own, and we rejected the followers, the impotent, those whose careers consisted of picking up a few crumbs of originality from here and there.

CÉZANNE *The Artist's Father* 1866

Did you realize that we were revolutionaries, without being aware of it? I have just been able to say to the public what we had been telling each other for ten years. You have heard the reverberations of the ensuing outcry, have you? And you have seen the warm welcome given to our cherished thoughts? It makes one wonder about the poor boys who once lived such a healthy life in the glorious sunshine of Provence, and who even in those days believed in such folly, such hypocrisy.

For – you probably did not know this – I am a hypocrite. The public has already ordered a number of straitjackets for my use when I'm confined in the asylum at Charenton. Apparently I have good things to say only about my relatives and friends. I am a foolish and evil man, writing with a poisoned pen.

This inspires pity, and it is very sad. Will it always be the same story? Will we always have to talk like everybody else, or stay dumb? Do you remember our long conversations? We said that even the slightest new truth could not be revealed without arousing anger and protest. Now it is my turn to be jeered and insulted.

But it is a good experience; and it is very sad. Will it always be the same? For nothing in the world would I wish to destroy these pages; they are not much in themselves, but they have been my touchstone of public reactions. We now know how unpopular our cherished thoughts are. But I believe in them, and I am sure that in a few years everyone will agree with me. I do not fear that they will be thrown in my face in the future.

Renoir is turned down by the Salon _1866_

In 1865 Renoir had his Portrait of M.W.S. (William Sisley) *accepted at the Salon, and was overjoyed, especially as it secured him another portrait commission. He submitted two in the following year. On 17 May Marie Le Coeur, sister of Jules – an affluent painter who had houses in Paris, Marlotte near Fontainebleau, and Boulogne, and had befriended Renoir – reported to a friend:*

M. Renoir, poor man, has been rejected. Just imagine, he had done two pictures; a landscape with two figures – everyone says that one is good, and that the whole work has its strengths and weaknesses – the other was done at Marlotte in two weeks. He calls it a sketch, and he only sent it to the exhibition because he had the other one which was a more important work, otherwise he wouldn't have decided to exhibit it.

On Friday, since nobody could tell him whether he'd been accepted or rejected, he

went to wait for a member of the jury to come out of the exhibition, and when he saw Corot and Daubigny emerging, asked them if they knew if the paintings of a friend of his named Renoir had been accepted. Whereupon Daubigny said he remembered the work, and described Renoir's painting to him, going on to say, 'We're very sorry about your friend, but his work was rejected. We did all we could to prevent this, and indeed got the painting reconsidered ten times without any success. What could we do? There were six of us in favour of it, against all the others. Tell your friend not to get discouraged; there are great qualities in his painting. He should get up a petition and ask for an exhibition of rejected paintings.'

So in his misfortune he has had the consolation of having been congratulated by two artists whose talents he admires.

In the evening he went into a café and overheard some painters talking about the exhibition, and one of them said, 'There's a painting by somebody named Renoir, that is very good and was rejected.'

Now what annoys him most is that he learned yesterday that his Marlotte painting was accepted. The other having been rejected, he would have preferred that this one had been rejected too.

Monet meets Manet _1866_

Still pursuing his career in Paris, Monet had met Johan Barthold Jongkind, who became his virtual master: 'it was to him that I owed the final education of my eye.' In 1866 two of Monet's seascapes were accepted by the Salon, and it was at this time he met Manet. His own account, remembered some thirty years later, appeared in the interview published by Le Temps *in November 1900 (cf. p. 16)*

The two seascapes that I sent were received with highest approval, and were hung on the line. It was a great success. The same unanimity of praise was accorded in 1866 to a large portrait the *Woman in Green*. The papers even carried my name back to Le Havre. My family at last began to take me seriously, and with this my allowance started to come in again. I floated in my wealth – temporarily at least, for later we were to quarrel again. I threw myself body and soul into *plein air* painting.

It was a dangerous innovation. Till then nobody had indulged in it; not even Manet, who attempted it only some years later, after me. His painting then was still very classical, and I have never forgotten the contempt he showed for my painting at that time. It was in 1867; my style had become definite, but it was still not really revolutionary in character. I was still a long way off adopting the principle of the subdivision of colour that set so many against me, but I was beginning to make some attempts at it, and I was experimenting with effects of light and colour that flouted conventions. The Salon jury, which had once been so favourable to me, turned against me, and I was blackballed when I presented this picture to them.

Still I found a way to exhibit elsewhere. Touched by my entreaties, a dealer in the rue Auber agreed to display in his window the seascape which the Salon had rejected. One evening when I had stopped in the street amongst a group of onlookers to hear what was being said about my picture I saw Manet coming along with some of his friends. They stopped to look, and Manet, in a contemptuous tone, remarked, shrugging his shoulders, 'Just look at this young man who tries to do *plein air* painting. As if the old masters would have thought of such a thing!'

Manet, moreover, had an old grudge against me. At the Salon of 1866 he had been received, on entering the *vernissage*, by a chorus of acclaim at the success of his painting. He was delighted. Then imagine his consternation when he discovered that the picture about which he was being congratulated was actually by me! It was my *Woman in Green*. The saddest part of all was that on leaving the building he came across a group which included Bazille and me. 'How goes it?' one of them asked. 'Awful,' replied Manet; 'I am disgusted. I am being complimented on a painting which is not mine.'

Next day when Astruc told him that he had given expression to his anger before the man who had painted the picture, and offered to effect an introduction, Manet refused absolutely. He felt bitter because of the trick I had unintentionally played on him . . . .

It was only in 1869 that I saw him again, and then we at once became firm friends. At our first meeting he invited me to join him every evening at a café in the Batignolles district, where he and his friends gathered at the end of the day to talk. There I met Fantin-Latour, Cézanne, Degas, who had recently returned from Italy, the art critic Duranty, Emile Zola, who was then making his first foray into literature, and several

MONET *Camille, or The Lady in a Green Dress* 1866

others. For my part I used to take Sisley, Bazille and Renoir there. Nothing could have been more interesting than the discussions we had, with their perpetual clash of opinions. They kept our wits sharpened, encouraged us to press ahead with our own experiments, and provided us with enough enthusiasm to keep at it for weeks on end until our ideas became clear and coherent. From them we emerged more finely tempered, our wills firmer, our thoughts clearer and less confused.

Cézanne appeals for a chance to exhibit 1866

At the age of twenty-seven, despite the championship of Zola, of Manet – and, of Daubigny, who tried very hard to get his work accepted in the Salon of 1866, for which he was a juror – Cézanne had been singularly unsuccessful in achieving any kind of official acceptance. Daubigny suggested that he write to Comte Nieuwerkerke, director-general of museums, superintendent of Fine Arts, and ex-officio chairman of the Salon jury, proposing a renewal of the Salon des Refusés which had been set up in 1863. This he did, but received no reply. On 19 April he wrote again.

I recently had the honour of writing to you about the two paintings of mine which the jury of the Salon turned down.

Since you have not yet replied to me, I feel that I must insist on reiterating the reasons which made me write to you. However, since you must have received my letter, there is no reason for me to repeat here the arguments which I felt I must put before you. I shall content myself with pointing out to you again that I cannot accept the unlawful judgment of colleagues to whom I have not myself given the task of assessing me.

I am writing to you therefore to underline my demand. I wish to make a direct appeal to the public, and to have my work exhibited without any restriction. My wish does not seem to contain anything exorbitant, and if you make enquiries of all the painters who are in the same position as myself, they will all reply to you that they reject the jury, and that they want, in one way or another to take part in an exhibition which should be compelled to be open to any serious worker.

Therefore, let the Salon des Refusés be set up again. And should it happen, that I were to be the sole exhibitor, I ardently wish that the public would thereby realize that I do not wish to be identified with those gentlemen of the jury any more than they wish to be identified with me.

I hope, Monsieur, that you will not maintain your silence. It seems to me that any reasonable letter deserves a reply.

Manet: sincerity not protest 1867

The jury which chose pictures for the Universal Exhibition of 1867 'shut the door on all those who take the new road', according to Zola. Manet decided to hold a one-man show in a wooden building at the junction of the Avenues de l'Alma and de Montaigne. For the catalogue Zacharie Astruc wrote an introduction, 'Reasons for holding a private exhibition', in which he emphasized the fact that Manet did not see himself as a revolutionary. The exhibition was poorly attended and was not a success.

Official recognition, encouragement and prizes are in fact regarded as proofs of talent; the public has been informed, in advance, what to admire, what to avoid, according as to whether the works are accepted or rejected. On the other hand, the artist is told that it is the public's spontaneous reaction to his works which makes them so unwelcome to the various selection committees. In these circumstances the artist is advised to be patient and wait. But wait for what?

Until there are no selection committees? He would be much better off if he could make direct contact with the public, and find out its reactions. Today the artist is not saying 'Come and see some perfect paintings', but 'Come and see some sincere ones'.

It is sincerity which gives to works of art a character which seems to convert them into acts of protest, when all the painter is trying to do is to express his own impressions. Monsieur Manet has never wished to protest. On the contrary, the protest, which he never expected has been directed against himself; this is because there is a traditional way of teaching form, techniques and appreciation, and because those who have been brought up to believe in these principles will admit no others, a fact which makes them childishly intolerant. Any works which do not conform to these formulae they regard as worthless. They not only arouse criticism, but provoke hostility, even *active* hositility. To be able to exhibit is the all-important thing, the *sine qua non* for the artist, because what happens is that, after looking at a thing for a length of time, what at first seemed to be surprising, or even shocking, becomes familiar. Gradually it comes to be understood and accepted. Time itself imperceptibly refines and softens the original hardness of a picture.

By exhibiting an artist finds friends and allies in his struggle for recognition. Monsieur Manet has always recognized talent when he has seen it; he has had no intention to overthrow old methods of painting, or to create new ones. He has merely tried to be himself and nobody else.

his parents explaining some of the ideas which were being canvassed. At this point they did not come to anything and in any case in the following year he had his The Artist's Family on a Terrace *accepted by a* Salon *which also contained works by Manet, Renoir, Pissarro, Monet, Sisley and Degas.*

I have bad news to tell you; my paintings were rejected for the exhibition. Don't be too upset about this; there is nothing discouraging about it; on the contrary, my works share this fate with everything that was good in the Salon this year. A petition is being signed at this moment demanding an exhibition of the *Refusés*. This petition is being supported by all the painters of Paris who are of any value. However it won't get anywhere. In any case the annoyance I suffered this year won't happen again, for I will no longer send anything to the jury. It's much too ridiculous, when one knows one isn't a fool, to be exposed to these administrative whims, above all when one doesn't care about medals and prizegiving. As for what I'm telling you, a dozen talented young people think the same way as I do about it. We have therefore resolved to rent a big studio each year when we will show as many of our paintings as we want. We will invite the painters whom we like to send paintings. Courbet, Corot, Diaz, Daubigny, and many others with whom perhaps you are not familiar, have promised to send paintings, and highly approve of our idea. With the latter, and Monet who is better than all of us, we are sure to succeed.

Bazille at the birth of an idea   1867

Reluctantly an increasing number of artists began to conclude that they had no hope of having their pictures accepted by the Salon, however much they may have wanted to, and in May 1867 Frédéric Bazille wrote to

Being painted by Manet   1868

In February 1868, two years after he had first met Manet, and sprung to his defence in the columns of L'Evénement, *Zola wrote to Théodore Duret: 'Manet is doing my portrait for the Salon' (John Rewald,* Cézanne et Zola, *Paris 1936, p. 61), and the finished work was exhibited at the Salon that year. It was generally highly praised, and Manet gave it to Zola, who kept it in his house at Médan. On the writer's death in 1902 his widow kept it for some time, but on her death in 1925 it went to the Louvre. Two months after the painting was finished Zola contributed to L'Evénement (10 May 1868) an account of what it was like to be painted by Manet, as part of a general review of the Salon.*

One of my friends asked me yesterday if I would say something about this picture of myself. 'Why not?' I replied. 'I would like to have ten columns of print to be able to describe what was going through my mind as I watched Edouard Manet struggle inch by inch with nature. But do not think for a moment that I get any personal pleasure in entertaining people with the appearance of my own countenance. Naturally I will say something about the portrait, and any ill-natured people who think they find it a subject for snide remarks are fools'.

I remember the long hours I sat for him. As my limbs became numb from not moving, and my eyes tired from looking straight ahead, a number of thoughts kept passing through my mind.

The nonsense that is spread about, the lies and platitudes about all manner of things, all this human hubbub which streams on uselessly like so much dirty water, seemed very far away. It seemed to me that I had been transported outside this world into an atmosphere of truth and justice, and I was filled with pity for the poor wretches floundering about below.

From time to time as I posed, half-asleep, I looked at the artist standing by his easel, his features drawn, clear-eyed, absorbed in what he was doing. He had entirely forgotten me; he no longer realized that I was there; he simply copied me, as if I were some human animal, with a sense of concentration and artistic integrity that I have seen nowhere else. Then I thought of the

slovenly dauber of legend, of this Manet who was a figment of the imagination of caricaturists, who paints cats as a kind of joke. It must be admitted that wit of this kind can be very stupid.

I thought for hours on end about the fate of individual artists, a fate which forces them to live apart in the loneliness of their art. Around me hung on the walls of the studio those forceful and characteristic paintings which the public had decided not to understand. All you have to do to be regarded as a monster is to be talented, and think your own thoughts. If you do you are accused of ignoring your art, of ridiculing common sense, simply because your eye and your inclinations lead you to individual results. As soon as you no longer swim along with the commonplace, fools stone you and see you as either mad or arrogant. It was while I was thinking along these lines that I saw the canvas take shape. What astonished me more than anything else was the extreme conscientiousness of the painter.

Often, when he was coping with some detail of minor importance I wanted to stop posing, and suggested to him that he should make it up.

'No,' he answered me, 'I can do nothing without Nature. I do not know how to make things up. As long as I have tried to paint something in accordance with the lessons I have been taught, I have never produced anything worthwhile. If my work has any real value today, it is because of the exact interpretation and truthful analysis.'

That is the secret of all his talent. Above all else he is a naturalist. His eye sees things and records them with elegant simplicity. I know that I shan't be able to make blind people like his pictures, but real artists will know what I mean when I talk of the slightly bitter charm of his works. Their colour is both extremely harmonious and extremely intense. And this, mark you, is the picture of a man who is accused of being able neither to paint, nor to draw. I defy any other painter to place a figure in an interior, as he has done with mine, and yet avoid making the surrounding still-life objects conflict with the head.

This portrait of me is a combination of difficulties overcome. From the frames in the background, from the lovely Japanese screen which stands on the left, right up to the very smallest details of the figure, everything holds together in clear, masterly, striking tones, so realistic that the eye forgets the multiplicity of objects and sees only one harmonious unity.

I do not speak of the still-lifes – the accessories, and the books scattered on the table. Manet is a past-master where this is concerned. But I particularly draw your attention to the hand resting on the knee. It is a marvel of skill. In short, here is skin, but real skin, without ridiculous *trompe-l'œil*. If all parts of the picture had been worked upon as much as the hand, the mob itself would have acclaimed it a masterpiece.

An election at the Salon   c. 1868

The annual exhibitions of the Salon which were held in the Palais de l'Industrie were a dominant feature of French artistic life, and one to which the Impressionists were by no means indifferent. They were, on the whole, organized on democratic principles, with exhibitors electing the hanging committee. In L'Oeuvre, Zola gives a vivid account of the atmosphere prevailing in these elections, when the hero of the book is invited to assist at the counting of votes.

At four in the afternoon, when the voting was over, Claude could not resist a fit of curiosity to go and have a look. The staircase was now free, and anyone could enter. Upstairs he came upon the huge gallery, overlooking the Champs-Elyseés, which was set aside for the hanging committee. A table forty feet long filled the centre of this gallery, and entire trees were burning in the monumental fireplace at one end of it.

Some four or five hundred voters, who had remained to see the votes counted, stood there mingling with friends and acquaintances and inquisitive strangers, talking, laughing and creating a storm of noise under the lofty ceiling. Around the tables groups of people who had volunteered to count the votes were already sitting hard at work. There were some fifteen of these groups, each with its own chairman and two scrutineers. There were still three or four to be organized, and nobody was coming forward; indeed, most were reluctant to accept a job which would keep them stuck there for most of the night.

It just happened that Fagerolle [a friend of Claude's and a candidate for the committee], who had been in the thick of things since the morning, was gesticulating and shouting, 'Come on, gentlemen, we need one more volunteer here!'

At that moment, noticing Claude, he dashed over to him and pulled him away. 'There you are. The very man we wanted. Oblige me by sitting down here and helping us. It's all in a good cause, isn't it?'

So Claude suddenly found himself chairman of one of the counting committees, and began to carry out his duties with all the gravity of a shy person, secretly experiencing a good deal of emotion, as if the hanging of his own picture depended on the degree of conscientiousness he displayed. He called out the names inscribed on the voting papers, which were passed to him in little bundles, while the scrutineers noted each successive vote obtained by candidates on lists especially prepared for the purpose. This went on to the background of a horrible uproar, twenty or thirty names being called out at the same time by different voices against the general rumbling noise of the crowd. As Claude could never do anything without becoming passionate about it, he got very agitated, becoming despondent whenever a paper appeared without Fagerolle's name on it, and deliriously happy whenever he had to shout out that name again. Moreover, he often tasted that delight, because his friend had made himself very popular, showing his face everywhere, frequenting the cafés where influential groups of artists assembled, even venturing to expound his opinions there, and binding himself to young artists, without failing to kowtow to members of the *Institut*. Thus there was a general current of sympathy in his favour. He was everybody's favourite son.

Darkness fell that rainy March day at about six o'clock. The assistants brought lamps, and some mistrustful artists, who, gloomy and silent, were watching the counting, got closer to the tables. Others began to get playful, mimicked the cries of animals or started yodelling. But it was only at eight o'clock, when a buffet of cold meats and wine appeared, that the gaiety reached its climax. The bottles were quickly emptied, people stuffed themselves with whatever they could get hold of, and there was a free and easy *Kermesse* in that hall, in which the logs in the fireplace lit everything up with a glow which seemed to come from a smithy. Everybody was smoking, and the tobacco smoke created a kind of mist around the yellow light from the lamps, whilst scattered all over the floor were spoilt voting papers from the polling; indeed there was a whole layer covering the floor composed of dirty paper, bits of bread, corks, and a few broken plates; even those sitting at the tables were up to their ankles in it. Restraint was cast aside; a little sculptor with a pale face jumped on a chair to harangue the assembly, whilst a painter with a hooked nose and waxed moustaches sat astride a chair and galloped, bowing, round the table, in imitation of the Emperor.

Little by little, however, a good many grew tired and went off. At eleven o'clock there were not more than a couple of hundred people present. Past midnight, however, some more people arrived, loungers in tails and white ties, who had come from

some theatre or soirée, and wished to know the result of the voting before all Paris knew it. Journalists also arrived, and they could be seen darting from room to room trying to find out how the voting was going.

Claude, though hoarse by now, still kept on calling out names. The smoke and heat had become intolerable; a smell like that of a byre rose from the filth on the floor. One o'clock, two o'clock struck, and he was still unfolding voting papers, his conscientiousness holding him up to such a point that the other groups had already finished their work, while his was still in a mass of figures. At last all the totals were added up, and the results proclaimed. Fagerolles was elected, coming fifteenth among forty places. Daylight was breaking when Claude got home to the rue Tourlaque, feeling both tired and happy.

Boudin on a proper subject for painting 1868

One of the innovations which people remarked on at the time about the new forms of painting in France was that they dealt with the bourgeois and city workers. Boudin, who so strongly influenced Monet, and who was close to the Impressionists in many ways, wrote on 3 September 1868 to one of his friends at Le Havre.

Your letter arrived at the very moment when I was showing Ribot, Bureau and another person my little studies of fashionable seaside resorts. They congratulated me especially on the fact that I had dared to put into paint the things and people of our time, and for gaining pictorial acceptance of the gentleman in his overcoat and his wife in her raincoat – thanks to the sauce and the spice I season them with.

This is no new thing however; the Italians and the Flemings simply painted the people of their own time, either in interiors or in large architectural settings. This approach is now making headway again, and a number of young painters, chief amongst whom I would put Monet, find that it is a subject that has hitherto been too much neglected. The peasants have had painters who have specialized in painting them; men such as Millet, Jacque, Breton, and that is a good thing. These men produce sincere and serious work. They take part in the work of the Creator, and help Him to make Himself manifest in a manner fruitful for man. That is good, but quite honestly, between ourselves, don't those middle-class men and women walking along the pier towards the setting sun also have a right to be fixed on canvas, *to be brought to light*? Don't you agree that these people, getting away from the daily grind, are seeking relaxation after hard work? There may be some parasites amongst them, but there are others who really do work hard. – This is a serious argument, and I think that it is irrefutable.

Under no circumstances could I see myself spending the rest of my career painting fancy costumes. Isn't it pitiful to see serious men like Isabey, Meissonier and so many others, collecting carnival costumes, and under the pretext of achieving a picturesque effect dressing up models who don't know what to do under their borrowed finery?

MONET *The Sea at Le Havre* 1868

The Poitevin [Meissonier] has made his fortune with an old felt hat and a feather along with a pair of musketeer's boots which he has painted time and time again, under all possible pretexts. I should very much like to have one of these gentlemen explain to me what interest such subjects will have in the future, and whether the picturesque quality of these paintings will make any impression on our grandchildren.

Monet in Le Havre   1868

Monet's early years as an artist were beset with financial and other problems, and at one point in 1868 he made a rather futile gesture of attempting (or pretending) to drown himself. Early in September, however, one of his patrons, a M. Gaudibert of Le Havre, called on him to do a portrait of his wife, and Monet wrote happily to his friend and supporter Bazille.

I am surrounded here by everything that I love. I pass my time out of doors on the pier when anything is happening, such as when the fishing fleet sets out; otherwise I go into the country which is very beautiful around

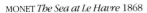

here, and which I find more pleasant in winter than in summer. After dinner, dear friend, I find in my cottage a good fire and a wonderful little family. If only you could see how cute your little godson is now! This little creature absolutely fascinates me, and believe me, dear friend, I am glad to have him. I'm going to do a painting of him surrounded by other figures for the Salon. This year I'm going to do two figure paintings; an interior with the baby and two women, and some sailors out of doors. I want to do this in a spectacular manner. Thank heavens for this gentleman from Le Havre, who came to my aid. I would like to stay for ever in a corner of the world as tranquil as this. Consequently I don't envy your being in Paris. Don't you think that one is better off with Nature? In Paris one is concerned with nothing but what one sees and hears, if one is to remain strong. What I do here will at least have the merit of not resembling the work of anyone else, because it will simply be the expression of my own personal feelings. The more I live, the more I regret how little I know. That's what makes me so uncomfortable. I hope that you are still fired by ambition and that you are working hard. People who are well off like you should be producing miracles. Tell me what you have got ready for the Salon, and if you are satisfied with it. I suggest that you send me all the works of mine that are now with you. I have lost so many that I cling to those which remain. Also, if you want to do me a favour, will you have a look in the cupboards for the unused canvases that I left behind, and also for any pictures which are unfinished, like your standing portrait, and another work from 1860 in which I painted some very unsuccessful flowers. Send me everything you can find which I might be able to use, and you will do me a great service, as I'm working so hard that I've used nearly all the canvases I have, and Charpentier, the local colour merchant, is stopping my credit. He's making me pay cash, and you never know how much things are going to cost.

Manet and the Maximilian affair   1869

Between 1867 and 1869 Manet had been preoccupied with the theme of the execution of Napoleon III's protégé, Maximilian, Emperor of Mexico. He painted three canvases and produced a lithograph on the subject. But he had not allowed for the stringent censorship exercised by the government, and in January 1869 received a letter from the Ministry of the Interior stating that the paintings would not be accepted at the Salon, and that the publication or printing of the lithograph would be forbidden. He immediately informed Zola.

My dear Zola, have a look at the enclosed letter, and return it to me in an envelope along with your opinion.

It seems to me that the authorities are bent on making me take action over my lithograph, which has been causing me considerable worry. I thought they could stop the publication, but not the printing. Still it speaks well for the work since there's no caption of any kind underneath it. I was waiting for a publisher to have the stone inscribed 'Death of Max. etc.'

I feel that a word about this ridiculously high-handed little act would not be out of place. What do you think?   ·

Zola reacted promptly, and La Tribune *for 4 February 1869 contained the following piece by him under the heading 'Coups d'épingle' (Pinpricks).*
I read in the most recent issue of *La Tribune* that M. Manet has just been refused permission to print a lithograph representing the execution of Maximilian.

This is the sort of measure that can save a government. Is its authority in such a bad way that those who serve it feel bound to save it the slightest annoyance?

The censors, no doubt, thought: 'If we allow Maximilian to be shot in public, his shade will go wandering with ominous cries in the corridors of the Tuileries. There's a ghost that it is our duty to put behind bars.'

I know exactly what kind of lithograph these gentlemen would be delighted to authorize, and if M. Manet wants to have a real success in their eyes, I advise him to depict Maximilian alive and well, with his happy, smiling wife at his side. Moreover the artist would have to make it clear that Mexico has never suffered a bloodbath, and that it is living, and will continue to live, under the blessed rule of Napoleon III's protégé. Historic truth, thus interpreted, will bring tears of joy to the censor's eyes.

The fact is, I could not at first understand the censor's severity to M. Manet's work. I remembered having seen, in all the newspaper vendors' windows, a penny print produced, I believe, by the Epinal workshops, which represented with terrifying naïveté the last moments of Maximilian. Why should an accomplished artist be refused what an industrial artisan was permitted? I believe today I have found the key to the enigma, and it is truly a gem.

On examining a proof of the condemned lithograph I noticed that the soldiers shooting Maximilian were wearing a uniform almost identical to that of our own troops. Fanciful artists give the Mexicans costumes from comic opera. M. Manet, who truly loves truth, has drawn their real costumes, which resemble those of the Vincennes infantrymen.

You can understand the anger of the censors. What now! An artist has dared to put before their eyes such a cruel irony: France shooting Maximilian!

In M. Manet's place, I would regret not having intended to add a biting epigram, an intention with which, no doubt, the censor credited him.

MANET *The Execution of Maximilian* 1868

MANET *The Balcony* 1868-69

BAZILLE *View of a Village* 1868

Berthe Morisot at the Salon 1869

In 1869 Manet exhibited at the Salon The Balcony, *which included a portrait of the twenty-eight-year-old Berthe Morisot, an artist who, having had lessons from Corot and Fantin-Latour, had achieved a precocious success at the Salon of 1864. Manet had known her since 1866, when he had admired her work in the Salon. She was to become a frequent exhibitor at the various Impressionist exhibitions, and her lively letters throw a great deal of light on the personalities and activities of her fellow artists. Here is her account of a visit to the Salon at which* The Balcony *was on view.*

The first thing we saw as we went up the main staircase was Puvis' painting. It looked well. Jacquemard was standing in front of it, and seemed lost in admiration, but what he seemed to admire less was myself. There is nothing worse than a former admirer. We next met Carolus Duran, who was with his wife, and who, on seeing us, blushed violently. I shook hands with him, but he did not have a word to say to me. His wife is a tall and handsome woman. He is exhibiting a portrait of her, which I think will be a success, although it is more than a little vulgar. It's not absolutely bad, but mannered, and flat. I need hardly tell you that the first thing I did was to go to Room M. There I found Manet, with his hat on, standing in bright sunshine, and looking dazed. He begged me to go and see the painting, as he did not dare move a step.

I have never seen a face as expressive as his; he was laughing at one moment, and looking worried at the next, assuring everybody that his picture was no good, and then adding in the same breath that it was bound to be a success. I think he has a very charming temperament, which I greatly like.

His works give the impression of a wild, or even an unripe, fruit. I do not dislike them, though I prefer his portrait of Zola.

I myself look more strange than ugly. It

seems that people are using the phrase *femme fatale* about the painting, but I realize that if I tell you everything at once I shall use up all my paper, so I had better talk another time about my impression of the paintings, especially as I could hardly see them. However I did look for our friend Fantin. His insignificant little work was hung incredibly high, and looked incredibly forlorn. I finally discovered him, but he disappeared before I could say a word about his exhibit. I do not know whether he was avoiding me, or whether he was sensitive about the worthlessness of his work.

I certainly think that his frequent visits to the Louvre, and to Mlle Dubourg, don't do him any good. M. Degas seemed happy, but guess for whom he abandoned me? Mlle Lille and Mlle Loubens. I must say that I was a little annoyed when a man whom I think is very intelligent abandoned me to pay compliments to two silly women.

I was beginning to find all this rather dull. For about an hour Manet, in high spirits, was leading his mother and wife and me all over the place, when I bumped into Puvis de Chavannes. He seemed delighted to see me, and told me that he had come largely on my account, as he was beginning to lose hope of seeing me at the Stevenses, and asked if he might accompany me for a few minutes. I wanted to see the pictures, but he implored me so eagerly, 'I beg of you, let us just talk. We have plenty of time to look at the paintings on other occasions.' Such conversation might have appealed to me had I not been confronted on every side with familiar faces. What is more I had completely lost sight of Manet and his wife, which further increased my embarrassment. I did not think it proper to walk round alone. When I finally found Manet again I reproached him for his behaviour; he answered that I could rely on his complete devotion, but he was nevertheless not prepared to act as my nanny . . . .

On 5 May, she continued in another letter:
On Monday I met Carolus Duran. It seemed

silly not to compliment him on his painting, which seems to be having a certain success, but he seemed surprised and responded with an endless stream of compliments about Manet's painting. Degas has a very pretty little portrait of a very ugly woman in black with a hat and a cashmere shawl falling from her shoulders. The background is that of a very light interior, showing a corner of a mantelpiece in half tones; it is very subtle and distinguished. Antonin [Proust]'s entries look well, despite the fact that he is very badly hung, but landscapes bore me, though I did see one by Lépine that I find charming. It is, as ever, a view of the banks of the Seine, near Bercy. I didn't see any of Oudinot's paintings. Those of Daubigny, father and son, tire me, and seem heavy and vulgar. Corot is very poetic as usual. I think that he has spoiled the sketch we saw at his home by working at it too much in his studio.

The tall Bazille has painted something that is very good. It is a little girl in a light dress seated in the shade of a tree, with a glimpse of a village in the background. There is much light and sun in it. He has tried to do what we have so often attempted – a figure in the outdoor light – and he seems to have been successful.

Here I stop to laugh at myself for passing these judgments. It seems to me that our friends would laugh even more if they could hear me dealing out censure and praise. I met Bracquemond, who was very friendly, paid me compliments on the pieces I exhibited last year, and reproached me for not showing this year. It seems that he has a painting in the exhibition; I shall look out for it, and give you my opinions about it.

The Fantin is decidedly weak. It is reminiscent of Veronese, and certainly has a certain charm of colour when looked at closely. Because it is hung so high the insignificance of the composition is accented. It is a portrait of a woman, surrounded by others in costumes à la Titian, or à la

43

Veronese, and is called *Le Lever*. The Tissots look quite Chinese, and the Toulmoches are intolerable.

Monet in penury   1869

Economic problems pressed on everybody. Monet was especially hard hit, and had been asking Bazille for help. The latter wrote suggesting work of some other kind. On 25 September 1869 Monet replied rather sharply, although he mellowed at the prospect of getting some wine.

This letter is to tell you that I have not followed your unforgivable advice of walking to Le Havre. I've been a bit happier this month in comparison with the preceding ones, for I'm still in a pretty hopeless state. I've sold a still-life, and I've been able to work a little. But as usual here I'm held up for lack of materials. Happy mortal, you will have stacks of canvases. I alone this year will have done nothing. This makes me angry at everyone; I'm jealous and wicked; furious with everybody. If only I could work, everything would be all right. You tell me that neither fifty francs nor a hundred will get me out of this jam; that's possible, but in that case there's nothing for me to do but bang my head against the wall, for I can't look forward to any immediate windfall, and if all those who spoke to me as you did had each sent me forty or fifty francs I most certainly wouldn't be in this spot. I am re-reading your letter, dear friend. It is certainly very comical, if I didn't know you, I would take it as a joke. You tell me in all seriousness, because that is your opinion, that if you were in my place you would chop wood. Only people in your position believe such things, and if you were in my position you would be even more baffled. It is tougher than you think, and I don't believe that you would cut much wood. No, don't you see that advice is very difficult to give, and, if I may say so without offending you, useless.

All this, however, doesn't change the fact that my troubles probably aren't over. Winter is near, not a good season for the unfortunate. Then comes the Salon. Alas, I shan't be represented there as I haven't done anything. I do have a dream, the swimming pool at La Grenouillère, for which I've done a few bad, rough sketches, but it is a dream. Renoir, who has just spent two months here, also wants to do this painting. Talking of Renoir reminds me that at his brother's house I drank some wine that he had just received from Montpellier, which was awfully good. This also reminds me that it's absurd to have a friend in Montpellier, and not be able to get a shipment of wine from him. Come now, Bazille, this is a time of the year when there should be no shortage of wine in Montpellier. Couldn't you send us a barrel, the price of which you can deduct from the money you still owe me? At least we would drink water less often, and it would be cheap. You can't realize what a favour that would be to us, because it's a big expense, and I would be much obliged to you.

An English refuge   1870-71

The Franco-Prussian war of 1870, and the disturbances which followed it, drove many artists out of Paris. Monet recalled the time in his 1900 interview (see p. 16).

War was declared on Germany. I had just married. We went over to London, where I met Pissarro and Bonvin. I endured much poverty, for my works were not popular there. Life was difficult. Quite accidentally I met Daubigny, who had formerly shown some interest in me. He was then painting scenes on the Thames, which were having considerable success. He was moved by my distress. 'I know what you need,' he said, 'I'm going to get you a dealer.' The next day I met M. Durand-Ruel.

Durand-Ruel in London   1870-71

Paul Durand-Ruel (1831-1922) was one of the most adventurous dealers of his time, and had vigorously supported Corot, Courbet and the Barbizon School at a time when they were not very popular. Settling temporarily in London, he opened a gallery at 168 New Bond Street, where he sold predominantly French paintings through a largely fictitious 'Society of French Artists'. He included works by Monet and by Pissarro, who had arrived in Paris from the Virgin Islands in 1855. In the art world Pissarro had become, and was to remain, an ever-active catalyst. In London he was in constant contact with Durand-Ruel and Monet. (But Durand-Ruel is wrong in saying that Monet introduced him to Pissarro; it seems to have been Durand-Ruel himself who put the two painters in touch with each other.)

The superb exhibitions organized during the five years I ran this gallery, which housed a considerable number of the masterpieces of some of our most illustrious painters, attracted a great deal of attention. The press was most favourable, and art critics published long and flattering articles in their magazines. A number of collectors, Messrs Murietta, Forbes, Ionides, Mieville, Louis Hutts and others from London and Glasgow, became my clients and made purchases at prices which were very satisfying for me, but which bore no relation to those which they would fetch today. The painter Legros, who had been living in London for some time, was very helpful in this context.

My intention had been to bring my wife and children to London as soon as I had settled down here, and to accommodate them I rented a small house with a garden in Brompton Crescent near the South Kensington Museum, and my wife joined me there with our four eldest children, leaving my little Jeanne with her nurse in my pa-

rents' home at Périgueux. Their journey to London was not an easy one, as the direct railway line had been cut at various points, but all ended well, and I was delighted to greet my family at the station. We lived in this modest house till the end of September, and had a very happy time there compared with that which we would have led had we been living in Paris during the siege and the Commune.

I had brought with me a number of remarkable works by all our best painters, which I was able to present in a number of exhibitions which are still remembered by all men of good taste living in London, and which greatly helped to reveal to the English the talent of our great artists. The money which I made from these enabled me to pay all my expenses, support my family, as well as some painters who had taken refuge in London, and also to send some money to Millet, who had taken refuge in Cherbourg, to J. Dupré, who was at Cayeux, to Fromentin at La Rochelle, to Diaz at Bonvin and to Van Marcke at Brussels. For their part they sent me paintings. Millet especially, who without me would have been entirely without resources, sent me many paintings which he had been able to produce at Cherbourg, and for which he asked ridiculously low prices, adding that if I found them too high I could reduce them. He was greatly surprised when, on the contrary, I increased them . . . .

1868 1st official guide for art dealers

Continued on p. 65.

45

PISSARRO *Lower Norwood under Snow* 1870

PISSARRO *The Crystal Palace* 1871

MONET *The Thames below Westminster* 1871

London

MONET *View of Green Park* 1871

Monet and Pissarro, living in obscurity in London for the duration of the Franco-Prussian War and the Commune, captured in very different ways the air and light of the mid-Victorian city and its suburbs.

Colour

This sequence of details in colour affords an opportunity to look for some pointers to the nature of Impressionism itself. Manet never exhibited under the Impressionist banner; but his willingness to use informal brushwork, and prismatic and often complementary colour in shadow, brought him closer and closer to the core of the Impressionist aim. That aim, which was itself at least partly the result of his own stimulus, was the painting of light and atmosphere. The beer carried by his Waitress is a beacon, concentrating the light in the painting. 'When the sun lets certain parts of a landscape appear soft,' wrote Sisley, 'it lifts others into sharp relief. These effects of light, which have an almost material expression in nature, must be rendered in material fashion on the canvas.' Monet's desire to paint 'the beauty of the air in which . . . objects are located' leads him to create an all-over effect with small brushstrokes. 'The eye', said Pissarro, 'should not be fixed on one spot but should take in everything, observing the reflections which the colours produce on their surroundings.' Renoir's nude becomes part of the dappled woodland light, and the grass on which Monet's turkeys feed takes on a bluish tinge under the skies of Northern France. Renoir's future wife Aline reflects and adorns the convivial shade of a lunch-party at Bougival; and in his very late Bathers the warm tones of a fertile Provençal scene are echoed in the models' ruddy skin with its complementary hints of green, so that they become symbolic representatives of a generous Nature.

In the atmosphere of her sunlit dining-room Berthe Morisot places an almost too pretty parlourmaid; looked at closely, the brushwork is more restless and summary even than in Monet's La Grenouillère. Mary Cassatt shared the Impressionist knack of making a figure – without losing its individuality – part of a scene, but her subtle colour recalls above all that of her friend Degas. The bonnets in his At the Milliner's, with their use of a pink-mauve contrast to create a layered space, are among the supreme examples of the Impressionist love of virtuosity in still-life, which was part of the legacy of Manet's Emile Zola.

At the end of the Impressionist era, Degas and Monet with their failing sight, and Renoir with his crippled hand, took Impressionism into a new period of undiminished vitality and originality. Monet chose the skies and times of day when he could see best for the magnificent all-over patterns of his late Waterlilies – a restriction which produces a completely different reflection of sky from the painting of Red Boats of forty years before. The tonality has shifted from reflections dominated by sharp greenery to a complex interaction of ochre, pink and magenta. In late Degas the forms become broad, almost crude. One senses the fascination of painting massive shapes, but also the perennial Impressionist love of the overall optical impression.

Everything holds together in clear, masterly, striking tones, so realistic that the eye forgets the multiplicity of objects and sees only one harmonious unity. I do not speak of the still-lifes – the accessories, and the books scattered on the table. Manet is a past master . . . . It is all a marvel of skill.

Emile Zola

MANET *Emile Zola* 1868

PISSARRO *Factory near Pontoise* 1873

SISLEY *The Seine at Port-Marly, the Sand Heaps* 1875

MONET *La Grenouillère* 1869

First of all, of course, there may seem to be some difficulty in distinguishing between the works of Monet, those of Sisley, and the style of the last of them, Pissarro. After a little study, however, one comes to realize that M. Monet is the most skilful and the most daring, M. Sisley the most harmonious, and the most timid, M. Pissarro the most direct and naive.

Their pictures are done in a singularly bright tonal range.... Their canvases... are windows opening on the joyous countryside, on rivers full of pleasure boats stretching into the distance, on a sky which shines with light mists, on the outdoor life, panoramic and charming.   Armand Silvestre

He loves to juxtapose on the lightly ruffled surface of the water the multicoloured reflections of
the setting sun, of brightly coloured boats, of
changing clouds.... The image of the shore is
mutable – the houses are broken up as they are in
a jigsaw puzzle.   Armand Silvestre

Surely broken brushwork and violet shadows
lead to only one possible goal: – the prismatic
colours.   George Moore

MONET *Red Boats at Argenteuil c.* 1875

While I could no longer go on playing about with shades or landscape in delicate colours, I could see as well as ever when it came to vivid colours, isolated in a mass of dark tones.... I said to myself, as I made sketches, that a sense of general impressions captured at the times of day when I had the best chances of seeing correctly would not be without interest.   Claude Monet

MONET *Waterlilies, Sunset, Left-hand Section* n.d.

His celebrated group of life-size turkeys . . . the high grass that the turkeys are nibbling is flooded with sunlight so intense that for a moment the illusion is complete. George Moore

Cézanne's landscapes . . . grandiose and yet so painted, so supple. Why? Sensation is there.
Camille Pissarro

MONET *The Turkeys* 1877

CÉZANNE *Le Château de Médan c.* 1880

Duranty . . . had constituted himself champion of the 'New Painting' though his praise was not without reservations. He complained of Cézanne, for instance, that he painted with a bricklayer's trowel.   Ambroise Vollard

One might say that he [Cézanne] wishes to restore intact to each object, in its primitive force unattenuated by the practices of art, its true and essential radiance.   André Mellerio

CÉZANNE *Still-life with Soup Tureen*

His celebrated group of life-size turkeys . . . the high grass that the turkeys are nibbling is flooded with sunlight so intense that for a moment the illusion is complete. George Moore

Cézanne's landscapes . . . grandiose and yet so painted, so supple. Why? Sensation is there.
Camille Pissarro

MONET *The Turkeys* 1877

CÉZANNE *Le Château de Médan* c. 1880

Duranty . . . had constituted himself champion of the 'New Painting' though his praise was not without reservations. He complained of Cézanne, for instance, that he painted with a bricklayer's trowel. Ambroise Vollard

One might say that he [Cézanne] wishes to restore intact to each object, in its primitive force unattenuated by the practices of art, its true and essential radiance. André Mellerio

CÉZANNE *Still-life with Soup Tureen*

As to the details of the picture, nothing should be absolutely fixed, in order that we may feel that the bright gleam which lights the picture, or the diaphanous shadow which veils it, are only seen in passing, and just when the spectator beholds the represented subject, which being composed of a harmony of reflected and ever-changing lights, cannot be supposed always to look the same, but palpitates with movement, light, and life.

Stéphane Mallarmé

MANET *Waitress Serving Bocks* 1879

poet to
attempting what
makes these
paintings
avant
garde

She is called Berthe Morizot [sic], and she makes an interesting spectacle. With her, feminine grace is retained amidst the outpourings of a mind in delirium.   Albert Wolff

Morisot seems to paint with her nerves on edge, providing a few scanty traces to create complete, disquieting evocations.   Octave Mirbeau

Try to explain to M. Renoir that a woman's torso is not a mass of decomposing flesh with those purplish green stains which denote a state of complete putrefaction in a corpse.   Albert Wolff

There was a half-length nude picture of a girl. How the round fresh breasts palpitate in the light! Such a glorious glow of whiteness was never observed before.   George Moore

MORISOT *In the Dining-room* 1886

RENOIR *Nude in Sunlight* 1876

A smiling woman, dressed in rose coloured clothes, sits in a chair, holding in her gloved hands a cup of tea . . . . These works accentuate the same note of tenderness, and exude a delicate fragrance of Parisian elegance.   J.-K. Huysmans

CASSATT *The Cup of Tea* 1879

The shifting shimmer of gleam and shadow which
the changing reflected lights, themselves influenced by every neighbouring thing, cast upon
each advancing or departing figure, and the
fleeting combinations in which these dissimilar
reflections form one harmony or many, such are
the favourite effects of Renoir – nor can we wonder that this infinite complexity of execution induces him to seek more hazardous success in
things widely opposed to nature.

Stéphane Mallarmé

RENOIR *Luncheon of the Boating Party* 1880-81

The naked woman has become impossible in
modern art; it required Degas' genius to infuse
new life into the well-worn theme.... With cynicism Degas has rendered the nude again an artistic possibility. George Moore

'I take all the colour out of [my pastels] that I can,
by putting them in the sun.'
'But what do you use, then, to get colours of such
brightness?'
'Opaque colour, Monsieur.'
Edgar Degas, to Ambroise Vollard

DEGAS *After the Bath* 1895-98

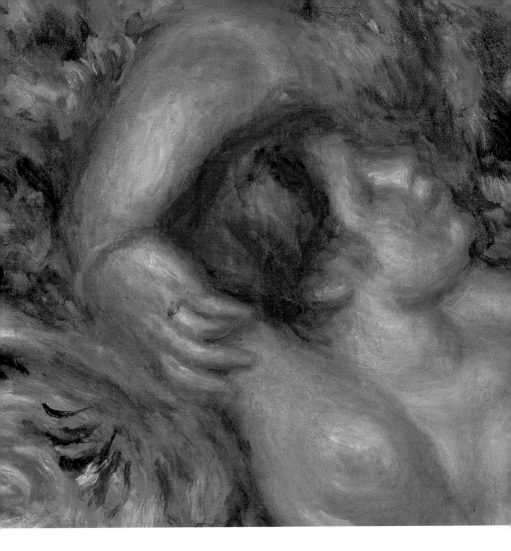

I have a horror of the word 'flesh' which has become so over-used.... What I love is skin: a young girl's skin that is pink, and shows that she has a good circulation. But above all else I love serenity.

Auguste Renoir

Young people today who prefer the later work of Degas and Renoir hardly realize how much of its looser character was due to their failing sight.

William Rothenstein

RENOIR *The Large Bathers* 1917

His skill as a colourist, and as one who can suggest – we can hardly say who can elaborately
paint – texture, is shown in another design, the
astonishing picture of two young women trying
on bonnets in a milliner's shop. Half of the design
is occupied by the milliner's table on which lies a
store of her finery. Silks and feathers, satin and
straw, are indicated swiftly, decisively, with the
most brilliant touch.   Frederick Wedmore

DEGAS *At the Milliner's* 1882

Continued from p. 45.

It was in my London gallery that, at the beginning of 1871 I met Monet, whose works in the Salon had already attracted my attention, but whom I had not actually met as he was hardly ever in Paris. He was brought to me by Daubigny, who had a high opinion of his talent. I immediately bought all the paintings he produced in London. In his turn Monet introduced me to Pissarro, who was also in London, and had recently produced some most interesting works. Monet's paintings cost me 300 francs each, those of Pissarro 200 francs. This was the price I continued to pay them for several years. Nobody else would have been so generous, as I had to sell them at 100 or even 50 francs, and even less.

Shortly afterwards I started to introduce some of their works into my exhibitions, and did in fact sell a few, though with great difficulty.

Renoir and the Commune   *1871*

Not all the Impressionists left Paris. Renoir was there during the war and the subsequent civil disturbances of the Commune, and managed to continue his landscape painting for reasons which Paul Valéry explained in an article first published in La Revue Hebdomadaire *on 2 January 1920.*

About the middle of the year 1869 he went sketching in the forest of Fontainebleau. One day he suddenly realized that he was being watched. On turning round, rather angrily, he confronted a bearded gentleman, leaning on his stick, who bowed politely and asked if he could watch him painting. It was difficult to refuse.

When Renoir had finished and packed up his kit, the man began to follow him as he went away. He persisted in this, despite the painter's obvious annoyance, and it seemed as though he wanted to say something. At last Renoir broke out, 'Look, Monsieur, which way are you going? Do you want me to guide you?'

'I do,' the man replied, 'but I didn't like to ask you. I am looking for the road that *doesn't* lead to Mazas.'

'To Mazas,' said Renoir uneasily, conscious of how lonely the place was, and fearing for his watch.

'Yes,' said the man, 'I was sentenced to six months yesterday morning. I write for Rochefort's paper [a strongly republican publication]. They're after me, and I don't want to spend this fine summer in the Imperial gaols. I've managed to get this far, but I can't stay under cover for ever. I saw you coming some time ago, and deciding where you were going to sketch, and so I thought, painters are decent fellows. He must know the area well. So I've been waiting for a chance to ask for your advice.'

Renoir had a resourceful mind. In classical times he would have been known as the Ulysses of painting; a smile crept over his face as an idea occurred to him.

'Ever dabbled with the brush?' he asked his journalist follower.

'A bit, when I was twelve.'

'Anyway,' Renoir continued, 'it doesn't make much difference. If I were you, I'd get hold of a box of paints, rent a room in Barbizon, and spend the days sitting in the forest sketching, and smoking cigarettes. There's not a policeman in the world who'd dream of coming to look here.'

The man brightened up immediately. He gripped Renoir by both hands, and assuring him of his eternal gratitude, made him promise that they would meet again, and before making off into the undergrowth, insisted on giving him his card on which was written 'Raoul Rigault, Correspondent for *La Marseillaise*'. 'Never heard of him,' thought Renoir.

Came the war, and then the Commune. The latter coincided with the arrival of spring. Renoir, who adored his work, and managed to make a living out of it, felt a wild longing for the countryside, and an urgent need to paint a few landscapes which he could sell. But the gates of the city were well guarded. From outside the Versailles troops, and from within those of the Commune, had put an interdict on Nature. Where was there to set up an easel? How could a painter manage not to look like a spy, even if he did manage to slip past the sentries and the barricades and set up his easel in the no man's land between the two rival camps?

Renoir had to make do with what the parks offered in the· way of spring. One morning he was walking along the rue de Castiglione on his way to the Tuileries to watch the young chestnut leaves sprouting – his heart in the woods of Meudon but his eye, as ever, alert to the instantaneous dialogue between light and objects – when a photographer's shop window caught his attention.

How good photographs were during the Second Empire, and even for some time after! They had not yet started to ape the misty charms of a charcoal sketch or those of lithography, but were simply photographs, delicate and clear with lovely sepia depths; and they did not fade.

On display were photographs of all the leading officials of the Commune; Rossel, Dombrowski, Ferre – and amongst them was the all-powerful *procureur* [public prosecutor], Raoul Rigault. Renoir recognized his old friend from the forest. What a marvellous opportunity to obtain a simple permit to go out into the open country! He stood for a moment thinking the idea over, and then, with youthful energy, he set out to follow it up. Turning left along the rue de Rivoli, just past the Châtelet, he made for his destination.

Entering the Préfecture de Police, he made his way upstairs. A resplendent doorkeeper, whose function and majestic appearance might well have remained unchanged since the heyday of the Empire,

ushered him into the waiting-room. It was crowded with nervous petitioners of every kind. The doorkeeper vanished, taking with him Rigault's card given to Renoir in the forest of Fontainebleau, on which the painter had scribbled his name. He reappeared. 'Citizen Renoir,' he shouted, in a voice which still had an Imperial ring about it.

When Renoir used to describe his own entry, he would say that never before in his life had he had such a reception. Rigault, sashed and booted, surrounded by a numerous staff, welcomed him with open arms. He introduced him as 'the citizen painter, who saved my life' to all present. 'The *Marseillaise*,' he commanded, 'for Citizen Renoir.' After the *Marseillaise* came the toasts in champagne. To the Commune, To Painting, To Citizen Renoir .... But neither the toasts, nor the cheers were enough to make our citizen artist forget his vernal mission. In between one glass and another he gently gave *M. le Procureur* to understand that a triumphal welcome was not exactly the thing he had come for. Rigault, no doubt expecting some request in proportion to his vast powers, and wanting nothing better than to give his visitor an indication of their extent, lavishly offered him his favours. 'Anything you like, dear citizen; all you have to do is to ask me.'

It came as a surprise to him when Renoir explained how much he would like to have a *laisser-passer*, which would allow him, without let or hindrance, to go and paint a few studies on the slopes of the fortifications. When Renoir left, he had in his possession a marvellous document, expressed in terms highly laudatory of his talents and his civic spirit. All the gates of Paris were opened through its powerful agency, stamped as it was with all the seals of the Prefecture, and adorned with all the requisite signatures and flourishes.

Degas in America   1872

Edgar Degas, who had been trained in the style of Ingres, had met Manet in the 1860s, and was gradually drawn into the circle of artists who were more concerned with aspects of contemporary life than with the accepted subjects of academic art. He became one of a group including Fantin-Latour, Renoir, Zola, Bazille, Nadar, Monet and Pissarro, who met in the Café Guerbois or (later) the Nouvelle-Athènes. During the war he fought in the artillery with the rank of Captain, and on demobilization started his series of ballet-pictures. In 1872, at the age of thirty-eight, he went to America to visit his brother René, who was in the cotton trade in New Orleans. When he was there he wrote a number of letters to friends in Europe, including the following to the Danish painter Lorentz Frölich, which was written in the November of that year.

The *Scotia* on which I travelled is an English boat, fast and safe. It got us here (I am with my brother René) in ten days, actually twelve, from Liverpool to New York, 'The Empire City'. It was a rather unfortunate journey. I couldn't speak English – I still can't – and on English soil, even when it's on the sea – there is a coldness, and a dislike of ordinary social conventions that you have already experienced.

New York is a huge city, a huge port. The citizens are very conscious of the water. They even describe going to Europe as crossing over the water. They are an entirely new people; they have forgotten their English origins even more than I expected.

Four days' journey by train eventually got us here [New Orleans]. Borrow an atlas from your dear little daughter, and look at the distance. I'm fatter now than when I left. The air, there is nothing but air. What new things I have seen, what ideas for paintings they have put in my mind! But I've already given them up, and decided I must religiously cultivate my own particular bent.

Art does not extend itself, it just abridges itself. And if you insist on comparisons at any price, I could say to you that to get good fruits you have to use an espalier. One spends the whole of one's life with open arms and an open mouth to assimilate what is happening, what is around you, and to live on it.

Have you read the *Confessions* of Jean-Jacques Rousseau? You almost certainly have. Do you remember his way of describing the real depth of his humour when he retired to the island in the middle of the Swiss lake of Saint-Pierre (it is towards the end of the book), and how he feels that he had examined everything without being conscious of it, that he espoused undertakings which would take ten years, and abandoned them without regret at the end of ten minutes? That is precisely where I am now. Everything here fascinates me; I stare at everything, and shall describe it all to you exactly when I come back. Nothing delights me so much as the Negresses of all shades, carrying small white children in their arms; they look so white, in front of white houses with their pillars of wickerwork like wood, in gardens full of orange trees; women in white muslin standing in front of their houses, the steamboats with two funnels each as high as factory chimneys; the fruit sellers with their stalls full and overflowing, and the contrast between the business offices with their bustle and order and this immense, black, animal vitality. And the lovely women of white blood, and the beautiful quadroons, and the statuesque Negresses.

I am amassing ideas which would take me ten years to realize. I shall abandon them in six weeks' time, without regret, to get back home again, and never to leave it.

I thank you a hundred times, my dear friend, for your letters and your friendship. They have meant so much to me when I've been so far away.

My eyes are much better. It is true that I am not doing much work, although what I am doing are rather difficult jobs. They are portraits of my family, and I have to make them suit family tastes, which means doing them in impossible light, and in a state of irritation, as the models, though fond of me, are a little too casual, and don't take me seriously because I am a member of the family, their nephew or cousin. I have just made a mess of a large pastel, to my intense annoyance. I hope if I have the time, to bring back some rough sketches, but only for myself, for my own room. One can't hover between the art of Paris and of Louisiana; that would end up as something for *Le Monde Illustré*. Another thing is that it needs a long stay to give you the manners of a people – and in that consists their charm. The instantaneous impression is what counts, and that is photography: nothing more.

Degas on the view from New Orleans 1873

Degas' relationship with the Impressionists was always a little ambiguous. At heart he saw himself as a disciple of Ingres, rejected the 'romanticism' of his fellows, and though courted by other members of his standing, both financial and artistic (though the former was to decline after his brother's bankruptcy), was not partial to the idea of artistic groups. On 18 February 1873 he wrote from New Orleans on paper headed 'De Gas Frères' to his friend the painter James Tissot, then living in London, giving him news of the Cotton Buyers' Office which he hoped to sell through Agnew's Manchester branch (for obvious reasons) and also enlarging upon the European art scene and his view of his own career.

Tissot, my dear friend, I had intended replying to your nice letter in person. I should have been in London or Paris round about 15 January (such distance has become immaterial to me; no distance must be consi-

dered great unless it is the ocean). But I'm still here, and shall be so till March. Yesterday my trunks and Achilles were ready, but there was a hitch which delayed everything. It's just as easy to miss the train here as it is at Passy. The *St Laurent* is leaving without us.

Having wasted time in the family trying to produce portraits under the worst possible conditions, I am concentrating on a fairly strong picture, which is destined for Agnew, and which he should sell in Manchester, for any cotton spinner who wants to have a painter should select me: *Intérieur d'un bureau d'acheteurs de coton à Nlle. Orléans, Cotton Buyers' Office.*

It contains about 15 individual figures crowded around a table, covered with the precious stuff, and two men, one leaning, and the other half sitting on it. They are the buyer and a broker discussing a sample. A vital picture if ever there were one, and I think from a better hand than many others. I am preparing another less complicated version, better artistically, where the people are all in summer clothes, the walls are white, and there is a sea of cotton on the table. If Agnew takes both from me, all the better. I do not, however, want to give up the Paris plan. In the fortnight that I intend remaining here I shall finish this picture, but it will not be possible for me to bring it with me. A canvas, hardly dry, shut up for a long time, away from light and air would, as you know, be changed into chrome-yellow no. 3. So I shall not be able to bring it to London myself or have it sent there before about April. Until then, preserve the good will of these gentlemen for me. In Manchester there is a wealthy spinner, who has a famous collection. A fellow like that would suit me perfectly, and Agnew even better. But let's be cautious about it, and not count our chickens too soon.

You seem to be getting on like a house on fire! Nine hundred pounds for a picture! That's a fortune! But why not? What a lot of good this absence from Paris has done me! In any case I have made the most of it. I have made certain good resolutions which (don't laugh) I honestly feel capable of carrying out. The exhibition at the Royal Academy will have to do without me, and I shall be more upset than it will. Millais does not understand my little Anglo-American excursion. Anyway we'll manage all right despite this. How much I want to tell you about my art! If I could have another twenty years' time to work I could produce things that would endure. Am I to end up like that, after racking my brains like somebody possessed, and after having experienced so many ways of seeing and doing? Remember the art of Le Nain, and of medieval France. Our race has something bold and simple to offer. The naturalist movement will draw in a manner worthy of the great masters of the past, and then its strength will be recognized. English art, which appeals so greatly to us, often seems just to be concerned with exploiting some trick. We can do better than that, and can still be just as strong.

I really have a lot of stuff in my head. I wish there were insurance companies who dealt in assets such as this, as there are for so many things here. That's one bale I would certainly insure. This youthful headpiece of mine is really my greatest asset.

I am very much afraid that Deschamps did not succeed in selling any of my pictures. From Hirsch I heard that Fantin

DEGAS *Cotton Buyer's Office* 1873

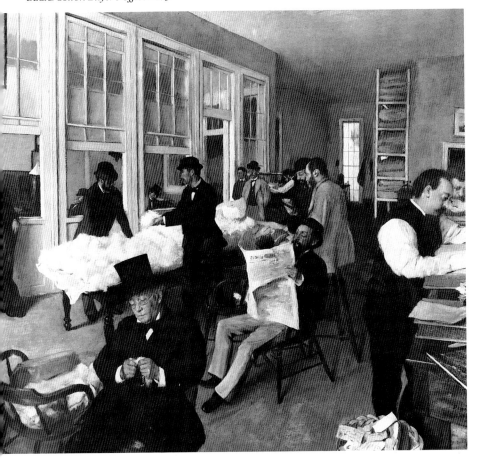

Latour's picture *Les Parnassiens* was sold in London. A very good thing too; he has skill and talent, has Fantin, but too little taste, too little variety, too few ideas. You keep on saying that in London we could do very well and that there's a place for us. I do believe you, but in my opinion we should go over there to sweep the said place a little, and clean it by hand.

What lovely things I could have done, and that quickly, if the bright daylight had not been so unbearable to me. I cannot go to Louisiana and keep my eyes open all the time. And yet I kept them sufficiently half-open to see my fill. The women are pretty, and unusually graceful. I have not had time to explore this black world completely, but there are some real treasures to be painted and drawn in these forests of ebony. I shall find it very surprising to be living amongst only white people once again in Paris. In any case I adore silhouettes, and these silhouettes walk.

Goodbye, see you soon. The moment I get to Paris I shall write. I intend to take a French boat, which goes to Brest. If I take an English one, we dock at Liverpool. In which case I shall see you in London.

The Café Guerbois c. *1873*

If Impressionism had a birthplace it was the Café Guerbois, where between 1869 and 1873 Manet, as it were, held court. There were regular meetings on Thursdays, but throughout the week Guillemet, Degas, Renoir, Cézanne, Monet, Pissarro, and Sisley were regular visitors, in addition to fringe figures such as Nadar, Fantin, Stevens, Bracquemond, Astruc, Duranty, Constantin Guys, and the writer Armand Silvestre. In the latter's Au Pays du Souvenir *(Paris 1892) he recounts his memories of the café in chapter XIII, though the unwary must note that there are two chapters with that numeration in the book.*

The Café Guerbois, which definitely deserves recognition as one of the leading literary cafés, is situated at the beginning of the avenue de Clichy, next door to the legendary restaurant of Père Lathuille. I know of few other places which are so thronged with passers-by at certain times of the day, when people are going to work and when they are coming home again. It is a working-class area, a world in which people, in Rabelais' words, 'scratch a poor living as best they may'. On fine summer evenings, as the sun is going down, and especially on Saturdays, it becomes a veritable fairground of people elated by the anticipation of Sunday as a day of rest. Beautiful bare-headed girls – for the girls of Montmartre are, by what remote strain of ancestry I know not, sisters to those of Athens – walk up and down in happy, carefree groups, their faces aglow with laughter, flowers hanging from their lips. All the artists of the quartier are familiar with this spectacle, and come here to choose models. Beauty is to be found here more frequently than virtue. But what a superb carriage these promenading girls have – a combination of classical dignity and Parisian gracefulness. And what a babble of fresh young voices, harshened though they are by the local accent.

I was attracted to the area shortly after the war by the combination of its material and intellectual advantages. Paris, still breathless from the final tremors of civil war, was yearning for tranquillity and forgetfulness of the past. Flowers were already beginning to grow from the blackened ruins, and to thrust their heads up amongst the blood-stained cobbles. Inanimate matter, no more than men, is not made to suffer protracted grief. It is true that one thought a bit about those who had been proscribed by the government, but youth, infatuated with the sunshine and spring, had reasserted its rights. Only philosophers wondered how long the shock of this recent upheaval would last. For, underneath these surfaces, which had been so rapidly calmed, like the waters of a

MANET *The Dead Toreador* c.1864

lake after a great storm, there seethed a ferment of hate and anger, and deep down in mysterious depths bubbled mad desires for revenge and expiation. What would happen to rational thought condemned to survive in these troubled waters? Would French art and its hallowed interests long survive this catastrophe? Uncertainty about all this exercised us when faced with the apparent indifference of a populace whose recent rebellion had been too violent to be so suddenly appeased . . . .

What I am trying to do is to capture glimpses of profiles, simple sketches which set out to give true impressions which are lifelike. I leave to others the task of judging Manet as a painter; his work is in any case sufficiently important for critics still to concern themselves with it. Recently indeed, at the Salon we have seen an ex-student of the French School at Rome, and not one of the less remarkable ones, M. Besnard, find his own road to Damascus on the route traced by the painter of *Olympia*. Manet was not the leader of a school – nobody ever had a temperament less suited for such a role, for I have never known anyone so free of the least touch of solemnity – but, without attempting to assess the full range of his influence, it is clearly considerable. He was one of the first to brighten the French palette and bring light back into it. Less intense, less magisterial than Baudelaire, but with a

much surer taste, he nevertheless affirmed in painting, what the writer had done in poetry, a sense of modernity, which though it was latent in many minds, had not till then seen the light of day. Both had the same horror of mythology and ancient legends, both the same passion for vitality, even at the expense of correctness. The name of Velázquez has often been cast in Manet's face, but those who do so can have little knowledge either of Velázquez or of Manet. *The Dead Toreador* is a miracle, but not the most typical of Manet's works. Those who are devoted to his real style and spirit will find them in his scenes of Parisian life, and his still-lifes, which I know are comparable to those of Chardin.

This revolutionary – the word is not too strong – had the manners of a perfect gentleman. With his often gaudy trousers, his short jacket, his flat-brimmed hat set on the back of his head, always wearing immaculate suede gloves, Manet did not look like a Bohemian, and in fact had nothing of the Bohemian in him. He was a kind of dandy. Blond, with a sparse, narrow beard which was forked at the end, he had in the extraordinary vivacity of his gaze, in the mocking expression on his lips – his mouth was narrow-lipped, his teeth irregular and uneven – a very strong dose of the Parisian street urchin. Although very generous, and very good-hearted, he was deliberately iro-

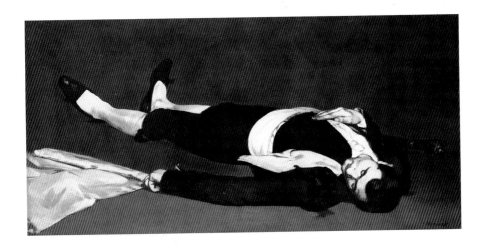

nic in conversation, and often cruel. He had a marvellous command of the annihilating and devastating phrase. But at the same time his expression was benevolent, the underlying idea always absolutely right. One of these, which would not have seemed out of place in the writings of La Rochefoucauld or Rivarol, comes back to me. Paul Baudry had just been exhibiting at the Ecole des Beaux-Arts the cartoons for his large figures in the decorations for the Opéra. I can assure you that they were very roughly handled in the discussions which took place in the meetings at the Café Guerbois. There was general agreement about their lack of personality – as though having had access to fine models was not enough – and the fact that entire pieces of the work were based on celebrated figures of the past. It was a real demolition job, in which the most virulent language was used. Manet said nothing, but nobody took his silence for approval. He was just waiting. Then everybody, having fiercely criticized the work, felt obliged to add: 'Even so, you have to have what it takes to do work like that.'

'One always has what it takes to fail,' said Manet. You must admit that this remark was both naive and profound . . . .

Amongst this group of painters and writers, brought together in time of crisis like sheep seeking refuge from the storm, one man attracted my attention particularly by the particularly attractive strangeness of his appearance. Tall, thin, a huge black fleece of hair adorning a wide and tormented-looking face; eyes like half-extinguished embers, since they were both black and glowing; an adolescent's beard which he kept twirling between his fingers, which were slender, intelligent, and adroit at the same time. A cheap hat adorned his head, seeming often enough to be riding on the crest of his billowing locks. His clothes were shabby, with a large cravat tied loosely round his neck. His shirt was unstarched, the cuffs adorned with a flurry of lace which hid the hands of a marquis. I have forgotten

to mention a pipe, small, black, well-seasoned, which never left his mouth, and was always giving out great clouds of smoke. But this is a useless exercise. If you really want to know what he looked like go and see Desboutin's own self-portrait in drypoint in the avenue de l'Opéra, a portrait large in scale, and probably the most marvellous drypoint etching which French art has ever produced.

Amongst the other figures to be detected in the gaslight of the Café Guerbois against the clicking of billiard balls on the table, I would like to pick out the painter Degaz [sic], who never used to stay seated for long; Degaz, with his very Parisian, very original looks, infinitely mocking and witty. It was he who, with Manet, first introduced Desboutin to us. The contemporary school owes a great deal to Degaz, and even the traditionalists, though grudgingly, have to admire the incontestable qualities of his draughtsmanship and the quality of his painting. These cannot be denied by anyone, not even by the most perfervid disciple of the academic tradition. He is a parlour revolutionary, the ironic modesty of his appearance saving him from the hate which firebrands draw on themselves . . . .

I know of no character more calm than that of Fantin-Latour, who was also a member of our circle, with his large child-like head and his passion for taciturnity. Glory came to him late, but when it did it was well-founded. He always seemed to be relaxing from the task he had performed during the day. Tall, gaunt, rather pale, with a quick darting eye, such at this time was the Impressionist Renoir who was also a formidable worker, and that in clear bright tonalities. His painting certainly did not resemble that of Fantin-Latour, but at the same time it had ties with it because of the particular way it wove the tones together, and blended them in fine threads like a textile. I have seen some marvellous pastels by him of nudes pulsating with the dazzling radiance of life itself.

MANET *The Café Guerbois* 1869

Café Life

*Places of endless and earnest conversation,
the artists' cafés provided scenes from 'modern life' such as Baudelaire had recom-
mended to painters.*

MANET *Le Bon Bock
– the Engraver Bellot
at the Café Guerbois*
1873

PHOTOGRAPH OF
THE NOUVELLE-ATHÈNES

DEGAS *Absinthe* 1876

MANET *George Moore in the Café* c.1879

Café Life

The Nouvelle-Athènes, in the Place Pigalle in Montmartre, succeeded the Guerbois as a meeting-place for painters, prostitutes, aesthetes and drunkards. Manet's view of the engraver Bellot (previous page), and Degas' of Marcellin Desboutin, posing with the actress Ellen Andrée for a scene (Absinthe) that almost looks like a warning against the Demon Drink, convey opposite extremes of the café atmosphere.

DEGAS *The Nouvelle-Athènes* 1878

DEGAS *Women on a Café Terrace* 1877

MANET *At the Café* 1878

MANET *At the Café* c.1880

The commercial amusements of the ville lumière *were and are legendary. Manet and Degas loved scenes of artificial light and public gaiety; unlike Renoir, they never showed them without their darker side, a hint of loneliness.*

Music and entertainment

MANET *Café du Théâtre-Français* 1881

DEGAS *Concert at the Ambassadeurs* c. 1875-7

Manet and Degas contrasted c. 1873

In the 1870s young George Moore, fresh from Dublin and Oscott, was living in Paris, frequenting artistic and literary circles, and creating within himself the resources which were to make him a novelist of distinction, an art critic of sensibility. In his Confessions of a Young Man, *published in 1888, he recorded the contrasting effects made on him by Manet and Degas, whom he used to meet frequently in the Nouvelle-Athènes, which had been popularized by the writer and painter Marcellin Desboutin. They had come to prefer this place to the Café Guerbois, which still remained the haunt of Monet, Sisley, Cézanne and Pissarro.*

At that moment the glass door of the café grated upon the sanded floor and Manet entered. Although by birth and art essentially a Parisian, there was something in his appearance and manner of speaking that often suggested an Englishman. Perhaps it was his dress – his clean-cut clothes and figure. That figure! those square shoulders that swaggered as he went across the room, and the thin waist; and that face, the beard and nose, satyr-like shall I say? No, for I would evoke an idea of beauty of line united to that of intellectual expression – frank words, frank passions in his convictions, loyal and simple phrases, clear as well-water, sometimes a little hard, sometimes as they flowed away, bitter, but at the fountainhead sweet and full of light. He sits next to Degas, that round-shouldered man in suit of pepper-and-salt. There is nothing very trenchantly French about him either, except the large neck-tie; his eyes are hard, and his words are sharp, ironical, cynical. These two men are the leaders of the Impressionist School. Their friendship has been jarred by inevitable rivalry. 'Degas was painting *Semiramis* when I was painting modern Paris,' says Manet. 'Manet is in despair because he cannot paint atrocious pic-

tures like Durand, and be fêted and decorated; he is an artist, not by inclination, but by force. He is a galley-slave chained to the oar,' says Degas. Different, too, are their methods of work. Manet paints his whole picture from Nature, trusting his instinct to lead him aright through the devious labyrinth of selection. Nor does his instinct ever fail him, there is a vision in his eyes which he calls Nature, and which he paints unconsciously as he digests his food, thinking and declaring vehemently that the artist should not seek a synthesis, but should paint merely what he sees. This extraordinary oneness of Nature and artistic vision does not exist in Degas, and even his portraits are composed from drawings and notes.

The new painting: an analysis 1873

In 1873 Durand-Ruel published a Recueil d'estampes, *prints of works of various artists whom he represented, with an introduction by Armand Silvestre, who set out to justify the inclusion of more 'contemporary' artists.*

At this point we come to discuss a group of artists who are even more contemporary, because they are younger – and whom it has been somewhat audacious to represent through several reproductions in this gallery, which is devoted to the authority of famous names. But after all this audacity is completely justified, because we have already been the first to recognize one of the great hopes of modern art, whose works are an investment for the future. First of all of course there may seem to be some difficulty in distinguishing between the works of Monet, those of Sisley, and the style of the last of them, Pissarro. After a little study, however, one comes to realize that M. Monet is the most skilful and the most daring, M. Sisley the most harmonious, and the most timid, M. Pissarro the most direct and naive. These nuances, however, are not our only concern. What is certain is that the painting of these three landscapists bears no resemblance at all to that of the other masters whose work we have been considering, and that we can trace its ancestry to a point which is distant and indirect, except for a closer temporal relationship to the works of M. Manet. It is a form of painting which states its premises with conviction, and a power which imposes upon us the duty of recognizing and defining what one may call its indeterminate direction.

What immediately strikes one when looking at painting of this kind is the immediate caress which the eye receives; above all else it is harmonious, and what really distinguishes it is the simplicity of the means whereby it achieves this harmony. In fact one very quickly discovers that its secret is based on a very fine and exact observation of the relation of one tone to another. In reality it is the scale of tones, reconstructed after the works of the great colourists of the century, a sort of analytical process which does not change the palette into a kind of banal percussion instrument, as one might first be tempted to believe. The meaning of these relationships, in their precise accuracy, is a very special gift, and one which constitutes the real genius of a painter. The art of landscape runs no risks of vulgarity in this sort of study. It receives from it qualities which by their very simplicity are nonetheless rare. When all those who sing out of tune have been banished from the choir, there will be less discord I should imagine. There will even be more room for those who arrive with good voices, and the three artists of whom I am speaking seem to me to have the principal merit of making the use of concert pitch seem commonplace.

It is M. Monet, who by the choice of the subjects themselves, betrays his preoccupations most clearly. He loves to juxtapose on the lightly ruffled surface of the water the multicoloured reflections of the setting sun, of brightly coloured boats, of changing clouds. Metallic tones, given off by the smoothness of the waves which splash over small, even surfaces, are recorded in his works, and the image of the shore is mutable – the houses are broken up as they are in a jigsaw puzzle. This effect, which is absolutely true to experience, and may have been borrowed from the Japanese school, strongly attracts the young painters, who surrender to it absolutely. However, its gains are more real than those of a jigsaw puzzle. The village interiors of M. Pissarro are considerably more complex than one might have expected. Do the painters cancel each other out? Certainly not, since nobody really knows who will insert, in its appropriate place, that stone which each of them contributes to the great edifice of art. This uncertainty gives to art its real unity. Each one has his part to play.

What could help to ensure the eventual success of these young painters is the fact that their pictures are done in a singularly bright tonal range. A blond light pervades them, and everything is gaiety, clarity, spring festivals, golden evenings, or apple trees in blossom – once again an inspiration from Japan. Their canvases, uncluttered, medium in size, are open in the surface they decorate; they are windows opening on the joyous countryside, on rivers full of pleasure boats stretching into the distance, on a sky which shines with light mists, on the outdoor life, panoramic and charming.

On the river

Parisian leisure had another side: the Seine and the leafy suburban resorts (now mostly swallowed up by the growth of the city) where people diverted themselves beside and on the water. Monet had a floating studio when he lived at Argenteuil, and Manet painted him working in the same light-filled setting.

MONET *The Studio Boat* 1876

MONET *Red Boats at Argenteuil* 1875

MANET *Monet Working on his Boat at Argenteuil* 1874

PIETTE *Pissarro at Work* c.1870

RENOIR *Monet Painting in his Garden* 1873

GEORGES MANZANA PISSARRO *Impressionist Picnic* 1881

Outdoor Life

Pissarro's son Georges Manzana has added to the visual record of Impressionists at work by showing, from memory, Guillaumin, Pissarro, Gauguin and M. and Mme Cézanne, all in varying degrees sur le motif. *The industrial background identifies this as a suburban landscape. Ludovic Piette, whose portrait of Pissarro contrasts with Renoir's of Monet, was a rich supporter of Pissarro as well as a painter who showed at the 1877 and 1879 Impressionist exhibitions.*

First English Impressions 1874

Durand-Ruel had been showing occasional works by Impressionists at his gallery at 168 New Bond Street from 1870 onwards. In the spring of 1874 he exhibited works by Manet, Sisley and Pissarro. On 27 April the anonymous art critic of The Times *had this to say about them.*

This exhibition should be visited by all who take an interest in French painting, as it illustrates some phases of the school not represented in the other collections of French paintings now open in London. M. Durand-Ruel . . . is a Frenchman influenced by contemporary French modes in art, and thus secures for some of the more daring and eccentric of these a representation which otherwise they would fail altogether to obtain in London.

There is now rising, or has risen, a recent school of French landscape which has gone as wide off the track of Dupré, Diaz, or their predecessors or Rousseau, as these from the classical landscape, against whose conventions they rose in revolt. If this latest sect of French landscapists have any prophet, it ought to be Courbet. It is difficult to see how its partisans can claim affinity with Corot, although his pictures usually hold a prominent part in exhibitions where the latter style appears in the ascendant. But Corot's present pictures – the work, be it remembered of his old age – with all their shortcomings, as we may think them, in the way of deliberate renunciation of all detail, and studious sacrifice of all but certain subdued and sober chords of nature's inexhaustible scale, have no more distinctive qualities than tenderness and delicacy. In the work of the school we are now considering, we find a harshness in the juxtaposition of tints, a crudeness of local colouring, a heaviness of hand, what seems a studied avoidance of delicate workmanship, and in short, what in France would be called a *franchise naïve et brutale*, which

we should suppose the very antipodes of anything suggested or sought by Corot. For illustration we may refer to the landscapes here, with the names of Monet, Sisbey [*sic*], Pissarro, G. Bellenger, and Bellet-du-Poisat. It is difficult to understand how such work as we see in these pictures, and, more or less, in a large portion of the contents of the Bond Street Gallery, can find acceptance from critics trained in that reverence for completeness and thoroughness of workmanship, and that artistic sense of subordination and reserve which never under any temptation loses sight of the right relation of parts and whole, which we are accustomed to consider leading characteristics of French taste. One seems to see in such work evidence of as wild a spirit of anarchy at work in French painting as in French politics.

Manet is a conspicuous representative of the school in figure painting. In what his admirers, we suppose, would call simplicity and frankness, he far out-Courbets Courbet. There is only one example of Manet here, a full-length of a Spanish *majo*.

Happily for those whose artistic digestion is not equal to such very raw and strong diet as this young school serves up to us, there are not wanting examples of a more delicate kind of work in this gallery.

The merits of the Salon 1874

Despite their ideological opposition to the idea of official art as exemplified by the annual Salon, then held at the Palais de l'Industrie, most of the Impressionists realized that it was the best market-place available, and often made attempts to get into it, sometimes successfully. In 1874, the year of their own first private exhibition at Nadar's, Théodore Duret – who was probably the most intelligent of the critics supporting the group – summed up the position in a letter to Pissarro.

You still have one further step to take, and that is getting known to the public and being accepted by all the big dealers and art-lovers. For that purpose there are only the auctions at the Hôtel Drouot and the big exhibition in the Palais de l'Industrie. You now have a group of art-lovers and collectors who are devoted to you and support you. Your name is familiar to art critics and artists – a special public. But you must take one more step, and become more widely known. You won't achieve this by showing your works at exhibitions of private societies. The general public doesn't go to these exhibitions, only that nucleus of artists and art-lovers who already know your work.

The Hoschedé sale did you more good and advanced you further along the way than all the private exhibitions imaginable. It brought you before a regular and numerous public. I urge you strongly to carry on with that process by exhibiting this year at the Salon. Considering what the general attitude seems to be this year, your name now being known, they won't turn you down. Besides you can send three pictures – of the three, one or two will certainly be accepted. Amongst the 40,000 people or so who visit the Salon, you will be seen by 50 dealers, art collectors, critics, who would never otherwise seek you out and discover you. Even if you only achieve that, that would be enough. But you will gain more, because you are now in a special position in a group which is being discussed, and which, with some reservations, is now coming to be accepted.

I urge you to select pictures that have a subject, something resembling a composition; pictures that are not too freshly painted, and have some finish to them.

I urge you to exhibit; you must succeed in making a noise, in defying and attracting criticism, in coming face to face with the big public. You can only achieve that at the Palais de l'Industrie.

The first group exhibition: 'appalling'   1874

Duret was perhaps over-sanguine. The Impressionists were loathed by most of those who visited the Salon. From March to May 1874 they held an exhibition at the photographer Nadar's premises in the boulevard des Capucines. The reaction quoted on p. 100 is fairly typical of the critics; and, as for the artists, Berthe Morisot's former teacher Pierre Guichard wrote to her mother in tones of horror. (An incidental reference to Manet suggests that he too might have felt compromised by association with the Impressionist group.)

The kind welcome which you gave me this morning moved me deeply. I felt younger by fifteen years, for I was suddenly transported back to those days when, as teacher and friend, I guided your delightful daughters in the arts.

I have seen Nadar's exhibition rooms, and wish to tell you my frank opinion immediately. When I entered, Madame, and saw your daughter's works in this appalling setting, my heart sank. I said to myself, 'One does not associate with madmen except at some peril. Manet was right in trying to dissuade her from exhibiting.'

To be sure, contemplating and examining these paintings, it is possible to find some excellent things, but for the most part all the exhibitors are a bit touched in the head. If Mlle Berthe is set on doing something violent she should pour petrol on these things and set them alight rather than destroy all she has done so far. How could she exhibit a work of art as delicate as hers next to *The Bachelor's Dream*? The two paintings actually touch each other!

That a young girl should destroy letters reminding her of a sad episode in her past life I can understand; such ashes are justifiable. But to deny all the efforts, the aspirations, the dreams that have filled one's life is sheer insanity. Worse, it is a sacrilege.

A gallery of Impressionists

PHOTOGRAPH OF DEGAS c.1862

PHOTOGRAPH OF MANET BY NADAR

PHOTOGRAPH OF MONET *c.*1877

RENOIR *Self-portrait* *c.*1875

RENOIR *Portrait of Monet* 1875

CÉZANNE *Self-portrait* 1875-6

87

As a painter, a friend and a physician, here is my prescription. She must go to the Louvre twice a week, stand in front of the Correggio for three hours, and ask his forgiveness for having attempted to express in oil what can only be said in watercolour. To be the first watercolourist of one's own time is a pretty enviable position. I hope, Madame, that you will be kind enough to answer this well-meant letter, which comes straight from the heart, for I am greatly interested in this promising artist. She must absolutely break with this new school, this self-styled school of the future.

Manet in Venice   1874

In 1874 the painter Charles Troché became friendly with Manet, who was then staying in Venice with his wife. Some years afterwards he recounted his impressions of the experience to the dealer Ambroise Vollard.

I remember dining with him in a little restaurant opposite the Giudecca. The table was laid in an arbour covered with vines. A little opening in this arbour framed the

church of San Salvatore [Redentore?] whose pink tones contrasted with the glaucous green of the water and the black spindle shapes of the gondolas. Manet observed and analysed the different colours taken on by each object as the light faded. He defined their values, and told us how he would try to reproduce them, steeped in this ashy twilight greyness. Suddenly he got up, and taking his paint-box and a little canvas, he ran down to the quay. There, with a few strokes of the brush, he set up the distant church . . . .

One day I was expatiating on the possibility of combining poetry and reality in a picture when Manet exclaimed: 'If that ass Courbet were to hear you! His idea of reality was . . . Well look at his *Burial at Ornans*, for instance, in which he has succeeded in burying everybody, priests, gravediggers, mourners and all. The horizon itself is six feet underground.'

I used to go and join him almost every day. The lagoons, the palaces, the old houses, scaled and mellowed by time, offered him an inexhaustible variety of subjects. But his preference was for out-of-the-way corners. I asked him if I might follow him in my gondola. 'As much as you like,' he told me. 'When I am working, I pay no attention to anything but my subject.' Now and then he would make a gesture of annoyance that set his boat rocking, and I would see his palette knife scraping away with ferocity. But all at once I would hear the refrain of a song, or a few notes whistled gaily. Then Manet would call out to me, 'I'm getting on, I'm getting on! When things are going well I have to express myself out loud.'. . .

One morning I was looking with him at *The Glory of Venice* in the Ducal Palace. 'There's something about it that leaves one cold,' he said. 'So much useless effort, so much wasted space in it. Not a shadow of an emotion. I like the Carpaccios, they have the naive grace of illuminations in a missal. And I rank highest of all the Titians and Tintorettos of the Scuola di San Rocco. But I always come back, you know, to Velázquez and Goya.'

Tiepolo irritated him. 'These Italians bore after a time,' he would say, 'with their allegories and their *Gerusalemme Liberata* and their *Orlando Furioso* and all that noisy rubbish. A painter can say all he wants to with fruits, or flowers, or even clouds.'

I remember wandering with him round the stalls of the Pescheria Vecchia under the bridge of the Rialto. Manet was intoxicated by light. He bubbled over with delight at the sight of the enormous fish with their silver bellies. 'That,' he said, 'is what I would like to have painted if the Paris city council had not rejected my decorative scheme for the Hôtel de Ville. You know I would like to be the St Francis of still-life.'

Another time we went to the vegetable market. Manet, a slender figure in blue, his straw hat tilted to the back of his head, went striding over heaps of provisions and vegetables. He stopped suddenly before a row of pumpkins, the kind that grows only on the shore of the Brenta. 'Turks' heads in turbans!' he cried. 'Trophies from the victories of Lepanto and Corfu.'

When Manet had been working hard, he would set out by way of relaxation to 'discover' Venice. Madame Manet would accompany him, and they would wander through the most tortuous of the little streets, or taking the first gondola that came, explore the little *canaletti*. Manet was mad on old tumbledown houses with rags hanging from the windows catching the light. He would stop to look at the handsome shock-headed girls, bare-necked in their flowered gowns, who sat at their doors stringing beads from Murano, or knitting stockings of vivid colours. In the fishing quarter of San Pietro di Castello, he would stop before the great piles topped with enormous eel-pots made of withies, which the light turned to amethyst. He marvelled at the children, burnt golden by the sun, shaking off their fleas on the crumbling steps of old staircases and quarrelling among themselves,

their faces smeared with polenta and watermelon. The afternoon would end up with visits to second-hand dealers, in whose miserable booths there was no hint of the sumptuous antique shops that were to arise on the same sites fifty years later. Nothing delighted him so much as to ferret out an old piece of lace, a finely worked jewel, a valuable engraving.

He would often arrange to meet me in the evening. Venice is particularly pleasant in the evening, and Manet liked going out after dinner. He became talkative on these occasions, and did not scruple to tease Madame Manet in my presence, usually on the subject of her family, and particularly of her father, a typical Dutch *bourgeois*, sullen, fault-finding, thrifty and incapable of understanding an artist. But a fisherman had only to start singing a barcarolle, or a guitar to throb, and instantly Manet would fall silent, caught by the charm of nocturnal Venice.

Carolus-Duran teaches portraiture   1870s

Carolus-Duran, the successful portrait-painter, was a close friend of Manet, and like him had been influenced by Velázquez. In the 1870s he was regarded as a modernist, and his work had some affinities with Manet's early style, which through his teaching he passed on to artists such as Sargent. R. A. M. Stevenson, who was also his pupil, describes his technique and ideals which in many ways came close to those practised by painters who were regarded at the time as 'real' Impressionists.

No preparation in colour or monochrome was allowed, but the main planes of the face must be laid directly on the unprepared canvas with a broad brush. These few surfaces – three or four in the forehead, as many in the nose and so forth – must be studied in shape and place, and particularly in the relative value of light that their various inclinations produce. They were painted quite broadly in tones of flesh tint, and stood side by side like pieces of mosaic, without fusion of their adjacent edges. No brushing of the edge of the hair into the face was permitted, no conventional bounding of eyes and features with lines that might deceive the student by their expression into the belief that false structure was truthful . . . you must make a tone for each step of a gradation. Thus you might never attempt to realize a tone or a passage by some hazardous, uncontrollable process.

Trials of a dealer   1875

In an interview given to Gustave Cocquiot, which was printed in the paper Excelsior *on 28 November 1910, Durand-Ruel recalled his connections with the Impressionists, and in particular his attempts to sell their work at auction in the mid-1870s.*

Monet was the first one I met. Daubigny introduced him to me in London in 1870 [but see p. 45], and on his recommendation I became immediately interested in this artist, who had great talent. Solidly built and sturdy, he looked as though he could go on painting effortlessly for more years than I was likely to live. It is true of course that I was older than Monet and Renoir; by nine years! When we got back to Paris Monet came and brought me pictures, and I became his official dealer.

Two years later I got to know Renoir, and also about the same time Manet; then I established relations with Pissarro, Degas, Puvis de Chavannes and Sisley. I was then established in my present galleries in the rue Lafitte, and had been there since 1869. What a ghastly time for painting it was! Had I not been the son of a picture-dealer, who had started off as a stationer, if I had not, in a word been brought up in the trade, I could not have continued the battle I had to fight against public taste.

Just as my father had had great difficulty in obtaining recognition for the great school of 1830, Delacroix, Descamps and Corot, so I found exactly the same hazards in wishing to sell the works of Monet and Renoir.

I was looked upon as a fool, a maniac. I was given a certain credit – but of course after the victory – for having some fine Delacroixs and Corots, but to see me now extolling Renoir and Monet, what a lack of common sense on my part! They barely managed to avoid insulting me in public.

All the same I was covered with abuse; in 1875, in particular, when I was organizing at the Hôtel Drouot a sale of the works of Monet and Renoir, which I had as a precaution presented in superb frames. In the course of the sale there was a fine commotion, I must say. The insults which were hurled at us – especially Monet and Renoir! The public howled, and treated us as imbeciles, as people with no sense of decency. Works were sold for as little as 50 francs – and that was only because of the frames. I bought in many of them myself. Afterwards it seemed as though I would be on the point of being taken to a lunatic asylum. It was fortunate that I was on good terms with my family.

But my revenge was complete. A painting which I bought in at 110 francs later made 70,000 francs at a public auction. Another, sold for 50 francs, and then resold goodness knows how many times, has recently risen to 100,000 francs.

And you were able to persist to the bitter end?

Yes, but without America I would have been ruined, after having bought so many Monets and Renoirs! Two exhibitions which I arranged there in 1886 saved me. The American public did not poke fun; it bought, in moderation, admittedly, but thanks to it Renoir and Monet were able to live, and since then, as you know, the French public has followed the American lead; you have to be firm with it.

Berthe Morisot in the open air   1875

In the summer after her marriage in 1874 to Eugène Manet, Berthe Morisot spent a holiday at Cowes on the Isle of Wight, and a letter to her sister Edma is a pleasant reminder of the Impressionist as tourist.

Nothing is nicer than the children in the streets, with their arms bare in the English style. I should like to get some of them to pose for me, but this is all very difficult, as my English is atrocious, and Eugène's worse.

The little river here is full of boats, rather like Dartmouth in the photographs Tiburce [her brother] sent us. I am sure that you would like all this very much, and that it would encourage you to start painting again. The beach is like an English park, with the addition of the sea. I shall have to make a watercolour of it, for I could never have the courage to set up my easel to do it in oil. At Ryde everything takes place on the pier, which is interminably long. It is a place for bathing, and promenading, and boats berth there too. I found a superb Reynolds in Ryde for a little less than two francs. My black hat with the lace bow made the sailors in the port burst out laughing . . . .

I have worked a little, but it has rained for a whole week! Today we have been to Ryde again. I set out with my sack and portfolio, determined to do a watercolour, but when I got there, my hat blew off, and my hair got in my eyes. Eugène was in a bad humour, as he always is when my hair is out of place, and three hours after leaving, we were back again in Globe Cottage. Nevertheless I took the time to have a short walk through the town, which I find even drearier than Cowes. There are more people in the streets, but not so many boats on the water, and the pretty little river adds a lot of charm to the place. Anyway I am happy with our choice, which is quite a rare thing.

At Ryde there are many shops, even a picture-dealer's. I went in, and he showed me some watercolours by a painter, who, he said, is quite well known. They sell for no less than four hundred francs each, and they are dreadful. No feeling for nature; these people who live beside the water do not even seem to see it. Anyway this has made me give up any hopes I may have had about being successful in England. In the whole shop the only thing that was possible or at all pretty was by a Frenchman, and the dealer says that this sort of thing does not sell . . .

Cowes has recently become very animated. The other day a whole party landed from a yacht. The garden of the Yacht Club is full of ladies of fashion. At high tide there is an extraordinary bustle. But all this is not for us; we are humble folk, too insignificant to mingle in high society. Anyway I don't know how one would go about it, unless you had a fortune of several million pounds, a yacht and were a member of the Club. I am completely indifferent to all this. I do not care for new acquaintances, and this society, from what I have seen of it, seems as dull as it is affluent. At the Goodwood races I was struck by the elegance and the bored airs of the women. On the other hand the ordinary people seem very gay; they possess a vitality which entirely contradicts the image we have of these northerners.

I am horribly depressed tonight, tired and edgy, I feel out of sorts, having once more proved that the joys of motherhood are not for me. This is a misfortune to which you would never resign yourself, and despite all my philosophy, there are days when I am inclined to complain bitterly about the injustice of fate.

My work is going badly, and this is no consolation. It's always the same story. I don't know where to start. I made a start in a field, but the minute I'd set up my easel more than fifty boys and girls came swarming about me, shouting and gesticulating.

All this ended in confusion and fighting, and the owner of the field came to tell me rudely that I should have asked for permission to work here, and that my presence attracted the village children who caused a great deal of damage.

On a boat one has another kind of problem. Everything sways; one has the sun and the wind to cope with; the boat changes position every minute and so on. The view from my window is very pretty, but not to paint. Views from above are almost always incomprehensible. As a result of all this I am not doing much, and what I am doing seems dreadful.

A generous gesture from Manet   1875

In spite of occasional differences and flare-ups, the Impressionists as a group were supportive and helpful to each other. In 1875 Monet was in great financial trouble, and depressed. Manet, who with Zola had helped him before, put this proposal to their mutual friend, the critic Théodore Duret.

I went to·see Monet yesterday. I found him in great distress, and at his wits' end. He asked me if I could find someone who would buy at choice ten or twenty of his paintings at 100 francs each. Do you think that we could fix him up between ourselves, each of us contributing 500 francs?

Of course it must be understood that nobody, and he least of all, should know that we are arranging it ourselves. I had thought of a dealer or a collector, but I have been frightened of a refusal.

It is unfortunately necessary to be as well abreast as we are, despite any repugnance we may have, to do an excellent bit of business, and at the same time render a service to a man of talent. Reply as quickly as you can, or arrange to meet me.

The meditative and the decorative: a contemporary view   c. 1876

George Moore's Modern Painting, first published in 1893, demonstrated a visual sensibility and a sense of discrimination based on his intimate personal knowledge of many of the Impressionists as well as of their works.

My first acquaintance with Monet's painting was made in '75 or '76, the year he exhibited his first steam-engine, and his celebrated troop of life-size turkeys, gobbling the tall grass at the end of a meadow, at the other end of which stood, high up in the picture, a French château . . . . Since that year I have seen Monets by the score, and have hardly observed any change or alteration in his manner of seeing or executing, or any development in his art. At the end of the season, he comes up from the country with thirty or forty landscapes, all equally perfect, all painted in precisely the same way, and not one shows the least sign of hesitation, not one suggests the unattainable, the beyond; one and all show us a man who is sure of his effect, and who is always in a hurry. Any corner of nature will do equally well for his purpose, nor is he disposed to change the disposition of any line of tree or river or hill; so long as a certain reverberation of colour is obtained, all is well. An unceasing production, and an almost unvarying degree of excellence, has placed Monet at the head of his school; his pictures command high prices, and nothing goes now with the erudite American but Monet's landscapes. But does Monet merit this excessive patronage, and if so, what are the qualities in his work that make it superior to Sisley's and Pissarro's?

Sisley is less decorative, less on the surface, and though he follows Monet in his pursuit of colour, nature is, perhaps on account of his English origin, something more to him than a brilliant appearance. It has of course happened to Monet to set his

SISLEY *Fog* 1874

SISLEY *Boats at Bougival Lock* 1873

easel before the suburban atmosphere that Sisley loves, but he has always treated it rather in the decorative than in the meditative spirit. He has never been touched by the humility of a lane's end, and the sentiment of the humble life that collects there has never appeared on the canvas. Yet Sisley, being more in sympathy with such nature, has often been able to produce a much superior, though much less pretentious picture than the ordinary stereotyped Monet. But if Sisley is more meditative than Monet, Pissarro is more meditative than either.

Monet had arrived at his style before I saw anything of his work; of his earlier canvases I know nothing. Possibly he once painted in the Corot manner; it is hardly possible that he should not have done so. However this may be, Pissarro did not rid himself for many years of the influence of Corot. His earliest pictures were all composed in pensive greys and violets, and exhaled the weary sadness of tilth and grange and scant orchard trees. The pale road winds through meagre uplands, and through the blown and gnarled and shiftless fruit-trees the shiftless silhouette of the town drifts across the land. The violet spaces between the houses are of the very saddest, and the spare furrows are patiently drawn, and so the execution is in harmony with and accentuates the unutterable monotony of the peasant's lot. The sky, too, is vague and empty, and out of its death-like, creamy hollow the first shadows are blown into the pallid face of a void evening. The picture tells of the melancholy of ordinary life, of our poor transitory tenements, our miserable scrapings among the little mildew that has gathered on the surface of an insignificant planet.

I will not attempt to explain why the grey-toned and meditative Pissarro should have consented to countenance – I cannot say to lead (for unlike every other *chef d'école* Pissarro imitated the disciples, instead of the disciples imitating Pissarro) – the many fantastic revolutions in pictorial art which have agitated Montmartre during the last dozen years. The Pissarro psychology I must leave to take care of itself, confining myself strictly to the narrative of these revolutions.

Authority for the broken brushwork of Monet is to be found in Manet's last pictures, and I remember Manet's reply when I questioned him about the pure violet shadows which, just before his death, he was beginning to introduce into his pictures. 'One year one paints violet and people scream, and the following year one paints a great deal more violet.' If Manet's answer throws no light whatever on the new principle, it shows very clearly the direction, if not the goal, towards which his last style was moving. But perhaps I am speaking too cautiously, for surely broken brushwork and violet shadows lead to only one possible goal – the prismatic colours.

Manet died, and this side, and this side only, of his art was taken up by Monet, Sisley and Renoir. Or was it that Manet had begun to yield to an influence – that of Monet, Sisley and Renoir – which was just beginning to make itself felt? Be that as it may, browns and blacks disappeared from the palettes of those who did not wish to be considered *l'école des beaux-arts et en plein air*. Venetian reds, siennas and ochres were in process of abandonment, and the palette came to be very much composed in the following fashion: violet, white, blue, white, green, white, red, white, yellow, white, orange, white; the three primary and the three secondary colours, with white placed between each, so as to keep everything as distinct as possible, and avoid in the mixing all soiling of the tones. Monet, Sisley and Renoir contented themselves with abolition of all blacks and browns, for they were but half-hearted reformers, and it was clearly the duty of all who came after to rid the palette of all ochres, siennas, Venetian, Indian and light reds.

Blanc d'argent.
Jaune de Chrôme
Jaune de Naples, —
Ocre Jaune,
Terre de Sienne Naturelle —
Vermillon
Laque de Garance
Vert Véronèse
Vert Emeraude
Bleu de Cobalt
Bleu Outremer.

couteau à palette
grattoir
epreuve
a qu'il faut pour peindre

L'ocre Jaune le Jaune de Naples
et la terre de Sienne ne sont
que des tons intermédiaires. dont
on peut se passer puisque vous
pouvez les faire avec les autres couleurs

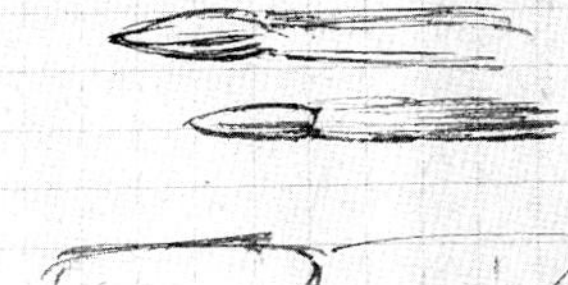

Pinceaux de Martin

Brosses plates en soie.

BAZILLE *The Studio in the Rue de la Condamine* 1870

MANET *An Exhibition of Paintings* 1876

Comforts of studio life

In Bazille's view of his studio in Les Batignolles, painted a few months before his death in battle, the figure of the artist himself has been painted (out of scale) by Manet, who is seen to the left of the easel. A still-life, one of the works Bazille bought from the struggling Monet, hangs above the piano. Next to the fireplace, in another studio used by Bazille, hung a portrait of Monet by Séverac. Nearby was Manet's studio, which we know from a finished painting by Fantin-Latour – a static array of portraits – and from this livelier sketch.

ML

BAZILLE *The Artist's Studio,
Rue Furstenberg* 1866

FANTIN-LATOUR *Manet's Studio
in Les Batignolles* 1870

97

Not Impressionists but independents 1876

In the spring of 1876 the second Impress-
ionist exhibition was held at 11 rue Le Pele-
tier. There were nineteen participants, with
24 works by Degas, 12 by Pissarro, 18 by
Monet, 15 each by Renoir and Sisley. In La
Presse of 31 March Alexandre Pothey made
some interesting comments and a fruitful
suggestion.

It was two years ago, in April 1874, if my
memory serves me aright, that a group of
artists got together to offer a selection of
their works directly to the appreciation of
the public. They demanded from the State
and the Administration neither favours, nor
rewards nor purchases, not even free exhibition space. It was with their own resources alone that they organized this exhibition, which took place in Nadar's old
studio in the Boulevard des Capucines. This
initiative deserved to be encouraged by all
who like or are interested in the modern
movement in the Fine Arts, for it was under-
taken with simplicity, sincerity and good
faith. Nevertheless the critics did not show
themselves to be very kind; the exhibitors
were dubbed, with a certain amount of
irony, 'impressionists' and 'rebels', whilst
all they really wanted was to be indepen-
dents.

In actual fact for the most part they did
deviate from the accepted official style,
from accepted techniques, from hallowed
formulae; nevertheless a painter is somebody who makes a painting live, who gives
proof of a personal form of drawing, a virile
technique, and who knows how to find a
new mode of expression. Moreover the
group of which we are speaking is composed of artists who for some fifteen or
twenty years have been working with fervour, perseverance and self-denial, and
who have sought buyers amongst those collectors who have the most discriminating
taste.

This morning, Thursday, the *Impression-*
nalistes [*sic*] or, if you prefer it, the Indepen-
dents, have inaugurated their second exhibition. They have borrowed M. Durand-
Ruel's gallery in the rue Le Peletier, three
large rooms where, for a month, their
works will be submitted to the judgment of
connoisseurs. The catalogue, which has not
yet appeared, will contain some 250 entries.
A visit, alas too hurried, gives us the opportunity at least of indicating those paintings
which have particularly struck us, but we
think that we shall be the first to express
praise. For the exhibition is far more interesting than that on the Boulevard des
Capucines. Thanks to a fortunate system of
hanging, each artist's works are shown
together, which allows the viewer to move
on from details to the general impression,
and to make a judgment based on what the
artist's aims really are.

M. Monet's contribution consists of a
series of landscapes painted directly from
nature at Petit-Gennevilliers or near Argenteuil; they are all marked by the freshness of
their execution, their real feeling, and the
beautiful light which they display. But M.
Monet has been determined to prove that
he can do other things as well. He has produced a life-size portrait of the most startling kind. It is a young Parisienne, with a
roguish look on her face, and blond hair,
dressed in a Japanese robe of exceptional
richness. This robe of red swanskin is covered with silken and gold embroidery with
fantastic figures in startling relief. With a
gracious movement, the woman, who is
playing with a fan, turns towards the spectator. The figure stands out against a neutral
blue background, and is standing on a bamboo mat. Art lovers who are on the lookout
for solid colouring and emphatic impasto
will find this rather strange figure a real
feast for their eyes.

M. Degaz [*sic*] offers us a quite remarkable American scene. It is a shop in New
York [New Orleans] where samples of cotton are displayed and sold. The owner, his

MONET *Mme Monet in Japanese Costume* 1875-76

assistants and the customers, some fifteen or twenty people, are happily distributed around this interior, drawn with rare skill in a whole variety of poses. In another painting M. Degaz shows us two laundresses; one is leaning on her iron in a finely observed stance, and the other is yawning and stretching out her arms. It is as powerful and authentic as a Daumier.

M. Renoir is exhibiting a number of portraits, all of them very different in their techniques. First of all there is one of the painter Bazille, who was killed in the war, sitting at his easel. Then a portrait of M. Chocquet, a light-coloured and very refined work, and then one of M. Monet, much more vigorous and daring. M. Renoir's *Baigneuse* is a nude study of superb colouring.

Amongst the landscapes one will certainly pay attention to those of M. Cicely [*sic*] which are in the centre of his display, and those of M. Pissarro whose picturesque landscapes are very well composed.

RENOIR *Bazille at Work* 1867

Five or six lunatics   1876

It is now a truism that the Impressionists were badly received by the press. Typical of this is the article by the well-known journalist Albert Wolff on their second exhibition, which appeared in the columns of Figaro *on 3 April 1876.*

The rue Le Peletier is doomed to misfortune. First there was the fire at the Opera, and now another disaster has struck the *quartier*. An exhibition of so-called 'paintings' has opened at the Durand-Ruel gallery. The inoffensive passer-by, attracted by the flags which adorn the façade, may go in, and if he does, finds displayed to his affrighted eyes a horrifying spectacle. Five or six lunatics, of whom one is a woman, a group of unfortunates, afflicted with the madness of ambition, have got together there to exhibit their works.

There are those who will roar with laughter in front of these works. For my part I am heartbroken. These self-styled artists, who call themselves 'The Intransigents' or 'The Impressionists', take a canvas, some paint and brushes, throw some tones haphazardly on to the canvas, and then sign it. This is the way in which the lost souls of Ville-Evrard [*a famous psychiatric hospital*] pick up pebbles from the roadway, and believe that they have found diamonds. A frightening spectacle of human vanity so far adrift that it verges on sheer lunacy. Try to make M. Pissarro understand that trees are not violets; that the sky is not the colour of fresh butter, that the things he paints are not to be seen in any country on earth, and that no intelligent human being could countenance such aberrations. You might just as well waste your time trying to persuade a patient of Dr Blanche's, who believes himself to be the Pope, that he is living in Les Batignolles and not in the Vatican. Try to make M. Degas understand reason, tell him that there are in art certain qualities which are called drawing, colour, technique and

MANET *Albert Wolff* 1877

effort, and he will laugh in your face, and tell you that you are a reactionary. Try to explain to M. Renoir that a woman's torso is not a mass of decomposing flesh with those purplish green stains which denote a state of complete putrefaction in a corpse. There is also a woman in this group, as there nearly always is in any gang; she is called Berthe Morizot [*sic*], and she makes an interesting spectacle. With her, feminine grace is retained amidst the outpourings of a mind in delirium.

And this is the collection of botched-up things being exhibited to the public without any thought of the fatal consequences they may entail. Yesterday in the rue Le Peletier an unfortunate man was arrested because on coming out of the exhibition he had started to bite passers-by.

Seriously, one must pity these misguided people; a benevolent nature has endowed some of them with the basic qualities which make an artist. But in their mutual admiration of a shared sense of confusion, the members of this extremely mediocre, vain and flashy group have raised to the status of a doctrine the negation of all that has made art what it is. They have tied a bundle of straws to a broom-handle and made a flag of it. Knowing very well that a complete lack of artistic education precludes them from ever crossing the moat which divides an attempt at painting from the real thing, they take refuge in their own inadequacy, which is the same as their adequacy, and every year they come and present their wretched daubs in oil and watercolour as a form of protest against that magnificent French School of Painting so rich in great names. These poor deluded creatures make me think of those versifiers who produce doggerel for boxes of sweets, and who, without any skill in writing, without an idea in their heads, or a single thought, come along and say 'Lamartine has had his day. Make way for the intransigent poet.'

I know some of these infuriating Impressionists. They are charming young people, absolutely convinced of what they are doing, absolutely certain that they are on the right road. It is a spectacle which is as afflicting as the sight of that poor lunatic whom I saw at Bicêtre; he held in his left hand a coal shovel tucked under his chin like a violin, and with a stick, which he took for a bow, he kept playing, or so he said, *The Carnival of Venice*, which he claimed to have played before all the crowned heads of Europe. If you placed this virtuoso at the entrance to the charade in the rue Le Peletier, the scenario would be complete.

Synthesists, not analysts   1876

Not all the critics were hostile, and a more thoughtful reaction was expressed by Emile Blémont in Le Rappel for 9 April 1876.

What is an Impressionist painter? We have hardly been given a satisfactory definition, but it would seem to us that the painters who group themselves or are grouped under this heading pursue, with varying techniques of execution, the same goal; to render with absolute sincerity, without any arrangement or attenuation, by simple process, the impression aroused in them by the various aspects of reality.

For them art is not a minute and meticulous imitation of what we used to call *la belle nature*. They no longer labour under the compulsion to reproduce people and objects servilely, nor to reconstruct laboriously detail by detail an overall view of a subject. They do not imitate; they translate, they interpret, they apply themselves to disentangling the admixture of lines and diverse colours which assail the eye when first it looks at a subject.

They are synthesists, not analysts, and in this they are right, we believe; for if analysis is specifically the method of science, synthesis is that of art. There are no basic laws other than the relationship of things to each other, and like Diderot they feel that the idea of beauty lies in the perception of these relationships. And as there are probably no two men in the universe who see exactly the same relationships in the same object, they do not feel it necessary to alter their personal and direct sensations to comply with any particular convention.

In principle, in theory, therefore, we feel able to approve of them completely. In practice, however, it is another matter. People do not always achieve what they set out to do as it ought to be done; one does not always reach one's goal, however clearly one might see it.

Henry James on the Impressionists as cynics   1876

On 13 May 1876 Henry James contributed to The New York Tribune *a piece entitled* 'Parisian Festivity' *in which he had something of interest to say to the American public about the difference between the Pre-Raphaelites and the Impressionists – an issue which seems to have preoccupied Anglo-Saxon commentators for many years.*

An exhibition for which I can claim at least that it can give rise (at any rate in my own mind) to no dangerous perversities of taste is that of the little group of the Irreconcilables, otherwise known as the 'Impressionists' in painting. It is being held during the present month at Durand-Ruel's, and I have found it decidedly interesting. But the effect of it was to make me think better than ever of all the good old rules which decree that beauty is beauty and ugliness is ugliness, and warn us off from the sophistications of satiety. The contributors to the exhibition of which I speak are partisans of unadorned reality and absolute foes to arrangement, embellishment, selection, to the artist's allowing himself, as he has hitherto, since art began, found his best account in doing, to be preoccupied with the idea of the beautiful. The beautiful, to them, is what the supernatural is to the Positivists – a metaphysical notion which can only get one into a muddle, and is to be severely let alone. Let it alone, they say, and it will come at its own pleasure; the painter's proper field is the actual, and to give a vivid impression of how a thing happens to look, at a particular moment, is the essence of his mission. This attitude has something in common with the English Pre-Raphaelites, twenty years ago, but this little band is on grounds less interesting than the group out of which Millais and Holman Hunt rose to fame. None of its members show signs of possessing first-rate talent, and indeed the 'Impressionist' doctrines strike me as incompatible, in an artist's mind, with the existence of first-rate talent. To embrace them you must be provided with a plentiful absence of imagination. But the divergence in method between the English Pre-Raphaelites and this little group is especially striking, and very typical of the moral differences between the

French and English races. When the English realists 'went in', as the phrase is, for hard truth and stern fact, an irresistible instinct of righteousness caused them to try and purchase forgiveness for their infidelity to the old more or less moral proprieties and conventionalities, by an exquisite, patient, virtuous manipulation – by being above all other things laborious. But the Impressionists who are, I think, more consistent, abjure virtue altogether, and declare that a subject which has been crudely chosen shall be loosely treated. They send detail to the dogs, and concentrate themselves on general expression. Some of their generalizations of expression are in a high degree curious. The Englishmen, in a word, were pedants, and the Frenchman are cynics.

Duranty hails the 'New Painting'   1876

Louis-Emile-Edmond Duranty was a prolific novelist and man of letters in the tradition of French rationalism, who shared with the Goncourt brothers the leadership of the realist movement. He was a close friend of Degas, and as habitué of the Café Guerbois had become familiar with the others of the group. His posthumously published novel Le Pays des arts *(1881) expressed through the mouth of its hero, the painter Louis Martin, his ideas about painters such as Degas, Cézanne, Fantin-Latour and Manet; but more explicitly in 1876 he published* La Nouvelle Peinture. A Propos du groupe d'artistes qui expose dans les Galeries Durand-Ruel. *In it he expressed with clarity, for the benefit of a mass audience, the basic principles underlying the Impressionists' technique and outlook.*

As far as colouring is concerned, they have made a discovery of real originality, the sources of which cannot be found anywhere in the past, neither in the works of the Dutch school, nor in fresco painting, with its clear tones, nor in the light tonalities of the eighteenth century. They are not only concerned with that fine and subtle manipulation of colour which stems from the close and intimate observation of the most delicate tonal values which are contrary or complementary to each other. Their real discovery consists in the realization that a strong light *discolours* tones, that sunshine, reflected off objects, tends by virtue of its clarity to blend its seven prismatic rays into a single, uncoloured brilliance which is light. From one flash of intuition to another, they have succeeded in breaking up solar light into its rays, its elements, and to reconstruct it as a unity by the general harmony of the iridescence they spread on their canvases. From the viewpoint of the refinement of vision and the subtle penetration of colours, it produced an extraordinary result. The most astute physicist could find no fault with their analysis of colour.

The Romantics absolutely ignored all these facts about light which the Venetians, nonetheless, had already caught a glimpse of. And as for the Ecole des Beaux-Arts, *they* have never given the subject a thought, as they paint from old paintings, and have nothing at all to do with nature.

The Romantic, in his study of light, knew only the orange-coloured light of the setting sun against dark hills, or impastos of white, tinted with either yellow, chrome or pink, which he plastered over the bituminous darkness of the interiors of forests. There could be no light without bitumen, without ivory black, without Prussian blue, without contrasting tones, which so it was said, brought out even the warmest tone. He believed that light coloured and brightened the tonality, and he was certain that it existed only as long as it was surrounded with dark tones. A cave with a ray of light coming through a small aperture; this has always been the ideal which obsessed the Romantics. Even today, in all countries, landscape is treated as though it were an oven or the back of a shop.

DEGAS *Edmond Duranty* 1879

MANET *Théodore Duret* 1868

Men of letters

The Impressionists were fortunate in firing the
imagination of a number of gifted critics, whose
writings show how keen was their awareness that
nineteenth-century life called for a new art as
well as a new literature. Even so, enlightened
patrons such as Chocquet, and the Charpentiers
(p.106) of La Vie Moderne, were rare.

MANET *Stéphane Mallarmé* 1876

RENOIR *Victor Chocquet* 1876

MANET *George Moore* 1879

RENOIR *Mme Charpentier and Her Children* 1878

PHOTOGRAPH OF GEORGETTE AND PAUL
CHARPENTIER *c.* 1878

PHOTOGRAPH OF MME CHARPENTIER *c.* 1876

Yet at the same time everybody passes in midsummer through countless sections of landscape, and is able to see how hillocks, meadows, fields, are dissolved, so to speak, in a single luminous reflection which they receive from the sky and which they return to it: for such is the law which creates light in nature; side by side with the special blue, green or composite ray which every substance absorbs, and above it, it reflects the combination of all the rays and the colouring of the vault which covers the earth. Thus it is that painters have for the first time understood and reproduced, or tried to reproduce, these phenomena. In those works which have tried to achieve this, one feels the light and colour vibrating; one feels an ambiance of clarity, which for artists educated to be above, or against, nature, is an achievement without merit, without importance, much too bright, too sharp, too crude, too formal.

But how many things landscape has never tried to express! A feeling for the structure of the land seems to have escaped all landscape artists. If hills have a certain formation, and trees group themselves in a certain manner, then houses nestle together in a certain way amongst their surroundings, streams have particular varieties of banks, and so the characteristic pattern of a country develops. Nobody has yet discovered how to express the French version of nature. And since colour and all its refinements have been mastered, it should now be time to pay some attention to forms. It would seem at least preferable to paint a landscape on the spot rather than from a sketch which one takes back to the studio, and of which one gradually loses the first spontaneous feeling. You must realize that close to the hearts of all of them in this moment is a passion for a new approach and for freedom.

Truth in people and places   1876

In the British magazine The Art Monthly Review *for September 1876 an article by Stéphane Mallarmé appeared, entitled 'The Impressionists and Edouard Manet', in the course of which he discussed, amongst other things, the Impressionists' concern with the actual life of their time, and the justification for* plein-air *painting.*

As for the artist himself, his personal feeling, his peculiar tastes are for the time absorbed, ignored, or set aside for the enjoyment of his personal life. Such a result as this cannot be obtained all at once. To reach it the master must pass through many phrases ere this self-isolation can be acquired, and this new evolution of art be learnt; and I who have occupied myself a good deal in its study, can count but two who have gained it.

By and by, if he continues to paint long enough, and to educate the public eye – as yet veiled by conventionality – if that public will then consent to see the true beauties of the people, healthy and solid as they are, the graces which exist in the bourgeoisie will then be recognized and taken as worthy models in art, and then will come the time of peace. As yet it is but one of struggle – a struggle to render those truths in nature which for her are eternal, but which are as yet for the multitude but new.

The reproach that superficial people formulate against Manet, that whereas once he painted ugliness, now he paints vulgarity, falls harmlessly to the ground, when we recognize the fact that he paints the truth, and recollect those difficulties he encountered on his way to seek it, and how he conquered them. *Un déjeuner sur l'herbe, L'Exécution de Maximilien, Un coin de table, Des gens du monde à la fenêtre, Le bon bock, Un coin de bal de l'Opéra, Le chemin de fer,* and the two *Canotiers;* these are the pictures which, step by step have marked each rung on the ladder scaled by this bold innovator, and which have led him to the point achieved in his truly marvellous work, this year refused by the Salon, but exhibited to the public by itself, entitled *Le linge* – a work which marks a date in a lifetime perhaps, but certainly one in the history of art.

The whole of the series we have just above enumerated, with here and there an exception, demonstrate the painter's aim very exactly, and this aim was not to make a momentary escapade or sensation, but by steadily endeavouring to impress upon his work a natural and a general law, to seek out a type rather than a personality, and to flood it with light and air; and such air! air which despotically dominates over all else. At this point I should like to comment somewhat on that truism of tomorrow, that paradox of today, which in studio slang is called 'the theory of open air', or at least on that which it becomes with the authoritative evidence of the later efforts of Manet. But here is first of all an objection to be overcome. Why is it needful to represent the open air of gardens, shore or street, when it must be owned that the chief part of modern existence is passed within doors? There are many answers; among these I hold the first, that in the atmosphere of an interior, bare or furnished, the reflected lights are mixed and broken and too often discolour the flesh tints . . . . The complexion, the very special beauty which springs from the very source of life, changes with artificial lights, and it is probably from the desire to preserve this grace in all its integrity that painting – which concerns itself more about this flesh-pollen than any other human attraction – . . . demands daylight – that is space with the transparence of air alone . . . .

Open air; that is the beginning and end of the question we are now studying. Aesthetically it is answered by the simple fact that there in open air alone can the flesh tints of a model keep their fine qualities, being nearly equally lighted on all sides. On the other hand if one paints in the real or arti-

ficial half-light in use in the schools, it is this feature or that feature on which the light strikes and forces into undue relief, affording an easy means for a painter to dispose a face to suit his own fancy and return to bygone styles.

The search after truth peculiar to modern artists, which enables them to see nature, and reproduce her, such as she appears to just and pure eyes, must lead them to adopt air almost exclusively as their medium, or at all events to habituate themselves to work in it freely and without restraint; there should at least be in the revival of such a medium, if nothing more, an incentive to a new method of painting. This is the result of our reasoning, and the end I wish to establish. As no artist has on his palette a transparent and neutral colour answering to open air, the desired effect can only be obtained by lightness or heaviness of touch, or by the regulation of tone. Now Manet and his school use simple colour, fresh or lightly laid on, and their results seem to have been obtained at the first stroke, that the ever-present light blends with and vivifies all things. As to the details of the picture, nothing should be absolutely fixed, in order that we may feel that the bright gleam which lights the picture, or the diaphanous shadow which veils it, are only seen in passing, and just when the spectator beholds the represented subject, which being composed of a harmony of reflected and everchanging lights, cannot be supposed always to look the same, but palpitates with movement, light, and life.

No cause for mirth   1877

Reviled by Albert Wolff in Le Figaro, *the Impressionist exhibition of April 1877 inspired Philippe Burty to give the readers of* La République Française *(25 April) a lesson in discrimination.*

PHOTOGRAPH OF THE ACTRESS MÉRY LAURENT WITH MALLARMÉ AND MANET 1872

Although generally greeted with imprecations and anger, this exhibition cannot but attract the public, and the first reaction it arouses is one of lively surprise. The word 'Impressionist' is inadequate to express the ordinary approach of those who practise it. Without getting too deeply involved in a discussion of the technique, which would bore our readers, we can say that generally these painters try to catch the general appearance of people and things, the objective character of conventional appearances, and in pursuit of this goal they favour clear colours and proclaim the uselessness of black, or opaque tones. Is this a cause for mirth or indignation? Certainly not. It is no more than the rather unusual development of what Corot had been seeking to achieve by renouncing a clear definition of form, and by breaking up shadows with grey configurations of varying strengths.

Their works have long since taken up too definite a stance for the public as a whole to accept them. But they do have their supporters, and these are not the first to appear. In the right place and as decorations, these paintings have the merit of clarity, of freshness, and an impact which is undeniable. They have ceased trying to force their way into official exhibitions, but they are beginning to filter in unobtrusively.

The true Impressionist landscape painters are MM. Claude Monet, Cézanne, Pissarro and Cisley [sic]. Their landscapes, which cease to be confused with each other if you pay a little attention to them, have for me one unpardonable defect, which is that they reduce trees to the state of disembodied phantoms, depriving the trunks of the branches which constitute their real beauty, just like the limbs of a human body.

M. de Gas paints in the delicate medium of pastel for those with delicate tastes, but he paints with passion and zest, choosing singular aspects of Parisian life: the cafes of the boulevard, the *cafés-concerts* of the Champs-Elysées, the corridors and rehearsal rooms of the Opera. He goes about this as a man of feeling, of wit and sardonic observation, as a draughtsman of skill and quick observation. The Salons are too hidebound to exhibit these delicate studies, which in literature would be the equivalent of a short, incisive novel.

M. Renoir is very much an Impressionist, but to define his standing more precisely, one would call him a 'romantic Impressionist'. Endowed with an acute sensibility, he always draws back from making overaffirmative statements. With a few brushstrokes in *Un bal à Montmartre* he emphasizes the stationary objects, chairs, benches, tables. He endows the groups of dancers and of talkers with their own truth of action, and renders the rays of sunshine with palpitating brushstrokes.

Impressionists in competition 1877

Poverty and the comparative lack of patronage sharpened rivalries, and Hyacinthe-Eugène Murer, a patron of both Pissarro and Renoir, recorded how, at one of his dinners in 1877, when Pissarro was not present, Renoir started complaining.

Over the dessert Renoir told us that all day long he had been about from place to place with a picture under his arm trying to sell it. Everywhere he had been bowed out with the words: 'You have come too late. Pissarro has just been here. I've taken a picture from him as a matter of common humanity. You know, poor chap, with all those youngsters.' This 'poor chap', repeated at every door he knocked at, exasperated Renoir, who was very much put out at not having sold anything.

'What?' he cried, with that good-natured ogre's voice of his, and rubbing his nose nervously with his forefinger – a familiar gesture of his – 'because I'm a bachelor and have no children, am I to die of starvation? I'm in just as tight a corner as Pissarro, but nobody says "poor Renoir".'

Manet receives an academician 1878

In 1878 Manet's works were not accepted for the Fine Art Section of the International Exhibition in Paris. The occasion however brought to Paris a number of distinguished figures in the art world, including the English painter Sir Frederic Leighton, who was on the selection committee of the British section. Many years later Antonin Proust recorded the following conversation, which though not verbatim is probably accurate.

When we arrived at Manet's studio he asked the porter Aristide if anyone had called. 'Monsieur Leighton,' he replied.

'Ah yes,' said Manet, 'Sir Frederic Leighton, the President of the Royal Academy in London. He's already been here; he came yesterday with Henri Hecht [a banker and collector], who had introduced him to me a few days earlier. I was busy painting at the time, and his arrival rather irritated me. He wandered round the studio and then, stopping in front of the painting *The Skaters*, said to me, "That's very fine, but don't you think, M. Manet, that the figures look as though they were dancing, and that the contours aren't sufficiently well-defined?" I replied: "They're not dancing, they're skating. But you're quite right; they are *moving*, and when people are moving I can't paint them as though they were standing still. On the other hand I'm told that the contour of my *Olympia* is too hard – so that makes up for it." Leighton realized that he was irritating me, and went off. I wonder why he came back today?' . . .

Talking about his portrait of Mademoiselle Lemonnier he said, 'My main worry is always to have regular sittings. When I start something I'm always frightened that the sitter will let me down, or that I shan't be able to see them as often as I'd like. They come, they sit for me, and then they go off saying to themselves, "He can finish that when he likes on his own." No, nobody ever finishes anything "by himself", not unless he finishes it on the same day he started it; otherwise one has to make fresh starts, and take a long time over it. On the other hand there are some sitters who come back when I don't want them to, asking me to alter or retouch this or that. That's something I would never agree to.'

Japanese influences 1878

The influence of Japan on French painting in the second half of the nineteenth century is a widely known phenomenon. Less familiar is how early it received critical recognition. Théodore Duret, who published his Les Peintres Impressionistes *in 1878, had been one of the first to admire and collect Japanese art. A one-time habitué of the Café Guerbois, a friend of Manet and others, he had always been a supporter of Impressionism, and in this book he related the artistic practices of the movement to Japanese art.*

The Impressionists were not self-generated; they did not grow like mushrooms. They are a product of the organic growth of the modern school of French painting. *Natura non fecit saltum* [nature did not make a leap] in painting any more than in anything else. The Impressionists are descended from the naturalistic painters; their ancestors are Corot, Courbet and Manet. It is to these three masters that their painting owes that simple technique of painting with impulsive brushwork, consisting of large strokes and the building up of masses, which defies time. It is to them that we owe those bright colours in painting, which has now been freed from lead and bitumen, from chocolate and tobacco juice, from burnt fat and breadcrumbs. It is to them that we owe out-of-doors painting, the feeling not only of colours, but of those slight variations of colour which we call tones, and even more important than this the search for the connection between the atmosphere which illumines the painting

and the general tonality of the objects which are painted in it. To all that the Impressionists received from their predecessors was added the influence of Japanese art.

If you stroll along the banks of the Seine, at Asnières for example, you can take in at a single glance the red roof and brilliant white wall of a cottage, the tender green of a poplar, the yellow of the road, the blue of the river. In the summer at midday, every colour will seem harsh to you, intense, with no possible diminution of saturation, or shrouding in a general half-tone. This may seem strange, but it is still true, and we had to wait until the arrival of albums of Japanese prints before anybody dared to sit down on the bank of a river to juxtapose on canvas an unashamedly red roof, a white wall, a green poplar, a yellow road, and blue water. Before Japanese art arrived the painter always lied. Nature, with its bold colours was there for everybody to see, but on canvas all you ever saw was anaemic colours, swamped in a general half-tone.

As soon as people looked at Japanese pictures in which the most vivid, piercing colours were set side by side, they finally understood that there were new methods for reproducing certain effects of nature which had been till then considered impossible to render, and which were obviously worth having a try at. For these Japanese pictures, at first taken for mere crude mixtures of colour, are strikingly realistic . . . . Japanese art conveys the real appearance of nature by bold new methods of colouring. It cannot fail to interest inquiring artists, and so strongly influenced the Impressionists.

After the Impressionists had taken from their immediate predecessors in the French school their forthright manner of painting out of doors from the first impression with lively brushwork, and had grasped the bold new methods of Japanese colouring, they set out from these foundations to develop their own originality, and to abandon themselves to their own sensations.

MANET *Music at the Tuileries* 1862

PHOTOGRAPH OF COUPLES DANCING IN PARIS ON
14 JULY c. 1900

RENOIR *Moulin de la Galette* 1876

Public gaiety

*From the Tuileries to Montmartre, in natural or
in artificial light, the Parisian love of amusement
was a favoured theme of the Impressionists. It was
a symbol of their concern with living social reality (and incidentally, for Manet, an opportunity
to provoke unease with a spatial conundrum in
the centre of his composition).*

Degas makes an embarrassing confession   c. 1880

Degas had been drawing ballet dancers since the early 1870s, but perhaps he did not have as much first-hand experience of the Opera as appears. The following two un-dated letters to Albert Hecht, the banker and patron of Manet, Degas and others (he first appears as the figure holding opera glasses to his eyes in the Ballet de Robert le Diable, London, Victoria and Albert Museum), *seem to belong to the early 1880s.*

Have you the *power* to get the Opera to give me a pass to see the examination of the ballet dancers, which should be on Thursday, according to what I am told. I have done so many versions of the subject without ever having seen it that I am ashamed. Wednesday morning.

I still believe that I wrote my address without my name. But what a rigmarole. You were very kind to look everywhere for me.

I was thinking of slipping into the Opera with my little bit of paper amongst all the anxious mothers, and perhaps you could lead me to the feet of M. Vaucorbeil [Director of the Opera, 1879-84]. See you on Tuesday, and a thousand thanks. Sunday morning.

Degas, the horse and the camera   c. 1880

Although the camera had a great influence on art in the latter half of the nineteenth century, it was especially relevant to the Impressionists, who found it an invaluable tool for recording instant reactions, and analysing movement. Of all members of the movement, Degas, himself an enthusiastic photographer, used it most. Paul Valéry, who knew him well, recorded in the 1930s his memory of Degas' reactions to horses and the camera.

A horse walks on its toes. Four hoofs, like toenails, support it. No animal is closer to a *première danseuse*, a star of the *corps de ballet*, than a perfectly balanced thoroughbred, as it seems to pause in flight under the hand of its rider, and then trips forward in the bright sunshine. Degas painted it in a single line in a poem:

Tout nerveusement nu dans sa robe de soie.

'Nervously naked in its silken robe': the line occurs in a fine sonnet in which Degas has deployed all his skill to display every aspect and function of the racehorse; the training, the pace, the betting and cheating, the beauty, the supreme elegance.

He was amongst the first to study the real positions of the noble animal in movement, in the 'instantaneous' photographs taken by Major Muybridge. For he had a liking and appreciation for photography at a time when artists still despised it, or dared not admit they made use of it. He took some very fine ones himself, and I still treasure one particular enlargement he gave me.

It shows Mallarmé leaning against the wall, close by a mirror, with Renoir sitting opposite on a divan. In the mirror you can just make out, like phantoms, Degas and the camera, Mme and Mlle Mallarmé. This masterpiece of its kind involved the use of nine oil lamps, and a fearful quarter of an hour of immobility for the subjects. It was the finest portrait of Mallarmé I have ever seen, apart from Whistler's admirable lithograph.

Muybridge's photographs laid bare all the mistakes that sculptors and painters had made in their renderings of the various postures of the horse. They showed how inventive the eye is, or rather how much the sight elaborates on the data it gives us as the positive and impersonal result of observation. Between the state of vision as mere *patches of colour*, and as *things* or *objects*, a whole series of mysterious operations takes place, reducing to order, as best it can, the incoherence of raw perceptions, resolving contradictions, bringing to bear judgments

PHOTO SEQUENCE OF RACEHORSE BY EADWEARD MUYBRIDGE 1884-5   DEGAS *The False Start* c. 1870

DEGAS *Two Trotting Horses c.*1882

DEGAS *Jockey Leaning Back in the Saddle*
*c.*1884-8

Thoroughbreds

Degas loved the races and constantly painted horses. Devoted to the camera himself, he eagerly consulted the photographic evidence which was the first accurate record of the way a horse moves.

formed since early infancy, imposing continuity, connections, and the system of change which we group under the labels of *space, time, matter* and *movement*. This was why the horse was imagined to move in the way the eye seemed to see it, and it might be that if these old-style representations were examined with sufficient subtlety, the *law* of unconscious falsification might be discovered by which it seemed possible to picture the positions of a bird in flight, or a horse galloping as if they could be studied at leisure; but these interpolated pauses are imaginary. Only *probable* positions could be assigned to movement so rapid, and it might be worth while to try to define, by means of documentary comparisons, this kind of *creative* seeing by which the understanding fills the gaps in sense perception . . . .

In the racehorse Degas discovered a rare subject, which could satisfy the conditions imposed, both by his own temperament and his period, on his range of choice. Where was purity to be found in contemporary reality? Both realism and style, elegance and precision, were made luxuriously one in the pure form of the thoroughbred. Nothing was calculated to please an artist so refined, so fastidiously attentive to preliminary research, to the fine shades of discrimination, to the delicate labour of preparation, than this Anglo-Arab masterpiece. Degas' love and knowledge of the saddle horse were such that he could find merits in artists very unlike himself when he found they could make a carefully studied drawing of a horse. One day at Durand-Ruel's he kept me for long in front of a Meissonier statuette, an equestrian Napoleon in bronze, about an elbow length in height, detailing its beauties, or rather the exactness of rendering he could see in it. Shank bones, pasterns, fetlocks, seat, hindquarters – I had to listen to a thoroughly critical, and in the end complimentary, examination. He also commended the horse of Paul Dubois' *Jeanne d'Arc* in front of the church of Saint-Augustin, but forbore to mention the heroine, whose armour is so accurate.

Zola on the Philistine public   1880

The notion of a public really hostile to certain kinds of art was a new one. It had not existed in preceding centuries, but now it was a fact of artistic life. In 1880 Emile Zola in Mes Haines (My Hates) set out to examine the reactions and nature of this public, the one to which the Impressionists were exposed for most of their careers.

When the crowd laughs, it is nearly always over a trifle. Take the theatre, for example; an actor falls down, and the whole audience is convulsed with mirth, and the next day will laugh at remembering his fall. Put ten people of average intelligence in front of a new and original painting, and all ten will behave in the most childish way. They will nudge each other, and comment on the work in the most facetious manner. Curious idlers in their turn will arrive on the scene to swell the group, and soon it will turn into a real hubbub, a paroxysm of mad folly. I'm not just imagining this. The artistic history of our times gives ample proof of how such purblind fools and scoffers gathered in front of works by Descamps, Delacroix and Courbet. A writer told me some time ago how once, having had the misfortune to mention in some drawing-room or other that he found the works of Descamps not displeasing, he was immediately shown the door. Jesting is infectious, and every now and again Paris wakens to find that it has found a new subject for jest.

Then the situation becomes delirious. The public has something to keep it amused. A whole army exists for this purpose, and does its job very well. Caricaturists seize on the man and his work; journalists jeer even louder than the disinterested scoffers. In the main it is mere mockery, sheer hot air. There is not the slightest sense of conviction, not the least consideration for truth. Art is something serious and deeply boring. One has to laugh at it a bit, and some work must be found in the Salon which can be turned to ridicule, and it is always an original work, the mature fruit of some new personality which is picked for the purpose. Let us look at the work which causes all this hilarity. The pose is excruciatingly funny! The colouring makes you cry with laughter! The draughtsmanship has made more than a hundred people sick! All that the public can see is the subject – a subject treated in a certain manner. They look at pictures in the same way that children look at picture-books, to get some amusement out of them. Ignorant people laugh with complete assurance; knowledgeable people, those who have studied art in moribund schools, are irritated, on seeing new work, to discover that it lacks those qualities in which they believe, and to which their eyes have become accustomed. No one thinks of looking at it objectively. The ignorant understand nothing about it, the learned make comparisons. None of them can 'see', and hence they are aroused to mirth or anger. I repeat, it is simply the superficial way the work presents itself to the eye that is the cause of all this. The public never tries to probe further. They are stuck, as it were, on the surface. What is shocking and irritating to them is not the inner meaning of the work, but the general superficial aspect of it. If it were possible, the public would accept the same subject matter if it were presented differently.

It's the originality that shocks. We are all more or less creatures of habit, even if we are not aware of it; we follow the well trodden paths to which we are accustomed. Every new path alarms us, we shy at unknown prejudices, and refuse to go forward. We always want to have the same horizon ahead; we laugh at or are irritated by the things we fail to understand. That is why we are quite happy to accept originality when it is watered down, but violently reject anything which upsets our preconceived ideas. As soon as anybody with originality appears on the scene, we become defiant and scared, like nervous horses which rear at a fallen tree on the road because they cannot understand either the nature or the cause of this obstacle, and make no further attempt to explain it to themselves.

It is only a question of what you are used to. By dint of seeing and examining the obstacle, fear and suspicion are diminished. after that there is always some kind passer-by who will make us ashamed of our anger, and explain to us the reason for our fear . . . .

The public will never be fair to real artists as long as it fails to regard a work of art solely as a free and original interpretation of nature. Is it not sad today to remember that Delacroix was despised in his time, that his genius was rejected, and trimphed only after his death? What do his detractors think now, and why don't they speak out and admit that they were blind and unintelligent? That would be a lesson for them. Perhaps it would teach them to understand that there is no common-denominator, nor rules, nor obligations of any sort – only living men, bringing with them a liberal interpretation of life, giving their flesh and blood, becoming more glorious as they become more individualistic and perfect. In that case, one should go straight for the pictures which are strange and bold – those are the ones which should be attentively and seriously studied in order to discover if they show signs of human genius. Then one would dismiss the copies and incoherencies of spurious painters, and all those worthless pictures which are merely the products of a skilful hand. What one wants to look for above all else in a work of art is the human touch, a living corner of creation, a new manifestation of humanity brought face to face with the realities of nature.

LELOIR *Private View at the Salon* 1879

Exhibitions

The Salon, an eighteenth-century invention,
allowed a public of buyers and non-buyers the
opportunity to see and judge the latest painting
(above, at the vernissage or varnishing-day,
artists add a last touch). As Zola bitterly observed,
much of the resulting comment aimed only at a
cheap laugh. Comments by Draner at the 1879
Impressionist exhibition (right): Gloves going
cheap; Steam boating; Soap-and-water colour.

DRANER *Exhibits at the
Fourth Impressionist Exhibition*
1879

CHANTEUSE DE CAFÉ.
Unique occasion à 7 fr 50 la paire !
Huit boutons ! Quelle excellente
enseigne pour un commerce de
gants !

DEGAS *Singer with Glove* 1878

PARTIE DE BATEAU
... à vapeur.

CAILLEBOTTE *Rower in Top Hat* 1879

L'artiste a pris soin de délayer
du savon de Marseille dans
son eau.

CAILLEBOTTE *Diver* 1877

SISLEY *Snow at Veneux-Nadoux* 1879-82

Sisley on the 'life-giving factor' c. 1880

In an undated letter to an unknown friend, Alfred Sisley put down some of his ideas about art and landscape painting.

It is a ticklish thing to put down on paper what an artist calls his 'aesthetic'.

The aversion to indulgence in theory that Turner felt, I feel too, and I believe it's much easier to talk about masterpieces than to create them, whether with the brush or in any other way.

As you know, the charm of a painting is many-sided. The subject, the motif, must always be set down in a simple way, easily understood and grasped by the beholder. By the elimination of superfluous detail, the spectator should be led along the road that the artist indicates to him, and from the first be made to notice what the artist has felt.

Every picture shows a spot with which the artist has fallen in love. It is this, amongst other things, which gives the work of Corot and Jongkind its unsurpassed charm.

The animation of the canvas is one of the hardest problems of painting. To give life to the work of art is certainly one of the most necessary tasks of the true artist. Everything must serve this end; form, colour, surface. The artist's impression is the life-giving factor, and only this impression can free that of the spectator.

RENOIR *Alfred Sisley* 1879

And, though the artist must remain master of his craft, the surface, at times raised to the highest pitch of liveliness, should transmit to the beholder the sensation which possessed the artist.

You see that I am in favour of a variation of surface within the same picture. This does not correspond to customary opinion, but I believe it to be correct, particularly when it is a question of rendering a light effect. Because when the sun lets certain parts of a landscape appear soft, it lifts others into sharp relief. These effects of light, which have an almost material expression in nature, must be rendered in material fashion on the canvas.

Objects must be portrayed in their particular context, and they must, especially, be bathed in light, as is the case in nature. The progress to be achieved in the future will consist in this. The means will be the sky (the sky can never be merely a background). Not only does it give the picture depth through its successive planes (for the sky, like the ground, has planes) but through its form, and through its relations with the whole effect, or with the composition of the picture, it gives movement . . . .

I emphasize this part of a landscape because I would like you to understand the importance I attach to it.

An indication of this: I always begin a picture with the sky.

MANET *Self-portrait* 1878-9

MANET *Théodore Duret* 1868

Manet paints a single figure   1880

In 1880 Manet sent his portrait of Antonin Proust, his friend, who had recently entered the Chamber of Deputies, to the Salon. After the opening he wrote to his sitter.

For three weeks now your portrait has been at the Salon, badly hung on a divided exhibition-stand near a door, and criticized even more unfavourably than it's hung. But it is my fate to be vilified, and I accept it

MANET *Antonin Proust* 1880

philosophically. Nevertheless, dear friend, you would hardly believe how difficult it is to place a solitary figure on a canvas, and concentrate interest on this single figure, and still keep it vital. To paint two figures is child's play in comparison. Ah, the portrait in blue with the hat on! Well I'm still waiting for it; I don't think that I'll ever see it. But when I'm dead they will realize that I saw and thought with accuracy. I remember as if it were yesterday the summary way in which I treated the glove in your ungloved hand.

And when at that moment you said to me 'Please, not a touch more,' I felt that we were in such perfect harmony that I could hardly resist the impulse to embrace you. I do hope that nobody will have the idea of locking up this portrait in a public collection. I have always been horrified by this mania for piling up works of art in public collections, without even leaving space between the frames. It's just like goods in a department store. Well, time will tell, we are in the hands of fate.

125

5ᴹᴱ EXPOSITION
FAITE PAR UN GROUPE
D'ARTISTES INDÉPENDANTS

BRACQUEMOND	GUILLAUMIN	ROUART
CAILLEBOTTE	LEBOURG	TILLOT
DEGAS	LEVERT	EUG. VIDAL
FORAIN	PISSARRO	VIGNON
GAUGUIN	RAFFAELLI	ZANDOMENEGHI

10, Rue des Pyramides, 10
A L'ANGLE DE LA RUE SAINT-HONORE

Du 1ᵉʳ au 30 Avril, de 10 heures à 6 heures.

PRIX D'ENTRÉE, 1 FRANC.

1111   Paris. — Typographie MORRIS père et fils, rue Amelot, 64.

POSTER FOR THE FIFTH IMPRESSIONIST EXHIBITION

Conflicts at the fifth exhibition   1880

*Each of the Impressionist exhibitions cre-
ated problems connected with the often
prickly personalities of the artists involved.
In March 1880 Degas wrote to Bracquemond about the fifth exhibition, in which
Degas himself, Pissarro and Morisot were
represented, as well as Degas' friend Mary
Cassatt and a newcomer, Paul Gauguin.*

It will open on the first of April. The posters
are going up tomorrow or Monday. They
are in bright red letters on a green background. There has been a great struggle
with Caillebotte about whether or not to put
names on it. I had to give in and allow them
to do so. When will people stop wanting to
be *stars*.

Mlle Cassatt and Mme Morisot were quite
adamant about not having their names on
the posters. It has turned out exactly the
same as last year, and the name of Mme
Bracquemond is not shown. The whole
thing is ridiculous. Every reasonable argument, quite apart from good taste, has no
effect on the pigheadedness of Caillebotte,
and the inertia of the rest.

In comparison with all the wild fuss that
de Nittis and Monet will make at La Vie Moderne, our fifth exhibition should be your
chance of glory. I shall arrange things so
that this situation does not continue. I am
upset and humiliated.

Start bringing your exhibits. There will
be two panel screens, one in the middle of
the gallery, with four sections, and the other
in the entrance hall. You can hang on them
all your engravings.

See you soon.

[PS.] If you agree and if Mme Bracquemond
also does, we can take out her name on the
second printing of 1,000 posters which will
be distributed during the exhibition. Let me
know.

126

Signac seeks advice   1880

*In 1880 the sixteen-year-old Paul Signac –
later a leader of the Neo-Impressionist
movement which was to be the heir and sup-
planter of Impressionism – wrote to Monet,
whose works he greatly admired, seeking
the kind of advice which other art students
must also have needed.*

Dear Sir and Master,
First of all I would ask you, sir, to forgive the
great liberty I take in writing to you. This,
briefly is my situation; for two years I have
been painting, having had as models only
your works, and following the great pathway which you have opened up. I have always worked regularly and conscientiously,
but without any advice or help, for I know
no Impressionist painter who could guide
me, living as I do in a mainly unfriendly
environment.

I am therefore frightened of taking the
wrong path, and I ask you, as a favour to
allow me to pay you a short visit; I would be
so happy if I could show you five or six of
my sketches, from which you can come to a
decision about my abilities, and give me the
advice which I so much need, because in
short I am horribly uncertain of myself, having always worked alone, without a teacher,
without support, without any criticism.

I dare to hope, M. Monet, that you will not
refuse me this boon which would be a very
great honour for me, and a real encouragement.

Hoping for a favourable response on
your part, I am, sir, your respectful pupil.

Degas on the technique of
aquatint   1880

*Degas was not only very preoccupied with
the various techniques of print-making, but
ready to pass on his advice. Sometime in
1880 he wrote to Pissarro, with whom he
worked on several occasions in this
medium.*

I compliment you on your enthusiasm. I
hurried to Mlle Cassatt with your parcel.
She congratulates you, as do I in this matter.

Here are the proofs; the prevailing black-
ish or greyish shade comes from the zinc,
which is greasy in itself and retains the printer's black. The surface of the plate is not
smooth enough.

But in any case you can see what great
possibilities there are in the technique. You
must practise dusting the particles, in order,
for instance to obtain a sky of uniform grey,
smooth and fine. This is very difficult if one
is to believe Maître Bracquemond.

Here is the method. Take a very smooth
plate – this is absolutely essential. Remove
the grease thoroughly with whitening. Before doing this you will already have prepared a solution of resin in very concentrated alcohol. This liquid is poured in the
manner of photographers when they pour
collodion onto their glass plates (take care,
as they do, to drain the plate well by tilting
it). This liquid then evaporates leaving the
plate covered with a coat of varying thick-
ness, composed of small particles of resin.
In allowing it to bite, you obtain a network
of lines of varying depth according to how
deeply you let it bite. To obtain consistent
tone this is essential; to get more haphazard
effects you can obtain them with a stump, or
with your finger, or any other pressure on
the paper which covers the soft-ground.

Your soft-ground seems to be a little too
greasy. You have added a little too much
grease or tallow.

What did you blacken your ground with
to get that bistre tone behind the drawing? It
is very pretty.

Try something larger with a better plate.

PISSARRO *Effect of Rain* (2nd state) 1879

PISSARRO *Effect of Rain* (6th state) 1879

Aquatints

DEGAS *Mary Cassatt at the Louvre* 1879-80

Degas, whose press Pissarro used to use, may him-self have printed some of the states of Effect of Rain. *This and the Degas print of Mary Cassatt, who was herself a printmaker, are aquatints, a process which gives an apparently light-filled tex-ture. Degas repeatedly traced and re-used the figure of Cassatt in her geometrically exact pose.*

DEGAS *Mary Cassatt c.*1884

Mary Cassatt at the sixth exhibition   1881

Joris-Karl Huysmans (1848-1907), famous mainly for the 'decadent' novel A rebours, *so greatly admired by writers such as Oscar Wilde, was also an art critic who devoted a book to the Flemish primitives, wrote criticism of the Salons and other current exhibitions for various magazines, which he published in book form in 1883 as* L'Art moderne, *and expressed views about the Impressionists which were lucid and impressive. He was especially impressed by the work of the thirty-eight-year-old American Mary Cassatt, a close friend of Degas, who was also responsible for securing patronage for the Impressionists from families such as the Stillmans, the Havemeyers and the Whittemores. The following account of her work in the Impressionist exhibition of 1881 appeared in* L'Art moderne.

Last year I wrote that the paintings of Mlle Cassatt recalled for the most part the pastels of Degas, and that one of them gave strong indications of the influence of modern English painters.

From these two sources there has arisen an artist who now owes nothing to anybody; an artist who at the first attempt has established her personality.

Her works at the exhibition consist of portraits of children, also interiors, and they are a miracle, as Mlle Cassatt has managed to escape from that sentimentality which so often affects English painters when they undertake subjects like this, which are so popular with them.

Those babies! How often their portraits have appeared absolutely repellent to me. There is a whole crew of French and English daubers who have painted them in stupid and pretentious poses. For the first time in my life, thanks to Mlle Cassatt I have seen images of ravishing children, tranquil scenes of bourgeois life, painted with a kind of delicate tenderness which is completely charming. Moreover, this is a fact which one must repeat, only women can really paint childhood. There is in the process a particular sentiment which men cannot express, at least not unless they are especially sensitive and delicate in their apprehension; their fingers are too clumsy to avoid their being apt to leave awkward fingerprints on what they do. Only a woman can pose a child, dress it appropriately, use pins without pricking. But then she often reverts to affectation or lachrymosity as Mlle Elisa Koch does in France, or Mme Ward in England. But, thank heavens, Mlle Cassatt is not one of these. The walls where her paintings are hung contain a mother reading, surrounded by lively children, and another mother kissing her baby on the cheeks, which are undoubtedly pearls of the finest water. Here is family life, painted with distinction, and with love. Inevitably one thinks of those discreet family interiors of Dickens, of Esther Summerson, of Florence Dombey, of Agnes Copperfield and the Dorrit children; women nursing children on their knees, whilst in the quiet room a kettle simmers on the hob, and the light spread over the table illumines the teapot, the cups and saucers, and falls on the plate stacked up with slices of bread and butter. In this group of works by Mlle Cassatt there is an affectionate understanding of quiet domesticity, a heightened sense of intimacy. To find their equivalent one has to go back to Millais' painting *The Three Sisters* which was exhibited in the English section at the International Exhibition of 1878.

Two other paintings: one called *The Garden* shows in the foreground a woman reading, whilst at an angle behind her great green clumps are pricked out with red stars composed of geraniums, and bordered by the deep purple nettles which stretch out to the house, the lower part of which completes the painting. In the other one, called *Teatime*, a smiling woman, dressed in rose coloured clothes, sits in a chair, holding in her gloved hands a cup of tea. Both these works accentuate the same note of tenderness, and exude a delicate fragrance of Parisian elegance.

This indeed is the most characteristic quality of her talent, that Mlle Cassatt, who, I believe, is an American, paints French women, but manages somehow to introduce into her Parisian interiors an 'at home' feeling. She has succeeded in expressing, as none of our own painters have managed to do, the joyful peace, the tranquil friendliness of the domestic interior.

Renoir paints Wagner   *1882*

Renoir, like many of his generation, had long been an enthusiast for Wagner's music, and in January 1882, during a lengthy stay in Italy, he went to Palermo to paint a portrait of the composer, who was engaged on finishing Parsifal *in the Villa Gangi on the Piazza dei Porazzi. There he made a sketch, which he later worked up into the portrait now in the Musée d'Orsay. He described his experiences to an unknown correspondent on 14 January.*

I am a bit worried about a letter which I wrote to you, because after sealing it, I weighed it, being uncertain how many stamps to put on. But since I posted several letters at the same time, I may have put it in another envelope. Where in God's name did it go? Luckily I have a torn draft of it, so I'm going to try and reconstruct it, without even asking your permission. You know very well I can't write. So that's that.

After having resisted my brother for a long time, he eventually sends me a letter of introduction to Naples from M. de Brayer. I don't read the letter; not even the signature, and there I am on the boat with the prospect of being seasick for at least fourteen hours. It then occurs to me to look for it in my pocket. No letter! I probably left it at the hotel. I go through everything; no sign of it. You can see what a fix I was in by the time I got to Palermo. I find the city rather depressing, and wonder whether I shouldn't perhaps take the boat back in the evening. Then I go to the Post Office to try and find out where Wagner is staying. Nobody speaks French; nobody has ever heard of Wagner. But at the hotel where I am staying there are some Germans, and they tell me he is staying at the Hôtel des Palmes. I take a carriage and visit Monreale, where there are some fine mosaics, and on the way I indulge in a lot of melancholy thoughts. Before leaving I send a telegram to Naples, without any hope or optimism, however, and sit around waiting. Nothing happens so I decide to introduce myself on my own, so there I am writing a note, in which I ask permission to pay my respects to the Master, and end it by saying that I shall be glad to take news of him back to M. Lascoux and Mme. Mendès in Paris; I wasn't able to add the name of M. de Brayer, because I hadn't looked at the signature on the original letter of introduction. So here I am at the Hôtel des Palmes. A servant takes my letter, goes away, comes back and says 'Non salue il Maestro' and vanishes. Next day my original letter turns up from Naples. I take it round again; the same servant takes it, with obvious contempt. I wait under the carriage entrance, anxious not to be seen, and not in the mood to meet anyone, since I only

screwed myself up to this second attempt in order to prove that I hadn't just come to beg 40 sous.

Finally along comes a fair-haired young man, whom I take to be English. In fact he's a Russian, and his name is Joukovski. He says that he knows my work very well, that Mme Wagner regrets not being able to receive me now, and asks if I could stay in Palermo for one more day, as Wagner is putting the final touches to *Parsifal*, and is unwell and in a state of nerves, has lost his appetite and so on and so forth.

I beg him to give my apologies to Mme Wagner, and ask to be excused. We spend some minutes talking, and when I tell him the purpose of my visit, I can see by the smile on his face that he thinks it will be a failure. He confesses to me that he himself is a painter, that he too would like to do a portrait of the Master, and to achieve this has been following him everywhere for two years, in vain. But he advises me to stay, saying that what he had denied him, he may grant to me, and that anyway I can't go away without actually seeing Wagner. This Russian is charming; he ends up by consoling me, and we make an appointment for the next day at two o'clock. Next day I meet him at the post office. He tells me that yesterday, 13 February [*sic*], Wagner finished his opera, that he is very tired, and that he can't see me till five o'clock, but that he will be there, so I won't feel uneasy. I accept enthusiastically, and go away happy. I'm there at five o'clock sharp, and again meet the same servant, who greets me with a deep bow, asks me to follow him, takes me through a small greenhouse and into an adjoining sitting room, asks me to sit down in a huge armchair, and with a gracious smile asks me to wait a moment. I see Mlle Wagner, and a youth who must be a little Wagner, but no Russian. Mlle Wagner tells me that her mother is out, but that her father is coming, and then she disappears. I hear the sound of footsteps muffled by thick carpet. It's the Master, in his velvet dressing gown, the

RENOIR *Richard Wagner* 1882

wide sleeves lined with satin. He is very handsome, very courteous. He shakes my hand and begs me to sit down, and then the most extraordinary conversation takes place, half German, half French – with guttural endings.

'I am very content. You are coming from Paris.' 'No,' I say, 'from Naples.' I tell him about losing my letter, which makes him laugh a lot. We talk a great deal, though when I say we, all I did was to keep repeating 'Yes, dear Master,' 'Of course, dear Master.' I would get up to leave, and he would take my hands and keep pushing me back into the chair. 'Wait a little more. My wife will be coming soon. And that good Las-

coux, how is he?' I tell him that as I have been in Italy for some time I don't know, and he doesn't even know I'm here. We talk about *Tannhäuser* at the Opera, in short we keep at it for more than three quarters of an hour, whilst I keep looking anxiously for the arrival of the Russian. Finally he comes in with Mme Wagner, who asks me if I know M. de Breyer well. Not understanding her accent, I reply, 'Not at all, is he a musician?' 'So' she replies 'he is not the one who gave you the letter?' 'Oh, M. de Brayé, yes of course I know him. We do not pronounce the word the same way.' I apologize, blushing furiously. But I make up for my gaffe with Lascoux, whose voice I mimic.

133

She then told me to give their regards to their friends when I get back to Paris, especially to Lascoux, insisting on it, and repeating it before I left. We talked about the Impressionists of music. What a lot of nonsense I must have talked! I ended up all hot and bothered, in a state of utter confusion and red as a rooster. I was a typical example of the shy man who plunges in too far, and yet I think that he was very pleased with me. I don't know why. He detests the German Jews, among others the art critic Albert Wolff. He asked me whether we still liked *Les Diamants de la couronne* in France. I attacked Meyerbeer [actually this opera was written by Auber]. In the long run I was given the chance to utter all the nonsense I felt like.

Then, all of a sudden, he said to M. Joukovski, 'If I'm feeling all right at midday I'll give a sitting until lunch. You know you'll have to be understanding, but I will do what I can. If it doesn't last long, it won't be my fault. M. Renoir, please ask M. Joukovski if it's all right if you do me too, that is if it doesn't bother him.'

M. Joukovski replies, 'But, dear Master, I was just about to ask you, etc., etc.'.

'How would you like to do it?' I say full-face.

He says, 'That's fine,' because he wants to paint the back, whilst I do the front.

Then Wagner says to him, 'You're going to paint me turning my back on France, and M. Renoir will do me from the other side. Oh dear!'

Next day I was there at noon; you know the rest. He was very cheerful, but I felt very nervous, and regretted that I wasn't Ingres. In short I think that my time – 35 minutes, which was not much – was well spent. If I had stopped sooner it would in fact have been better, because my model started to lose some of his cheerfulness, and he was starting to get constrained. I recorded these changes a bit too closely. Anyway, you'll see.

At the end Wagner asked if he could have a look, and said 'Ach! I look like a Protestant minister' – which was true enough. Anyway I was glad not to have made a botch-up of it; I now have a little souvenir of that splendid head.

[PS.] I'm not re-reading my letter; if I did I would tear it up again, and that would be my fifteenth try. If there are things I've forgotten I'll tell you. He repeated several times that the French read art critics too much, this with a roar of laughter. 'Ach! Those German Jews! But, M. Renoir, I know there are a lot of fine French people, whom I do not confuse with them.' Unfortunately I cannot recreate the openness and gaiety of this conversation with the Master.

Renoir on art and politics   1882

Despite the traditional alliance between 'advanced' art and the Left – as epitomized, for instance, in the career of Courbet – most of the Impressionists were conservative in their political opinions, and more intent on achieving social and official recognition than popular ideas of the 'avant-garde' might lead one to expect. In the spring of 1882 Renoir, who was ill with a chest infection at L'Estaque, wrote to Durand-Ruel about Pissarro's plan to organize a group exhibition which would include Cézanne, Gauguin and others. Durand-Ruel himself was in favour, but Monet would participate only if Renoir did, and he gave a dusty answer.

To exhibit with Pissarro, Gauguin and Guillaumin would be as if I were exhibiting with some Socialist group. Before long Pissarro will be inviting Lavrof [a Russian anarchist] or some other revolutionary. The public doesn't like anything smelling of politics, and at my age I certainly don't want to become a revolutionary. To go on along with the Israelite Pissarro would be revolution. Moreover, these characters know that I took a great step forward in getting accepted by the Salon. It is a question of not losing what

RENOIR *Paul Durand-Ruel* 1910

I have gained. They will do anything, even at the price of dropping me once the show has failed. I don't want that! I don't want that! Get rid of these people, and give me artists like Monet, Sisley, Morisot, etc., and I am with you. It's not about politics any more; it's about pure art.

Praise in London   1882

During the summer of 1882 Durand-Ruel organized a small exhibition of work by Impressionists in London. It was followed in 1883 by a much larger one at Dowdeswell's Galleries in New Bond Street, and this may have been at least partly due to the favourable review which appeared in The Standard *of 1 July 1882. It was probably by Frederick Wedmore.*

Though the exhibition of certain French 'Impressionists' open for the moment at 13, King Street, St James's, is but a small one, it is thoroughly worth seeing; first because several of the pictures are excellent, and secondly because until now the Impressionists have been little known in England. That is to say, in the matter of the Impressionists, we have 'entertained angels unaware', for Mr Whistler and Mr Tissot have long been with us, and their work is like that of the Impressionists in two respects – it aims generally to record what the eye actually sees, and not what the mind knows the eye ought to see, and likewise it addresses itself with courage and confidence to the artistic problems of modern life, and our artificial society.

Continued on p. 139.

Mockery

Draner was paid to scoff, of course; but his reactions are still curious. He constantly refers to the sheer ugliness of the pictures. 'No danger of anyone taking advantage of her', he remarks of Renoir's Young Girl Sleeping.

RENOIR *Woman with a Fan* 1881

PISSARRO *La Mère Larchevêque* 1880

RENOIR *On the Terrace* 1881

RENOIR *Sleeping Girl with Cat* 1880

RENOIR *Young Girl Sleeping* 1880

MONET *Grainval near Fécamp* 1881

UNE VISITE AUX IMPRESSIONNISTES

PAR DRANER

MANET *A Bar at the Folies-Bergère* 1882

EDOUARD MANET.

40901

UNE MARCHANDE DE CONSOLATION AUX FOLIES-BERGÈRE. — (Son dos se reflète dans une glace; mais, sans doute par suite d'une distraction du peintre, un monsieur avec lequel elle cause et dont on voit l'image dans la glace, n'existe pas dans le tableau. — Nous croyons devoir réparer cette omission.)

STOP *Seller of Consolation at the Folies-Bergère* 1882
(with 'missing' figure of customer added)

To do both of these things is certainly a 'note' of the Impressionist, and he among them who does both of these things with the best effect is undoubtedly Mr Degas, a skilled draughtsman, a brilliant and dextrous colourist, and a perfectly unfettered and keen observer of the modern world. He has now four pictures at King Street, and we will speak of them first, not only because he is chief of the school, but because in his recent work the revolt from recognized subjects and recognized methods of treatment is the more pronounced. One of his pictures is a study of horses and jockeys in action, the horses restive, the riders resolute. The wonderful action – the action of a moment – so rapidly portrayed in both the animals and the figures evidences Mr Degas' prompt force of draughtsmanship, as well as the closeness of his observation. His skill as a colourist, and as one who can suggest – we can hardly say who can elaborately paint – texture, is shown in another design, the astonishing picture of two young women trying on bonnets in a milliner's shop. Half of the design is occupied by the milliner's table on which lies a store of her finery. Silks and feathers, satin and straw, are indicated swiftly, decisively with the most brilliant touch. Another work of Mr Degas is devoted entirely to the play of light and of shadow on the front of one opera box, and in the recesses of another. Every tone, every gradation, is followed with perfect skill, and the choice of the theme finds its justification in the success of the treatment. Mr Degas' remaining work – a perfectly original study of the scuttering ankles of certain ballet girls under the weird and vivid illumination of the stage – is unquestionably clever, but the amateurs are few to whom it will afford unmixed delight.

A highly accomplished pupil of Degas is a young American lady, Miss Mary Cassatt. Her most considerable contribution – and it has a grace and refinement which her master is not particularly anxious about – displays two gentlewomen, the one armed with a fan and the other with an opera glass, shoulder to shoulder at the Opera. Mr Renoir paints both landscape and the figure – a Parisian model, and a purple clover field edged by the sea. Mr Sisley's best work is that which represents a bridge over the Seine, with the shallowish water flowing quietly in pleasant glances and gleams. Mr Claude Monet, who is not for a moment to be confused with Manet, the figure painter, is at his finest in *Low Tide at Varengeville*, a coast picture of cliff, and beach and sky, full of glowing colour and liquid light, and attaining, after all, though by means absolutely different from Mr Hook's, something of Mr Hook's atmospheric effects. The artist has been bold enough to rely for the attractiveness of the picture on the unaided landscape. No figure is introduced to mar or mend the scene.

Sisley argues for group shows 1882

One of the things which exercised many of the artists involved in the movement was whether or not to maintain a corporate identity. The stronger their artistic personality, the more they tended to react against the idea, as did some of their supporters. In 1882 Durand-Ruel, who in that year had taken an active part in the organization of a seventh group show at 251 rue Saint-Honoré, began to believe that individual exhibitions were probably preferable, and also – as he was going through a difficult financial time – more profitable to him. Sisley, who had 27 works in the exhibition, did not agree, and wrote to him on 5 November from Moret close to the forest of Fontainebleau.

The more I think about the idea you put forward yesterday, the less enthusiastic I am about it.

All precedents prove that group exhibitions are nearly always successful, and generally individual ones aren't.

But not only would your idea involve a constant series of exhibitions, but also by its very nature it would become a kind of permanent exhibition, and what a dealer can do in his own gallery a group of painters cannot do without eventually making the public both bored and hostile. For, no matter whether we exhibit together, or one after the other (in the same place), to the public we shall always be *The Impressionists*. I could understand it if the central problem were knowing whether or not we ought to have a regular annual exhibition. But if we do exhibit annually, we must do it together as a group, in our own interest.

It is not, it seems to me, at the moment when we cease to be nomads and have a regular location for our exhibitions that we should think of initiating another type of exhibition, and explore possibilities in that direction. As far as I'm concerned both our interest and yours lies not so much in showing a lot of pictures, but in doing everything necessary to sell those we have actually painted. To arrive at this result a joint exhibition, composed of a small number of works by each member, would be much more effective, and would have a greater chance of success. These are my arguments against one-man exhibitions. What do you think of them?

Impressionists and aesthetes   1883

Durand-Ruel's London exhibition of 1883 included eleven works by Pissarro, nine by Renoir, eight by Sisley, seven each by Degas and Monet, three by Berthe Morisot, three by Manet (who died that year), and two by Mary Cassatt. None was sold, but the press was generally less hostile than might have been expected. It was seen as an exhibition of avant-garde art, and, as Lucien Pissarro – who was living in Holloway, North London, with his wife, Esther, – had predicted in a letter to his father, dated 28 February, there was now a tendency to confuse Im-

pressionism with the English 'Aesthetic' or Decadent movement, of which the leading artistic exponent was Whistler.

You're wrong to accuse me of not being interested in painting. That's what I talk about the most with Esther, or at Henry's. As for the National Gallery, I went through it rapidly with Esther, that's why I didn't want to talk to you about it – I had hardly seen anything of it. On the other hand on Saturday I saw the Whistler exhibition. He lifted the idea of coloured rooms from us. His is all white, bordered with lemon yellow; the drapes are yellow velvet with his butterfly embroidered on the corner. The chairs are yellow with white straw. On the floor there's a yellowish Indian mat, and vases in clay with some kind of yellow dandelions. Finally the servant is dressed in white and yellow. This arrangement makes the room seem very gay compared to the neighbouring rooms where the paintings of a dealer are on view. The English were rather critical of the room, and there were many people there the day I went .... I think that if you [the Impressionists] show in London, it is essential to have rooms like the ones you had in Paris. That will make people talk about you and you'll have a good turn-out. Newness is always attractive, and you'll be taken for the French aesthetes. Whistler hasn't gone into nuances, so there would be something to do in that direction. But it is important not to waste time, otherwise he'll do it first, and you would be called imitators.

Degas in need of money   1883

Most of the Impressionists were chronically hard up, and even so apparently secure a person as Degas had recurring money problems. This was largely because he had assumed responsibility for the debts his brother had incurred in his cotton-broking business. In 1883, at the age of forty-nine, he was still having to badger Durand-Ruel for money.

17 July 1883

You would give me great pleasure if you could send me all or part of what I asked you for the other day. I have not yet finished the pastels for which they are payment, and I could not take anything from you without offering something in return. But I am not allowed time to wait. I have a bill to pay *tomorrow morning.* I hope to send you two pieces in the course of tomorrow.

Undated

Send me a little more money by Prosper [his servant] immediately. *I need it for this afternoon.* There are 7 drawings heightened with pastel and a small painting at the framer's. You will have them all on Friday.

Undated

On Friday I sent you three drawings. You will have two more tomorrow, and Tuesday the two others and the paintings. The framer has let me down. On Monday I would be pleased if you could send me 300 francs in the morning. If you could go as far as 400 I would be even more relieved. I have more than 200 francs to pay out immediately.

You will have a painting in the course of the week.

Undated

Please have the goodness to send me something by Prosper tomorrow morning. I only got the picture in the small frame this morning, and there were some small changes I had to make to it. I am hurrying as much as I can, but I am not getting along as quickly as we would both wish.

It is *absolutely necessary*, that is why I am making this request.

Undated

I shall not have had the time to finish the little painting for the 2nd of this month, which was yesterday. I have therefore finished the pastel for you.

This evening I have to pay 300 francs. Send me therefore, I beg of you, the remaining 400 francs.

Advice from Degas   1883

In 1883 Lucien Pissarro was thinking of attending Alphonse Legros's drawing classes at the Slade School of Art in London. On 13 June his father Camille wrote to him.

I mentioned to Degas that you are thinking of taking Legros' course in drawing. Degas says there is one way of escaping from Legros' influence, the method is simply this: it is to reproduce, at home and from memory, the drawing you made in class. I suppose that you begin by making a sketch of the whole figure; when you get home, you prepare the sketch and try to do again from memory what you did from nature. The next day, in class, you finish a part of your figure; at home you go on with the work from memory. Little by little you finish both studies simultaneously, then you compare them. You will have your difficulties, but a moment will come when you will be astonished by the ease with which you retain forms, and, curiously enough, the observations you make from memory will have far more power and be much more original than those you owe to direct contact with nature. The drawing will have art; it will be your own; this is a good way of escaping slavish imitation.

You speak with some severity of the Academy exhibition. It is very likely that you are right, but one must not make the mistake of judging English art in the way French art is sometimes judged here, as if it were represented by Bastien-Lepage and Gervex. Remember England has Keene; he does not exhibit, he is not fashionable, and that is everything. England, like France, is rotten to the core; she knows only one art, the art of throwing sand in your eyes.

PISSARRO *Lucien Pissarro* 1883

And from Pissarro 1883

On 25 July Pissarro returned to the same theme in another letter to Lucien, in which he reinforced the advice given by Degas.

It is good to draw everything, anything. When you have trained yourself to see a tree truly, you know how to look at the human figure. Specialization is not necessary, it is the death of art, whose requirements are exactly opposed to those of industry. Once again I say, you can never waste your time if you are drawing landscapes conscientiously. The classroom is good only when you are strong enough not to be influenced.

I know Legros quite well. Monet and I had lunch with him when we were in London in 1870. He may remember me; he may have totally forgotten me. I could get you introduced to him, but I fear his influence.

You must follow Degas' advice to the letter, and with an iron will; it is much more important than you imagine; all the more so since I want you to be protected against Legros; he has lost sight of much that he did here, or so I am told. How much does he want? Write to me.

You wrote that there is a simple old fellow who just has an Academy, but is rather lax in running it. This would be just right, for, let me repeat, I fear Legros has a *preconceived method*.

Watercolour is not especially difficult, but I must warn you to steer clear of those pretty English watercolourists, so skilful and alas so weak, and often too *truthful*. Look at the little wash drawings of Turner. But the trick cannot be learned, you can do it when you know how to draw. Oil is much more difficult, but when you master it, you can do with it what you want to. Think of the watercolours of Delacroix, Jongkind. Who else? Degas, Manet – with the rest it is a technique, though there are some who bring talent to it. When you have occasion to, look at the Persians, the Chinese, the Japanese. Derive your taste from those who are truly strong, for you must always go to the source; in painting to the primitives, in sculpture to the Egyptians, in miniature to the Persians, etc., etc.

Pissarro contemplates his own works 1883

After the exhibition of Impressionist paintings in London in 1883, Lucien Pissarro tried to persuade his father to have a one-man exhibition there. The reply came from Rouen on 20 November.

You tell me that if I have a show in London I must send my best works. That sounds simple enough, but when I reflect and ask myself what are my best works, I am in all honesty greatly perplexed. Didn't I send to

PISSARRO *Peasant Girl Drinking Coffee* 1881

London my *Peasant Girl Drinking Coffee* and my *Peasant Girl With A Branch*? Alas, I shall never do more careful, more finished work; however these paintings were regarded as uncouth in London. So it is not an improper selection that explains why my work offends English taste. Remember that I have the temperament of a peasant, I am melancholy, harsh and savage in my works, it is only in the long run that I can expect to please, and then only those who have a grain of indulgence; but the eye of the passer-by is too hasty, and sees only the surface. Whoever is in a hurry will not stop for me. As for the young misses, touched alas with the modern neuroticism, they are even worse; the romantics were much less ferocious! If they looked into the past they would see to how slight a degree the old masters were – how shall I say? – precious, for they were indeed elegant in the artistic sense of the word.

I have just concluded my series of paintings, I look at them constantly. I who made them often find them horrible. I understand them only at rare moments, when I have forgotten all about them, on days when I feel kindly disposed and indulgent to their poor maker. Sometimes I am horribly afraid to turn round canvases which I have piled against the wall; I am constantly afraid of finding monsters where I believed there were precious gems! Thus it does not astonish me that the critics in London relegate me to the lowest rank. Alas, I fear that they are only too justified. However, at times I come across works of mine which are soundly done, and really in my style, and at such moments I find great solace. But no more of that. Painting, art in general, delights me. It is my life. What else matters? When you put all your soul into a work, all that is noble in you, you cannot fail to find a kindred soul who understands you, and you do not need a host of such spirits. Is not that all an artist should wish for?

PISSARRO *Peasant Girl with a Branch* 1881

Pissarro on the bourgeois 1883

Throughout his life anarchism was one of the strongest elements in Pissarro's thinking, and in a letter to Lucien written on 28 December 1883 he spits out his detestation of the bourgeoisie.

See, then, how stupid the bourgeoisie, the real bourgeoisie, have become; step by step they go lower and lower; in a word they are losing all notion of beauty, they are mistaken about everything. When there is something to admire they shout it down, they disapprove! Where there are stupid sentimentalities you want to turn away from in disgust, they jump for joy or swoon. Everything they have *admired for the last fifty years* is now forgotten, old-fashioned, ridiculous. For years they have had to be forcibly prodded from behind, shouted at: This is Delacroix! That's Berlioz! Here is Ingres! etc. And the same thing is held true in literature, in architecture, in science, in medicine, in every branch of human knowledge. They are Zulus in straw-yellow gloves, top hat and tails. They are like the falling, rolling rock, which we must ceaselessly roll back to avoid being crushed. Hence the sarcasms of Daumier, Gavarni, etc., etc. You are indeed young to want to convince a bourgeois – English or other!

Impressionist 'humbug' 1884

Many artists, in France and elsewhere, detested the very name of Impressionism. In 1884 the American landscape painter George Inness (1824-94) wrote the following letter to the editor of a paper (untraced) which in the course of an otherwise laudatory article had referred to him as an 'Impressionist'.

A copy of your paper has been handed to me, in which I find your art editor has classified my work amongst the 'Impressionists'. The article is all that I could ask in the way of compliment. I am sorry, however, that either of my works should have been so lacking in the necessary detail that from a legitimate landscape-painter I have come to be classed as a member of the new fad 'Impressionism'. As however no evil extreme enters the world except as an effort to restore the balance disturbed by some previous extreme, say in this instance Preraphaelitism, absurdities frequently prove to be the beginnings of uses ending in a clearer understanding of the legitimate as well as the rationale of the question involved.

We are all the subjects of impressions, and some of us seek to convey the impressions to others. In the art of communicating impressions lies the power of generalizing without losing that logical connection of parts to the whole which satisfies the mind.

The elements of this, therefore, are solidity of objects and transparency of shadows in a breathable atmosphere through which we are conscious of space and distances. By the rendering of these elements we suggest the invisible side of painting, and the want of that grammar gives to pictures either the flatness of a silhouette or the puddling twaddle of Preraphaelitism.

Every fad becomes so immediately involved in its application, in the want of understanding of its mental origin, and the great desire of people to label men and things, that one extreme is made to meet with the other in a muddle of unseen life application. And as no one is long what he labels himself, we see realists whose power is a strong poetic sense as with Corbet [*sic*]. And Impressionists, who from a desire to give a little objective interest to their pancake of color, seek aid from the weakness of Preraphaelitism, as with Monet. Monet was made through another kind of humbug. For when people tell me that the painter sees nature in the way the Impressionists paint it, I say 'Humbug' – from the lie of intent to the lie of ignorance.

Monet induces the humbug of the first form, and the stupidity of the second. Through malformed eyes we see imperfectly and are subjects for the optician. Though the naturally formed eye sees without degrees of distinctness, and without blur, we want for good art sound eyesight. It is well-known that we through the eye realize the objective only through the experiences of life.

Caillebotte on art and letters   1884

It is impossible adequately to recreate the kind of discussions which went on amongst the Impressionists at places such as the Nouvelle-Athènes. This letter from Gustave Caillebotte, artist and collector, at Trouville to Monet at Menton (18 July 1884) suggests the kind of literary interests that they shared.

I have just been reading the letters of Flaubert. What an interesting book, and what a prodigious artist! But even so there are a lot of things which I shall never be able to understand, to begin with, his admiration for George Sand. Have you ever read, or indeed could you, *La Petite Fadette*, and so many other bucolic bits of nonsense; *La Mare au Diable* for instance. They seem to me very far removed from Flaubert; it is rather depressing too. Perhaps eventually we shall discover that what he lacked, as he has said as much himself, is an Olympian sense of detachment. His whole art lacks calmness, and when one has read it only one really clear idea emerges; he wants to prove that man is brutish, and that all science, all religion, etc., are as nothing. After that just emptiness. It is all extremely discouraging, and reading it has absolutely annihilated me.

I suppose that a lot of great artists link you more closely with life itself. Compare, for instance, the work of Delacroix with that of Flaubert. He had just as much to complain

about in the way his contemporaries treated him, but there is no suggestion of it in his works. His work is above all that; it is Olympian. I suspect that Millet was an Olympian. This does not exclude pride, nor contempt for the stupidity of others. I only want to say that people shouldn't be so preoccupied with matters of no great significance. Take Degas, for instance; he's not Olympian, and this will be one of his great drawbacks. He has some good things to say about old Hugo. But how can he compare him with Zola and Daudet? And why this horror of Veuillot? A man, who, like Flaubert, has been preoccupied only with phraseology, with expressing as simply and clearly as possible what he wants to say, and so on and so forth. But it doesn't really make any difference; what a great craftsman he was, and so uninterested in anything apart from his art. Without these letters I doubt if one could understand how *L'Education sentimentale* and *Saint Antoine* could have been written by the same man. But I can tell that I'm becoming a bore.

Good night; all my best wishes.

Renoir unfolds a plan   c. 1884-85

Having at least partially cut themselves off from official art, and the doctrines of the Ecole des Beaux-Arts, many painters connected with Impressionism seem to have hankered after some other social and aesthetic structure to support them. Amongst Durand-Ruel's papers was this memorandum from Renoir, dating apparently from the 1880s, setting out a strange project.

The Society of Irregularists

In all the controversies which arise every day about questions relating to art, the one which is generally disregarded and to which we wish to draw attention and discuss is this: irregularity.

Nature abhors a vacuum, say the physicists, but they might complete their axiom by adding that she equally abhors regularity.

Observers have noted in fact that, despite the apparent laws which preside over their formation, the works of nature from the most important to the most insignificant are infinitely varied, no matter what type or species they belong to. The two eyes of even the most beautiful face are never exactly alike; no nose is ever situated immediately above the middle of the mouth; the segments of an orange, the leaves of a tree, the petals of a flower, are never exactly identical. It would seem that every type of beauty derives its charm from its diversity.

When one comes to examine from this point of view the most famous examples of the plastic arts, or of architecture, it is easy to see that the great artists who have created them, anxious to proceed like nature, whose respectful pupils they are, have taken great pains to avoid transgressing the fundamental law of irregularity. One has noticed, for instance that even works based on geometric principles, such as St Mark's, or the Cour de la Reine in Francis I's little palace [at Blois], as well as all the so-called Gothic churches, never make use of an absolutely straight line, and that round, square, or oval figures, which might without difficulty be made so as to be absolutely accurate, never are. One may therefore affirm, without fear of error, that every truly artistic production has been conceived and executed according to the principle of irregularity; in a word, if we may be excused a neologism, that it is the work of an irregularist.

At a time, therefore, when our French art, which till the beginning of the century had been so replete with penetrating charm and its imaginative fantasy, is about to perish through aridity, regularity, a misguided mania for a bogus perfection, stemming from the engineer's drawing-board, which has become the ideal, we think it is necessary to react promptly against these deadly doctrines which threaten to destroy French art, and to unite people in this cause, whatever may have been their previous reluctance to join groups.

An Association therefore is necessary.

Without wishing at this point to detail the actual structure of such an association, I would like to submit for consideration some general outlines. The Association will be called 'The Society of Irregularists', a title which explains the general ideas of its founders.

Its main purpose will be to organize, as soon as possible, exhibitions in which all artists, painters, decorators, architects, metal workers, embroiderers etc., and anybody who has irregularity as a basis of their aesthetic thinking, can participate.

Amongst other conditions of entry there will be one especially referring to architecture. All ornamentation must be based on nature, with no other element intruding; flowers, leaves, figures etc. must be reproduced exactly. Even the smallest outlines must be done by hand, without the help of any instruments, and as far as other plastic arts, such as metal work, embroidery and painting on porcelain are concerned, nothing can be exhibited unless it is accompanied in its finished state by the drawings or paintings from nature on which it has been based.

A complete grammar of art, dealing with the aesthetic principles of the Society, explaining its principles and showing its usefulness, will be published under the direction of its founders, and with the collaboration of members.

Photographs of monuments or famous decorative works which will reinforce the evidence for the principle of irregularity will be acquired at the expense of the Society, and put in a special gallery to be seen by the public.

MANET *The Folkestone Boat* 1869

The Manet auction 1884

In 1884, the year after Manet's death, an important exhibition of his paintings was held at the Ecole des Beaux-Arts, and the remnants of his studio were sold at the Hôtel Drouot. Berthe Morisot wrote two letters to her sister about the sale.

Here I am again, sending you not the catalogue of the Beaux-Arts exhibition but of the auction at the Hôtel Drouot. Do you want to buy any pictures? I am sure that your husband will jump out of his chair at the idea, and even you will think that I have gone crazy, but too much wisdom and caution cause one to miss golden opportunities. In the old days mother or father would

never have dreamt of spending a thousand francs – or even five hundred – for a purchase of this kind, but today Faure is offered 20,000 francs for *The Dead Man*, which he bought for a thousand; as a good speculator he is waiting for its value to increase still further.

I want to buy some if I can; I even have the ambition to own a large one, if the legacy from Grandma Manet materializes.

I have marked with a cross those of the smaller ones which I like best. All the heads in pastel are pretty, but I think that they will fetch high prices. If you reply to me about this, do make sure to indicate the catalogue numbers. I think that you should leave a margin of between 500 and 1,500. If you do not think this idea too absurd, let me know.

I am negotiating to sell my *Child with Cherries* by Edouard; it is a relatively average work, but it had a great success at the exhibition. I am asking 1,500 francs for it, and I'm sure that I'll get it. I have bought for 1,700 francs a picture of a small corner of the garden; it is a jewel, one of the prettiest things he ever did. I also have a magnificent sketch of Mme Manet in the garden.

I don't have an envelope for the catalogue, so I can't post it today; you won't get it till tomorrow. I think that everything would sell at very high prices were it not for the fact that we are in the middle of a recession. Don't mention my buying intentions to anybody, for if they were known they could harm the auction.

A few days later she reported on the sale.
It's all over. It was a fiasco. Following on the victory at the Beaux-Arts, it was a complete failure. For 620 francs I got you the picture of the departure of the steamboat. It is not a nocturne, but a daytime scene, with a crowd swarming on the dock. It is a very attractive work. If you want it, let me know immediately, and I shall have it packed for you. If not I shall keep it to resell at a profit. Not that I do not like it enormously, but in this débâcle the brothers thought that they had better step in and we spent 20,000 francs. In fact I have some of the big paintings; *The Linen, Madame de Caillas* and *Girl in a Garden*, as well as some of the smaller ones – a singer at a *café-concert*, two pastels, a torso of a woman and some oysters. It would certainly have been better to buy the small ones, even though they were going at comparatively high prices, than the larger ones, though we had to intervene with the latter, otherwise they would have fetched nothing at all. Anyway I am broken-hearted. The only consolation is that the works have gone to real art-lovers and artists.

In all the auction brought in 110,000 francs, whereas we had been counting on a minimum of 200,000. Times are bad, and it has been a severe blow. Do you remember

Madame de Caillas, which was in the studio, a woman in black lying on a sofa, with Japanese fans hanging in the background? It is a marvel, and it is going into the Louvre. As for *The Linen*, you know it. *The Girl in a Garden* is a girl sitting under rose bushes; it is the same size, but less finished. Anyway here I am with a whole gallery of pictures; our future inheritance from Madame Manet has been eaten into, but no matter; one can only laugh. Answer me about the picture of the boat; do exactly as you please.

Monet as a gardener   1885

In 1885 Monet moved to Giverny on the banks of the river Epte, 75 kilometres (47 miles) from Paris, 60 (38) from Rouen, and bought a house there with a large garden. Here he was to stay for most of the rest of his life. The garden becomes virtually an obsession with him, and the inspiration for most of his famous series of works, the Nymphéas *(Waterlilies). His stepson Jean-Pierre Hoschedé, who was then a child, described in 1960 the garden which Monet created there.*

The gardens of Claude Monet, his indubitable form of self-indulgence and his joy, were a triumph, and in saying this everybody will realize that I am thinking of the *Nymphéas*, a work which he consciously evolved from his garden, and the pictures that he dreamed of making of it.

His gardens were an even greater source of pleasure than his house, and they were to place Monet in the environment he loved best, amongst his flowers, which he seemed to caress with his eyes, happy too at being able, without thought of expense, to indulge all his fantasies. In actual fact the exercise was a profitable one, in that the flowers produced subjects for him, they became real paintings themselves, created by nature, but moulded by him to make in actual paintings some of his finest works.

Monet had got his first taste for gardens at Argenteuil, through contact with his friend Caillebotte, who himself was a great gardener; but he owed some of it, if we are to judge from the painting *The Terrace at Sainte-Adresse*, to his parents. The terrace which he painted, so beautifully adorned with flowers, shows that whilst he was living with them his parents had a taste for flowers. At Ville-d'Avray, Louveciennes, Argenteuil and Vétheuil, Monet had small gardens, but at Giverny he found himself in possession of a large orchard, and in front of the house various clumps of trees, with two long flower beds on either side of the main pathways which led down to the Chemin du Roy. These are still there today, but their structure has been completely altered. Along the centre of each of these beds there were pine trees and cypresses, and these together with the other groups of trees were surrounded with clipped box. All this did not appeal to Monet, although he liked the two yew-trees, which were on either side of the top of the drive in front of the house. First of all he had the box removed. He did not like the pines and the cypresses, which spoilt his beloved flowers, and intended having them chopped down, but my mother, who was devoted to trees, opposed the idea. It was an epic struggle. On the one side Monet knowing what he wanted to do; on the other, my mother refusing to allow them to be chopped down.To see a tree chopped down, she said, made her feel ill. The battle continued but mutual accommodations eventually took place. In the first place the uprooting of the cypresses was agreed. They were replaced by metal arches spanning the alley, and these were soon covered with climbing roses; despite their age they are still there. Then an agreement was reached about pruning the pines, whose lower branches were lopped off. But this wasn't enough to satisfy Monet, and then an even more bizarre compromise was reached, the pines were cut off half-way up, so that only the branchless half of their trunks were left standing, looking like pillars. Some roses were climbing all over them, but eventually the trees began to decay from the base, and were then taken away. What remained were the arches of roses, which created a delightful effect. Monet had been quite right, and had got his way. The central pathway, surrounded with flowers and bordered with nasturtiums invading the paving stones, was the admiration of all.

During this time, and bit by bit, Monet enlarged his garden, or rather he modified and harmonized it with great simplicity, and in marvellous taste. After dealing with that part of the garden surrounding the house, he turned his attention to the orchard. The west side became a lawn, laid out in the English style, constantly watered, and regularly cut. At various points in this lawn, Monet planted groups of irises and Oriental poppies. The fruit trees which had died or been grubbed up were replaced, but on a smaller scale, by flowering trees, wild cherries and Japanese apple trees. The borders were arranged in various successive steps, each one stocked with different plants; gladioli, larkspur, phlox, asters, large marguerites etc. Overhanging them were supports on which grew climbing clematis of the *montana rubens* type. Practically all the flower beds were surrounded by irises of every possible variety, for Monet had a special liking for this flower. Every year the number of varieties in his garden was increased, so that there was a large diversity of colours. On the whole, these flowers were of the single-petal type, for Monet did not like double ones. At the same time, annual plants were placed amongst the perennials in such a way that there was always a showing of flowers, and it was almost impossible to see any bare earth.

Finally, in the choosing of his flowers and plants Monet was well informed, with a wealth of horticultural magazines and growers' catalogues, as well as the visits which he made to their establishments. He was also helped by the contacts he maintained with a number of people, notably Georges Truffault, who was often a guest at our table at Giverny. Under these circumstances Monet knew exactly what he wanted from the plants he had bought and planted in specific places, not haphazardly, but with foreknowledge of what role they would play. In fact he knew well in advance that when they were in full flower they would have a certain relationship with their adjoining plants and with the garden as a whole. In this way he achieved exactly the effects he had intended, rather as he painted a picture, but in this case not with colours taken from his palette, but with flowers judiciously chosen for their individual colours, mixing them, or isolating them in clumps, the whole marvellously planned.

Monet's garden formed a unique combination of grass and flowers. It was entirely free from any large or overwhelming features of the kind you find planted with canna, surrounded with marigolds, interspersed with zinnias so rigid that they seem to be made out of zinc. Arrangements like this are usually the adornment of suburban houses. The pathways in the garden at Giverny were absolutely straight, without curves or labyrinths, without terminating in a kiosk or a cement fountain in imitation stone and its little jet of water, the accessories of what I might call a garden of pseudonature.

The property was circumscribed by a wall which bordered the end of the garden along the roadside. Monet took a dislike to this, for he loved having a view, and this stone horizon cut off half of it. He replaced it with an iron railing, and nasturtiums of a very bright red colour, of a variety which has now disappeared, grew around it.

Then there was the construction of a greenhouse extended by a number of frames. For many years Monet cultivated in this glass house a magnificent collection of orchids and exotic ferns, as well as a num-ber of other equally exotic plants, especially a climbing begonia, which he got from the botanical gardens at Rouen, and which grew so vigorously that it was always being pruned to stop it breaking through the glass. All this, however, was eventually neglected, and then fell into ruin through lack of proper care, before the glass was destroyed by the bombing in the last war.

I have been describing in some way the history of the garden which Monet created in front of the house, but I must also add a few words about another garden, that which surrounds, and forms part of the famous waterlily pond. This was entirely his own creation; he converted a patch of meadow into the most beautiful section of landscape, and filled it with water to mirror the sky and with plants: some red, yellow, pink and white waterlilies to float on this water as though it were on the surface of the sky; the others, irises, calatheas and arrowheads to mark the line of the banks, and above all else to give pleasure to the eyes. On the confines of the layout there were clumps of rhododendrons, azaleas and hydrangeas enclosed with hedges of roses, and then there is a Japanese-style arched bridge, covered with wistaria, some mauve, some white, which spans the pond. Beside this bridge there is a semicircular stone seat, and planted around it, to protect it from the wind, a veritable forest of bamboo. The whole area is a place for dreaming and resting, which creates the feeling that one is not in Normandy but has been transported to some Oriental country. Finally on the strips of grass bordering the pond there were peony bushes with their large, simple flowers in pink, white and wine-red. The whole was dominated by trees, weeping-willows and poplars, which had been there when the estate was bought and which were carefully preserved.

PHOTOGRAPH OF GERMAINE HOSCHEDÉ, LILI BUTLER,
MME JOSEPH DURAND-RUEL, GEORGES DURAND-RUEL
AND MONET IN MONET'S GARDEN AT GIVERNY, 1900

PHOTOGRAPH OF MONET IN HIS STUDIO *c.*1920

Monet and his waterlilies

*Throughout his life, but especially in his declining
years, Monet found in his garden and its ever-
changing beauties a constant source of inspiration. His canvases of waterlilies grew into vast
panoramas that fill the visual field.*

MONET *The Waterlily Pond* 1899

PISSARRO *Capital (Social Iniquities)* 1889

Pissarro on elections   1885

Camille Pissarro, the Anarchist, was far more involved with politics than any of his fellow Impressionists. On 12 December 1885 he wrote to his niece Esther Isaacson, who had written deploring the Tory victory at the recent British general election – and gave his opinion of electoral politics in general.

It matters little to people who work hard and are dying of hunger. You should know then, my little Esther, that the best way of being free is not to delegate any of your powers. England has reached the same degree of cretinism that we have, except that because of their idiotic and Protestant educational system, they are blinded by an appearance of false values, false morals, false liberties. France, or at least the Latin race, is more free of this rubbish, and will be more inclined to follow a new way.

On 22 December he returned to his theme. Was he thinking of the Impressionists' politician friend Antonin Proust, who eventually became minister responsible for the arts?

Universal suffrage, the instrument of domination of the capitalist bourgeoisie, let me tell you, has been condemned once and for all by the forces of progress; its day is over! It is only the big shots it serves effectively. You can imagine the absurdity of having everybody's interests represented by one man alone, no matter how marvellous he might be. Let me suppose that I, a painter, should nominate the Right Honourable Mr Blank. I ask you, how could he serve my interests? Will he ever understand, as a professor, the necessity of levelling those Bastilles of art, the Ecoles des Beaux-Arts, the Academies, the coalitions of art dealers, the capitalists who build up reputations; not likely, don't you agree ? Universal suffrage has served as a weapon whereby the bourgeoisie controls the economic situation. Therefore it must disappear; within ten or twenty years, perhaps sooner, this will be the general demand in addition to that for the expropriation of capital.

PISSARRO *Social Iniquities* 1889

Renoir on the nude   1886

On 11 January 1886 Berthe Morisot, who was building up a close friendship with Renoir, which was to play an important part in the latter part of her life, wrote in her journal.

A visit to Renoir. On the stand a red pencil and chalk drawing of a young mother nursing her child; charming and gracious in its subtlety. As I admired it, he showed me a whole series, done from the same model, and with the same degree of movement. He is a draughtsman of the first order. It would be most interesting to exhibit to the public all these preparatory studies for a painting, for they seem to think that Impressionists work in a very casual way. I don't think it possible to go further in the rendering of form. I saw two drawings of women going into the water, which I found as charming as any work by Ingres. He said that nudes seemed to be one of the essential forms of art.

RENOIR *Bathers* 1887

RENOIR *Study of Two Nudes* 1886-7

RENOIR *Study of Three Nudes c.* 1886-7

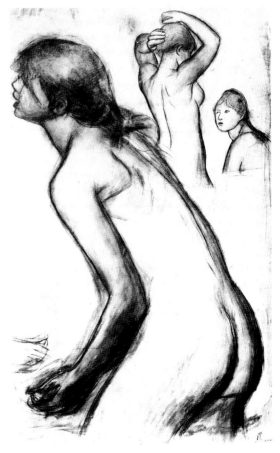

An American Judgment   1886

On 10 April 1886 Durand-Ruel opened an exhibition of Impressionist paintings in New York. Its success marks a turning-point in the movement's fortunes. It transferred in May to the National Academy of Design. In June a laudatory article by Luther Hamilton appeared in Cosmopolitan.

One of the most important artistic events that ever took place in this country, eminently the event of the season '85-6, was the exhibition in New York in April, under the auspices of the American Art Association, of a collection of works in oil and pastel of the Impressionists of Paris. . . .

This exhibition was composed of two classes of pictures, those that excited great admiration in everybody, and those that provoked equally great admiration in some, and surprising antagonism in others. Its supreme merit was that the beholder could be indifferent to none. It was a glorious protest against the everlasting commonplace, which is another way of saying that its pictures were that rarest thing, a record of the artists' own impressions, not, as usual, their reminiscences of other pictures.

Someone said, looking round the galleries, 'Yes, it is an effort after something new, anything to be novel.' But that was not it. These pictures are too really new to have come about in that way. They are the result of an effort on the part of the painters to break with tradition and to see things freshly with their own eyes.

That is the only way originality ever comes, and, for all the cheapness of the method, it comes rarely, and then to a crucifying world, as Millet, Carot [*sic*], Rousseau and Delacroix, in this field would once have testified.

The Impressionists will doubtless have their weak and merely imitative followers, people who catch the manner, and are incapable of more; and when they get to be the fashion, which promises to be soon, they will be followed by all the pot-boiling, time-serving crew who reap most of the pecuniary benefits of art, but now they are scarcely out from under the purifying influences of persecution. The first impulses of revolt and reformation, which brought them into existence, are still unexhausted, and as is sure to be in such a case, sincerity and originality (as we have seen in art these terms are all but synonymous) are still the rule among them.

It was this absence of concession to the market that made the exhibition in New York so refreshing and unique. Hence the much talked-of Morgan collection which preceded it was as a whole 'shoppy' by comparison.

'We have had in years no other chance to see a collection in which the necessarily vitiating element of saleability was unconsidered. Parenthetically it may be recalled that the American market, owing to our general ignorance of all aesthetic matters, must impose a generally low standard, at least, and when the risks of the picture dealer are augmented by a 'protective' tariff of thirty per cent, we may be sure that none of them are going to indulge themselves in the always expensive luxury of educating the public; but will on the contrary confine themselves to the most commonplace and popular canvases.

In the Impressionist exhibition were two hundred and eighty-nine pictures. This is said to be the most complete and first display of this school ever made. It contains such a collection of Monet's pictures as would, in themselves, make an artistic event if shown in Paris.

It is impossible here to go into any catalogue description of the paintings, and it is unnecessary, the aim of this little paper being to draw attention to the movement they represent, and to chronicle their appearance in New York as an event certain to have a very marked influence on our own art.

The collection embraced a very great variety of work, from immense, highly-finished pictures to the slightest sketches, only their general unconventional freshness of interest gave a homogeneous character to the whole.

Now, the pain of a new idea is proverbially severe, and such an avalanche of new ideas as was poured upon us here was sure to provoke such agonized protest. The punishment of the innovator is a conspicuous incident in all history, but there are reasons why the original painter has a particularly hard time of it.

Painting is an art in which imitation and symbolism are blended, and only of the lesser and lower element are the uncultivated in the least capable of judging. Moving water, for instance, cannot be imitated; it can only be suggested by certain symbols about which the painter and the public have a certain common understanding, the symbols, of course, approximating the appearance of the water.

Acquaintance with this symbolism and capacity for judging it can only result from special culture. The Impressionists believe in the possibility of making closer approximations to many appearances in nature than have been in vogue, and, even in the possibility of approximating in the symbolism of painting phases of nature that have not hitherto been attempted.

On these theories, one of them paints, say a man rowing on a lake, aiming to give the impression of the broken reflections produced by his oars, and, perhaps, doing it wonderfully; but between the painter and the observer there must be generally lacking that common understanding before referred to. The approximation may be far closer than that in various ambitious portrayals of Niagara Falls with which the observer is familiar. But long experience has taught him that certain woolly appearances do nominally represent Niagara Falls, while the yellow splashes of paint suggesting the broken reflections he sees in all their nakedness as yellow splashes of paint.

Moreover, the tendency is not even to compare the new approximation with Nature, but with other and different pictures, the measure of the nearness being also the measure of the condemnation meted out.

One of the greatest stumbling-blocks in the Impressionist work, as shown here, was the prevalence of violet shadows. In considering this, it must be remembered that there are more violets in the shadows in many parts of France than in this country, also the violet in out-of-doors pictures greatly brightens the effect of the yellow sunshine, and to give any impression of light and brilliancy, in the least suggesting nature's, is always the painter's most impossible problem. The Impressionists, with their violet shadows, have made by far the closest approximation we have yet had. We can well afford to take the little exaggeration, or even falsity for the sake of the far larger and more important truth thus attained.

This article is being written after the first display of these pictures is closed, but so great was its success and the interest it aroused that arrangements have been made for its repetition in the National Academy when the annual spring exhibition there is over.

Exhibits of the collection in other American cities before its return to Paris are contemplated, but all the movements of its managers are so encompassed with difficulties because of the jealous zeal of the regular dealers to prevent infringement of the tariff law on imported pictures, that it is doubtful whether or not they incline to prolong the struggle. The action of the dealers can hardly be blamed; but this case illustrates some of the disadvantages of our barbarous tariff on imported works of art. The original intent on bringing these pictures to America was for exhibition merely. For one thing it was not supposed that we would become educated to the point of wishing to buy them, but, in the natural course of things, it would have been so arranged as to make sales possible. To escape the crippling tariff of thirty per cent, however, it was necessary to pledge the pictures to exhibition only, and even then, the dealers did everything in their power to prevent their appearance here.

No sooner were they seen in New York, than various of the more intelligent critics and patrons of art cried out with zeal that this picture and that picture should be kept in the country ... but all plans for the purchase of any picture in this collection must, perforce, be of the character of ways that are dark, and, all too probably, in the line of tricks that are in vain.

Rifts   1886

There had been no group exhibition since 1882, and early in 1886 there was talk of inaugurating another, stimulated originally by Berthe Morisot and her husband Eugène Manet. But there were complications. On the one hand there were the more traditionalist elements, notably Degas and Morisot. On the other there were those who, reacting against the 'disorder' of Impressionist techniques, had evolved a more 'scientific' approach, painting with tiny dots applied over a flat coloured background, so that the colours merged, not on the canvas, but in the eye of the beholder who placed himself at the right distance from it. The structure and the general effect of their works were austere, classical, as opposed to the romantic effect of pure Impressionism. The main exponents of this style were Seurat, who in 1885 had just completed A Sunday Afternoon at the Island of La Grande Jatte, *Signac, and the much older Pissarro, who in his enthusiasm for this new departure was insistent, that Seurat and Signac be included in the show (which opened in May). In March Pissarro had written to Lucien explaining the situation.*

Because of Degas I missed the post last night. We went in a body to meet him to determine the number of paintings each

would be allowed to exhibit. As usual he arrived at an impossible hour. We had to stand in the street discussing the matter. Things are going well.

I went to dinner with the Impressionists. This time a great many came; Duret brought Burty, an influential critic, Moore, the English novelist, the poet Mallarmé, Huysmans, M. Deudon, and M. Bérard; it was a real gathering. Monet had been in Holland – he arrived from The Hague at eight o'clock; just in time for dinner. I had a long talk with Huysmans, he is very conversant with the new art and is anxious to break a lance for us. We spoke of the novel *L'Oeuvre* [Zola's *His Masterpiece*]. He is decidedly of my opinion. It seems that he had a quarrel with Zola, who is very worried. Guillemet, who is furious about the book, also wrote to Zola, but only to complain that Fagerolles (the painter hero of the book) is too easily identifiable. They are telling a charming anecdote in connection with this book: Guillemet, who worships Zola, and with good reason, wanted his name to appear on this book, which would certainly add to Zola's renown. He wrote Zola, requesting that the book be dedicated to him. Zola, very embarrassed, as you can imagine, by this expression of admiration, replied that he was reserving all dedications until the whole *Rougon-Macquart* series appeared. But since *L'Oeuvre* was published Guillemet's ardour has melted like butter in the sun; he wrote Zola a long letter of complaint. Zola assured him that it was Gervex he had described. Guillemet calmed down, completely satisfied with this explanation. As for Gervex, he takes a different attitude. He lets his friends call him 'Fagerolles'. At X's marriage he paraded this name.

What I have written to you should not be repeated.

Yesterday I had a violent run-in with M. Eugène Manet on the subject of Seurat and Signac. The latter was present, as was Guillaumin. You may be sure I rated Manet roundly; which will not please Renoir. But

SEURAT *The Lighthouse at Honfleur* 1886

SIGNAC *The Railway Junction at Bois-Colombes* 1886

anyhow, this is the point, I explained to M. Manet, who probably understood not a word I said, that Seurat has something new to contribute, which these gentlemen, despite their talent, are unable to appreciate; that I am personally convinced of the progressive character of his art, and certain that in time it will yield extraordinary results. Besides I am not concerned with the appreciation of artists, no matter whom. I do not accept the snobbish judgments of 'romantic Impressionists', in whose interest it is to combat new tendencies. I accept the challenge; that's all.

But before anything is done they want to stack the cards and ruin the exhibition. M. Manet was beside himself! I didn't calm down. They are all underhanded, but I won't give in.

Degas is a hundred times more straightforward. – I told Degas that Seurat's painting [La Grande Jatte] was very interesting. 'I would have noted that for myself, Pissarro, except that the painting is so big.' Very well, if Degas sees nothing in it, so much the worse for him. This simply means there is something precious which escapes him. We shall see. M. Manet would also like to have prevented Seurat showing his figure painting. I protested against this, telling Manet

that in such a case we would make no concessions, that we were willing, if space were lacking, *to limit our paintings* ourselves, but that we would fight anyone who tried to impose his choice on us.

But things will arrange themselves somehow.

A final fiasco   1886

In 1886 the last Impressionist exhibition was held at Durand-Ruel's and aroused a good deal of ill-feeling. Monet (who exhibited at Goupil's that year) wrote to Berthe Morisot complaining that 'young Durand' was putting in some paintings of his without his approval. Renoir did not participate, but Berthe Morisot sent in three oils, one pastel and a watercolour. After Monet had written congratulating her, she replied early in June.

Thank you very much for remembering me so kindly and for your words about my wretched paintings at Durand's. I am all the more touched because, as you know, the show is a complete fiasco, and it seems to me that all of us have had a share in the responsibility for this disaster, Renoir and

1, RUE LAFFITTE, 1
ANGLE DU BOULEVARD DES ITALIENS

8ᵐᵉ EXPOSITION
PAR

Mᵐᵉ MARIE BRACQUEMOND	Mᵐᵉ BERTHE MORISOT	MM. SCHUFFENECKER
MM. DEGAS	MM. C. PISSARRO	SEURAT
FORAIN	L. PISSARRO	SIGNAC
GAUGUIN	ODILON REDON	TILLOT
GUILLAUMIN	ROUART	VIGNON
	ZANDOMENEGHI	

Ouverte du 15 Mai au 15 Juin
DE 10 HEURES A 6 HEURES

PRIX D'ENTRÉE : 1 FRANC

Whistler of course less than the others. But all this is incomprehensible to the public at large.

As for you, you have conquered this recalcitrant public. At Goupil's one meets only people who have the highest admiration for your works, and I think that you are playing the coquette in asking for my opinion of them. In actual fact I am dazzled by them, a fact which you must know quite well. If you will insist, however, the one I like best is the picture with the little reddish-brown tree in the foreground. My husband and I stood in ecstasy in front of it for an hour.

I saw Mallarmé on Thursday. I would not be surprised if this charming man is in the process of writing a letter to you to express his admiration of the exhibition. Both of us are still very eager to visit you at Giverny, and I hope that next month the weather will be less unpleasant than it is now. Give my best regards to Mme Hoschedé.

George Moore at the last
Impressionist group show   1886

Moore's Confessions of a Young Man *(1888) includes a description of the exhibition in the rue Lafitte in May 1886, which he visited with his friend the Belgian painter Lewis Weldon Hawkins. Although he gives a perceptive and indeed flattering account of the exhibits, he ascribes to his narrator and to his fictitious companion the indignant reactions of the Philistines.*

And so we went to jeer a group of enthusiasts that willingly forfeit all delights of the world in the hope of realizing a new aestheticism; we went insolent with patent leather shoes, and bright kid gloves, and armed with all the jargon of the school . . . .

The history of Impressionist art is simple. In the beginning of this century the tradition of French art – the tradition of Boucher, of Fragonard and Watteau – had been com-

pletely lost; having produced genius, their art died. Ingres is the supreme flower of the classic art, which succeeded the art of the palace and the boudoir; further than Ingres it is impossible to go, and his art died. Then the Turners and the Constables came to France, and they begot Troyon, and Troyon begot Millet, Courbet, Corot and Rousseau, and these in turn begot Degas, Pissarro, Madame Morisot and Guillaumin. Degas is a pupil of Ingres, but he applies this marvellous acuteness of drawing he learned from his master to delineate the humblest aspects of modern life. Degas draws not by the masses, but by the character; his subjects are shopgirls, ballet-girls and washerwomen, but the qualities that endow them with immortality are precisely those which eternalize the virgins and saints of Leonardo da Vinci in the minds of men. You see the fat, vulgar woman in the long cloak trying on a hat in front of the pier-glass. So marvellously well are the lines of her face observed and rendered that you can tell exactly what her position in life is; you know what the furniture of her rooms is like; you know what she would say to you were she to speak. She is as typical of the nineteenth century as Fragonard's ladies are of the Court of Louis XV. To the right you see two shopgirls with bonnets. So accurately are the habitual movements of the heads and hands observed that you at once realize the years of bonnet-showing and servile words these women have lived through. We have seen Degas do this before – it is a welcome repetition of a familiar note, but it is not till we turn to the set of nude figures that we find the great artist revealing any new phase of his talent. The first, in an attitude which suggests the kneeling Venus, washes her thighs in a tin bath. The second, a back view full of the malformations of forty years, of children, of hard work, stands gripping her flanks with both hands. The naked woman has become impossible in modern art; it required Degas' genius to infuse new life into the worn-out theme. Cynicism was the great means of eloquence of the middle ages, and with cynicism Degas has rendered the nude again an artistic possibility. What Mr Horsley or the British matron would say, it is difficult to guess. Perhaps the hideousness depicted by M. Degas would frighten them more than the sensuality which they condemn in Sir Frederic Leighton. But, be this as it may, it is certain that the great, fat, short-legged creature, who in her humble and touching ugliness passes a chemise over her lumpy shoulders, is a triumph of art. Ugliness is trivial; the monstrous is terrible. Velasquez knew this when he painted his dwarfs.

Pissarro exhibited a group of girls gathering apples in a garden; sad greys and violets beautifully harmonized. The figures seem to move as in a dream; we are on the thither side of life, in a world of quiet colour and happy aspirations. These apples will never fall from the branches, those baskets that the stooping girls are filling will never be filled; that garden is the garden of the peace that life has not for giving, but which the painter has set in an eternal dream of violet and grey.

Madame Morisot exhibited a series of delicate fancies. Here are two young girls; the sweet atmosphere folds them as with a veil; they are all summer; their dreams are limitless, their days are fading, and their ideas follow the flight of the white butterflies through the standard roses. Take note too of the stand of fans; what delicious fancies are there; willows, balconies, gardens and terraces.

Then, contrasting with these distant tendernesses, there was the vigorous painting of Guillaumin. There life is rendered in violent and colourful brutality. The ladies fishing in the park, with the violet of the skies and the green of the trees descending on them, is a *chef d'oeuvre*. Nature seems to be closing about them like a tomb, and that hillside, – sunset flooding the skies with yellow and the earth with blue shadow, – is another piece that will one day find a place in one of the public galleries, and the same can be said of the portrait of the woman on a background of chintz flowers.

We could but utter cheap gibes and exclaim: 'What could have induced him to paint such things? Surely he must have seen that it was absurd. I wonder if the Impressionists are in earnest, or if it is only *une blague qu'on nous fait* – ?'[1] Then we stood and screamed at Monet, that most exquisite painter of blonde light. We stood before 'The Turkeys' and seriously we wondered if it were 'serious work', – that *chef d'oeuvre*; the high grass that the turkeys are nibbling is flooded with sunlight, so swift and intense that for a moment the illusion is complete. 'Just look at the house! why the turkeys couldn't walk in at the door. The perspective is all wrong.' Then followed other remarks of an educational kind, and when we came to those piercingly personal visions of railway stations by the same painter – those rapid sensations of steam and vapour, – our laughter knew no bounds. 'I say, Marshall, just look at this wheel; he dipped his brush into cadmium yellow, and whisked it round; that's all.' Nor did we understand any more Renoir's rich sensualities of tone; nor did the mastery with which he achieves an absence of shadow appeal to us. You see colour and light in his pictures as you do in nature, and the child's question, 'Why is one side of the face black?' is answered. There was a half-length nude figure of a girl. How the round fresh breasts palpitate in the light! such a glorious glow of whiteness was never observed before. But we saw nothing but that the eyes were out of drawing.

A dangerous craze stands condemned   1888

Probably the most successful painter in Victorian England was William Powell Frith, whose Derby Day *(1858) and* The Railway Station *(1862) had become icons of*

1 A joke they're playing on us.

the age. A prolific writer, who produced a three-volume autobiography, he wrote as well in the art press, and in an article on 'Crazes in Art' which appeared in The Magazine of Art *in June 1888 he addressed himself to Impressionism.*

We have now done, long ago, with the Pre-Raphaelitic, and another, and far more dangerous, craze has come upon us. Born and bred in France, what is called *Impressionism* has tainted the art of this country. It is singular that this phase of art, if it can be called art, is in exact opposition to the principles of the Pre-Raphaelites. In the one we had overwrought details, in the other no details at all. So far as my feeble powers enable me to understand the Impressionist, I take him to propose to himself to reproduce an *impression* – probably a momentary one – that Nature has made upon him. If the specimens of the impressions that I have seen are what have been made on any human being, his mind must be strangely formed .... There is an exhibition every year at Mr Wallis' Gallery in Pall Mall where admirable examples of foreign art may be studied, and a comparison of our own school with the examples of others ought to be a lesson to students and professors alike. And when there is so much to instruct and stimulate in a study of the best of these, it has always seemed to me strange in the extreme that painters can be found who seem only to strive to reproduce their faults. It is to be hoped that the 'Impressionists' will not be allowed to play their pranks in the Royal Academy exhibition; we have enough evidence there of the seeming forgetfulness of the good that may be obtained by foreign training in the occasional display of sooty flesh and dingy, unmeaning – not to say unpleasant – subjects. I have sometimes been surprised to find that a picture, of the subject of which – to use a vulgarism, I could make 'neither head nor tail', had found a purchaser. It might have had a strange roughness entirely incomprehensi-

ble to me, a kind of affectation of cleverness which the purchaser may have mistaken for genius. I fear my experience of public knowledge of art leads me to the conclusion that a picture simply true to Nature has no chance against one in which the painter has indulged in eccentricity, which the buyer thinks wonderful because he cannot understand it.

In the way of a final word to the gentlemen who record their momentary impressions of Nature, I venture to advise them to dwell longer on their impressions; let them keep Nature before their eyes for hours, days and weeks, and then perhaps their Impressions will be more what they ought to be. This advice is not likely to be taken and these artists(?) may do much mischief to our modern school, the effects of which may be disastrously permanent; but the craze itself will as assuredly pass away as everything foolish and false does sooner or later.

Degas, his models and his pastels   *c. 1890*

Ambroise Vollard arrived in Paris from his native Réunion in 1888. He became one of the great picture-dealers, whose career involved promoting the Impressionists and each succeeding generation of avant-garde painters in Paris. In his Recollections of a Picture Dealer, *published in 1934, he records a wealth of possibly embroidered anecdotes about the painters with whom he came into contact.*

I was just ten when I saw some of Degas' horses in the Museum on La Réunion. An event had just occurred which had caught my childish fancy. The curator of the Museum had received a box from France containing the egg of an aepyornis. As a matter of fact, it was only an imitation. I had happened to be present at the unpacking. Among the paper which had been packed round the object, I perceived a picture of horses torn from an illustrated review. I thought these horses as fine as those I used to admire every year at the races. One day in Paris, turning the pages of a review, I came across the same one that had struck me so forcibly in my childhood. This time I looked carefully at the artist's name; it was Degas. I mentioned my discovery to Lewis Brown.

'By Jove! Degas is the greatest of them all. His studio is quite close by. But you've seen Degas once as it is. Yesterday, when we were starting out together, the person with big black glasses I said good-morning to as we passed.'

I got into touch with Degas myself not long after. I had given the frame-maker Jacquet some planks of foreign wood from the Exhibition of 1889. I intended having frames made of them. One day Jacquet said to me 'You know, M. Degas is always scheming out frames. He has seen your wood, and told me to ask if you would let him have it.' I replied that I would not take any money for it, but that I would be delighted to accept the smallest sketch. Degas agreed. That was how I made my way into his studio.

When he moved from the rue Ballu to settle into the rue Victor Massé, everything for which there was no room in the new flat was taken up to the studio. Consequently the most heterogeneous objects were to be seen there side by side. A bath, little wooden horses with which the artist composed his pictures of racecourses, so marvellous for their colour and movement. Easels too, with canvases half-finished on them, for after he had started an oil-painting, he soon gave way to discouragement, not being able to fall back, as he did with his drawings, on tracing after tracing by way of correction. I remember too a tall desk at which he stood to write. Once an object had found its way into the studio, it never left it, nor changed its position, and gradually became covered with a layer of dust that no flick of a feather duster came to disturb. The painter would have been very astonished if he had been told that his stu-

dio was not perfectly tidy. One day I brought him a small picture that he had asked to see. As I undid the parcel a scrap of paper, no bigger than confetti, flew out and settled on a seam of the floor. Degas pounced on it. 'Do take care, Vollard! You will make my studio untidy.'

When I arrived, the painter was working on one of his pastels, those marvellous things that have been compared to butterflies' wings. I mentioned this in the hearing of the painter La Touche.

'Couldn't you,' he said, 'try to find out from Degas where he gets those pastels which give him the shades that no one else can obtain?'

When I saw Degas again, he happened to have a box of pastels in his hand, and was spreading them out on a board in front of the window. Seeing me watching him, he said: 'I take all the colour out of them that I can, by putting them in the sun.'

'But what do you use, then, to get colours of such brightness?'

'Opaque colour, Monsieur.'

When I reported this to La Touche, the way he looked at me showed me clearly that he thought I was laughing at him.

They were speaking of a former dancer in Degas' presence.

'You must have known her, M. Degas?'

'She even sat for me. I painted her waking up. There was nothing to be seen but her legs feeling about through the opening of the bed-curtains for her slippers, which had been thrown on an Oriental carpet. I even remember the reds and yellows. I can see her two green stockings too. I wanted to keep that painting, but it appeared to please the poor girl so much that I gave it to her.'

Dinners at the Café Riche

Between 1880 and 1894 many of the Impressionists used to have a monthly dinner at the Café Riche, attended by others connected with them. One of the latter was Gustave Geffroy (1855-1926) critic and novel-ist, of whom Cézanne painted a memorable portrait. In his Claude Monet *(Paris 1922) Geffroy gives an account of these meetings.*

These dinners were usually attended by Claude Monet, Camille Pissarro, Auguste Renoir, Alfred Sisley, Gustave Caillebotte, Dr de Bellio [a Romanian patron], Théodore Duret, Octave Mirbeau, and sometimes Stéphane Mallarmé.

They were evenings dedicated to talk and conversation, in which the happenings of the day were discussed with that freedom of spirit which was peculiar to artists who were free from any contact with official organizations. It must be admitted that the Impressionists' table was a very lively and noisy one, and that these men, relaxing from the burden of work, were rather like children just let out of school. The discussions sometimes got quite heated, especially between Renoir and Caillebotte. The former, nervous and sarcastic, with his mocking voice, and a kind of Mephistophelism which marked with irony and a strange mirth his face already ravaged by his illness, took a mischievous delight in irritating Caillebotte, a choleric and irascible man whose face would change in colour from red to violet, and even to black when his opinions were contradicted with that sprightly flow of words which Renoir loved to employ against them. He would then display a fierceness which turned to anger, though that was inoffensive enough. The discussions covered not only art, but every possible literary subject, politics, philosophy, subjects which appealed to Caillebotte's enthusiasm – for he was a great reader of books, reviews and newspapers. Renoir kept himself abreast by buying an encyclopaedia, out of which he culled arguments 'to floor Caillebotte'. Mirbeau would throw himself headlong into these intellectual combats, and he was always listened to, when he gave his considered decisions. Pissarro and Monet were also devotees of literature, both of them possessed of a sure and

CÉZANNE *Gustave Geffroy* 1895

refined taste. I well remember a real duel for and against Victor Hugo which unleashed a flood of passion, ardour and wisdom, and from which everybody emerged reconciled, to go and sit on a café terrace and contemplate the ever fairy-like appearance of Paris by night. On other occasions too, the arguments sometimes continued outside on the boulevard, and I am sure that there were some which were never resolved.

Degas writes to his landlord   1890

Practical affairs were always present. Even when actual poverty had been surmounted there were the mundane problems of everyday life. One of these is reflected in the letter which Degas wrote on 13 April 1890 from his apartment at 37 rue Victor Massé to his landlord M. Brebion.

Here are the few alterations which, on the advice of my solicitor, M. Bartholomé, I should be obliged if you could make in your lease.

Please add apropos the means of payment, *in gold and silver*, and not otherwise, or in notes of the Banque de France.

I should like to remain free from random visits from the agents of the insurance company, and it would be equally distasteful to me to have to submit my receipts for this to you, and thus to have to be double-checked.

I am content with a simple lease drawn up between us. If for specific reasons relating to your own business you need a legal, formal lease, it will be up to you to pay for it. There is no problem there.

You must make a brief survey of the current state of the property, indicating where it is not adequate. As soon as the repairs are completed, which should be in two or three days, I hope that we can make a little inspection together, and see on the spot the exact condition of the place. 'Entirely renovated' is a bit excessive. I did not ask for that much,

and I have made concessions. I should not like to make any more.

Finally, in the case of a break, that is non-renewal of the lease, three months must suffice. Why as long as six months?

I must confess, you really have helped me to enjoy a little tranquillity in your charming apartment. Do not let us quarrel any more, I beg of you. I am a quiet and solvent tenant. Do not ask any more of me.

I hope to see you soon. Let us get the whole thing settled in a day or two.

A social peril   1892

By the 1890s Impressionism had not only arrived, but its principles had attracted more people to painting than more academic forms of art ever had. In the Echo de Paris *for 17 May 1892, Octave Mirbeau drew attention to this phenomenon with more than a touch of irony.*

It must be said quite openly that painting, developing as it is at this speed, has become no longer just a menace to art but a veritable social menace. In the cities we see nothing but studios turning their large folding windows to the light from the north-west, that light which brings so much squalor. In the country and by the seaside, we meet nothing but people painting under the shade of umbrellas, which are more numerous than the trees. They look like whole armies standing at ease by their tents. The very landscape has started to disappear beneath the vast array of painting materials. Easels cut the sky with their triangular frames; canvases plaster their blemishes on the glorious background of light. In the purity of sylvan flowers paintboxes lie open; paint tubes pour out their contents, paintbrushes sully the virginity of the morning grass with their horrid, sticky hairs. Wild mint gives out rectified odours; violets absorb the tainted air of varnish; the dew, the mysterious mists rising from the soil – all that clear limpidity, all that dream of nature is ruined in contact with fixatives and confusing copals.

And what do they paint? They don't know, nor does anybody else. They plaster a canvas with red, blue, yellow and green; that's enough for them, and it sells. And not only do they paint, but they ·are *real painters*.

To be or not to be a painter? That's the great question of modern times. There's an itch to be a painter in every man, woman and child who has achieved our contemporary level of civilization, and it is also the most certain instigator of anarchist destruction. If this impulse goes on for another half century, in fifty years' time there will be nobody left but painters, and the social balance will have been completely upset. The economists of the day, if there are such things as economists left, will have to treat this problem seriously and depicturalize society. We shall be living in the age of oil paints, and there will be nothing else left to eat, to clothe ourselves with, or to house us. There will only be paintings.

Mary Cassatt in an unaccustomed role   1892

Mary Cassatt, at work in Paris on an allegorical mural for the south tympanum of the Women's Building of the 1893 Chicago World's Fair, started to feel out of her depth. She wrote to Mrs Palmer, president of the Board of Managers, on 1 December 1892.

Your telegram received today gave me the greatest pleasure. I am infinitely obliged to you for the kind thought which prompted you to send it.

The fact is I am beginning to feel the strain a little, and am apt to feel blue and despondent. Your cable came just at the right moment to act as a stimulant. I have been shut up so long now with one idea that

I am no longer capable of judging what I have done. I have been half a dozen times on the point of asking Degas to come and see my work, but if he happens to be in the mood he would demolish my work so completely that I could never pick myself up in time to finish for the exposition. Still he is the only man I know whose judgment would be a help to me. M. Durand-Ruel, poor man, was here with his daughter a week ago. It was most kind of him to come, they are all broken-hearted over the death of poor Charles. M. Durand was very kind and encouraging, said he would buy it if it were for sale, and of course from his point of view that was very complimentary, but it is not what I wanted. He seemed to be amazed at my thinking to strike for a very high degree of finish, but I found that he had never seen the frescoes of the early Italian masters, in fact he has never been to Italy, except to Florence for a day or two on business. I asked him if the border shocked him, and he said not at all, so it may not look eccentric, and at the height it is to be placed, vivid colouring seems to me necessary.

I have one of the sides well under way and I hope to have the whole finished in time for you to have it up and out of the way by the end of February.

You must be feeling the strain too, with all the responsibility on your shoulders. I hope you will have strength and health to see you through.

The Duret sale   1893

In 1893 the critic Duret sold his collection of Impressionist paintings. Sixteen-year-old Julie Manet, daughter of Berthe Morisot and Eugène Manet, went to see the paintings on 17 March, the day before the actual sale.

During the course of the day we went to see the exhibition of paintings belonging to M.

MONET *The Turkeys* 1877

Duret, which were on view before the sale. It is a very fine collection which includes a painting by Mummy of a woman in a low-cut dress with a garland of ravishing white flowers on it, several large paintings by Uncle Edouard [Manet]: *Repose* (a portrait of Mummy in white on a red couch with one foot sticking out), *Le Père Lathuile*, and another portrait of her, small in size, showing her with a bunch of violets on her black dress, a little hat and the whole composition seen against the light. I adore this portrait, the quality of the paint is so beautiful, the blacks are as magnificent as the whites in the other portrait. What a marvellous brush-stroke Uncle Edouard had. There is also in the collection a very fine work by M. Monet: white turkeys in a large meadow, and in the background a brick chateau, surrounded by pine trees, and also a hunt. As to the two

171

MANET *Repose (Berthe Morisot)* 1870

PHOTOGRAPH OF JULIE MANET 1894

PHOTOGRAPH OF BERTHE MORISOT *c.*1877

Morisot and daughter

Whether or not Berthe Morisot was ever in love with Edouard Manet, she was his most talented pupil and a major Impressionist whose looser, light-filled style influenced Manet's own late work. Later she and her daughter Julie (whose Journal *unfortunately ceased on her marriage to Degas' pupil Ernest Rouart) recorded many conversations with Renoir.*

canvases by M. Renoir, they are very fine, a landscape, and one of a nude drying herself with a towel; there is so much grace in this work, the head a little foreshortened is ravishing, the whole colouring is so delicate and agreeable. A painter who gives me great pleasure from what one can see of him here is Cézanne. Outstanding are some beautifully painted apples, which I found very nice indeed (these are the only works of his which I know), I am forgetting a portrait of Albert Wolff by my uncle Edouard (it is unfinished); it is a stunning portrait, a painting which is pure Manet, and it is extremely life-like. Looking at this portrait, one cannot help thinking what a wonderful thing to be created from so ugly and unpleasant-looking a man. Amongst other paintings I especially noted some racehorses by M. Degas, and some beautifully drawn dancers, the works of a great master of painting.

This evening Mummy had a lot of people to dinner, M. Degas, M. Mallarmé, M. Renoir, M. Bartholomé, Paul and Jeannie. M. Degas was very lively and engaging. As to M. Bartholomé, he seems very down in the dumps, and hardly spoke at all.

Degas and Renoir   1893

Although there was a good deal of comradely feeling amongst the Impressionists, it would be unrealistic to expect to find constant amity prevailing all the time. Vollard recorded some of Degas' judgments, and a row he had with his most constant friend, Renoir, in 1893.

The Café de la Nouvelle Athènes, in Montmartre, was a meeting place for Degas, Cézanne, Renoir, Manet, Desboutin and critics such as Duranty. The latter had constituted himself champion of the 'New Painting', though his praise was not without reservations. He complained of Cézanne, for instance, that he painted with a bricklayer's trowel. In his opinion Cézanne's reason for

putting so much paint on his painting was that he thought that a kilogram of green would look greener than a gram.

Nor did Manet, for his part, set much store by the painter from Aix. To Manet, the refined and elegant Parisian, the artist in Cézanne was but the counterpart of the 'foul-mouthed' man. But to tell the truth the vulgarity of speech he was reproached with was actually a pose adopted by Cézanne for Manet's benefit, irritated as he was by his stand-offish airs. Once, for instance, when the painter of *Le Bon Bock* asked his colleague if he was preparing anything for the Salon, he drew upon himself the retort 'Yes, some nice dung.'

It was sometimes said that Degas and Renoir, with their dissimilar natures, were not made to understand each other. As a matter of fact, although Degas disliked the fluffy texture of some of Renoir's paintings – 'He paints with balls of wool,' he would say when confronted with them – at other times, on the contrary, I have heard him exclaim, as he passed his hand amorously over one of his pictures, 'Lord, what a lovely texture!'

On the other hand, there was no greater admirer of Degas than Renoir, although secretly he deplored Degas' desertion of the art of the pastellist, in which he was so entirely himself, for that of the painter in oils.

Notwithstanding their esteem for each other as artists, Renoir and Degas did, however, manage to quarrel. It happened this way.

The painter Caillebotte, being about to die, wished to indemnify Renoir for purchases he had made of him he was now ashamed of. In his will therefore he bequeathed to Renoir any one of the paintings in his collection at the artist's choice.

Renoir was just beginning to 'sell', though his prices were not very high. Having heard that an admirer was prepared to pay 50,000 francs for the *Moulin de la Galette*, Renoir, very naturally would have liked to select this picture. But Caillebotte's executor pointed out that, as the collection was likely to go to the Luxembourg, it would be a pity if he were to beggar it of one of his most characteristic works. The same objection was made with regard to *The Swing*, on which his choice fell next, and finally, as the bequest included several pictures by Degas, Caillebotte's brother suggested to Renoir that he should take one of the *Dance Classes*, and Renoir agreed.

But Renoir soon tired of seeing the musician for ever bending over his violin, while the dancer, one leg in the air, awaited the chord that should give the signal for her pirouette. One day when Durand-Ruel said to him, 'I have a customer for a really finished Degas', Renoir did not wait to be told twice, but taking down the picture, handed it to him on the spot.

When Degas heard of it, he was beside himself with fury, and sent Renoir back a magnificent painting that the latter had once allowed him to carry off from his studio – a woman in a blue dress cut low in front, almost life-size. This picture belongs to the same period as the famous *La Dame au Sourire*. I was with Renoir when the painting was thus brutally returned to him. In his anger, seizing a palette knife, he began slashing at the canvas. Having reduced the dress to shreds, he was aiming the knife at the face.

'But, Monsieur Renoir!' I cried. He interrupted the gesture.

'Well, what's the matter?'

'Monsieur Renoir, you were saying in this very room only the other day that a painting is like a child one has begotten. And now you are going to destroy that face!'

'You're a nuisance with your wise tales.'

But his hand dropped, and he said suddenly:

'That head gave me such trouble to paint! *Ma foi!* I shall keep it.'

He cut out the upper part of the picture. That fragment, I believe, is now in Russia. Renoir threw the hacked strips furiously

DEGAS *Dancing Lesson* c. 1878

into the fire. Then taking a slip of paper, he wrote on it the single word *'Enfin'*, put it into an envelope addressed to Degas, and gave the letter to his servant to post. Happening to meet Degas some time after, I had the whole story from him again; and after a silence:

'What on earth can he have meant by that *"Enfin"?'*

'Probably that at last he had quarrelled with you.'

'Well I never,' exclaimed Degas. Obviously he could not get over his astonishment.

Bloodshot Cézanne   *1894*

In September 1894 Mary Cassatt was staying in the same inn at Giverny as Cézanne, who was visiting Monet. Her first reactions to him are of interest, not only in themselves but because her description of him as 'the first impressionist' throws some light on the vagueness with which even those deeply involved in the art world regarded Impressionism and its practitioners.

The circle has been increased by a celebrity in the person of the first impressionist, Monsieur Cézanne – the inventor of impressionism, as Madame D. calls him. M. Cézanne is from Provence, and is like the man whom Daudet describes; when I first saw him, he looked like a cut-throat with large red eyeballs standing out from his head in a most ferocious manner, a rather fierce-looking pointed beard, quite gray, and an excited way of talking that positively makes the dishes rattle. I found later on that I had misjudged his appearance, for far from being fierce or a cut-throat, he has the gentlest nature possible, *'comme un enfant'* as he would say. His manners at first rather startled me – he scrapes his soup-plate, he then lifts it and pours the remaining drops in his spoon; he even takes his chop in his fingers, and pulls the meat from the bone. He eats with his knife, and accompanies every gesture, every movement of his hand with that implement, which he grasps firmly when he commences his meal, and never puts down until he leaves the table. Yet in spite of the total disregard of the dictionary of manners, he shows a politeness towards us which no other man here would have shown. He will not allow Louis to serve him before us in the usual order of succession at table; he is even deferential to that stupid maid, and he pulls off the old tam-o-shanter which he wears to protect his bald head when he enters the room. I am gradually learning that appearances are not to be relied on here.

The conversation at lunch and dinner is mainly on art and cooking. Cézanne is one of the most liberal artists I have ever seen. He prefaces every remark with *'pour moi'* it is so and so, but he grants that everyone may be just as honest and faithful to nature from their own convictions; he doesn't believe that everybody should see alike.

PHOTOGRAPH OF CÉZANNE IN HIS STUDIO *c.* 1894

Degas intercedes for a model   1894

Degas was always solicitous about his models, and he wrote the following letter on 3 October 1894 to his friend, the playwright Ludovic Halévy who in 1877 had written a play, La Cigale, *in which the principal character was 'An Impressionist Painter', and for which Degas had done a set design.*

Here I am recommending an actress, dear friend. She is a Creole, named Schampsonn, though that name conceals another, belonging to a noble family of Guadeloupe. She has posed for me on several occasions. She wishes to be admitted to the Conservatoire for the examination on the 17th of this month. She is very keen on tragedies, and has had lessons from Guillemor and Paul Mounet. She would like to get into Worms' class. Had you been in Paris, I would have brought her to you, but I know my place and what is and what is not appropriate, and I could hardly bring her down to Sucy. Do you want to see her? Could you, when you leave the Academy on Thursday, let her take up a position, somewhere on the way you usually take in front of the Bastille or at the Vincennes Métro? She will come to hear your decision at the rue Ballu.

Degas at sixty   c. *1894*

In the early 1890s young William Rothenstein arrived in Paris from Bradford via the Slade School of Art, and cultivated Degas.

Degas was famous, and feared for his terrible *mots*. He was unsparing in his comments on men who failed in fidelity to the artistic conscience. Flattery, usefulness and subservience provided in some cases the key to intimacy with Whistler; with Degas integrity of character was a *sine qua non* of friendship. One thing he had in common with Whistler – a temperamental respect for the aristocratic tradition, the West Point code of honour, a French West Point, which included anti-Republican and anti-semitic tendencies which later made him a strong partisan of the Militarists and anti-Dreyfusards. He heartily disliked the cosmopolitanism which was ousting the narrower, but more finely tempered French culture – destroying it indeed, so he thought; hence he wanted to save what he could of French art from the rich American collector, then already beginning to cast his efficient nets, baited with dollars, in Parisian waters. Degas was buying as many drawings by Ingres as he could; he had also acquired half a dozen of his paintings, and many drawings by Daumier and Delacroix. Daumier he placed high among the nineteenth-century painters. 'If Raphael', he said, 'returned to life and looked at Gérôme's pictures he would say "*connu*",[1] but if he saw a drawing by Daumier, "*Tiens,*

c'est intéressant ça, et d'une puissante main"[2] he would say.' Degas owned various large slips of Manet's *Execution of Maximilian*, two of which are now in the National Gallery. A dealer bought the original painting, and being unable to dispose of so large a canvas, cut it up and sold the fragments separately; most of these Degas was able to acquire. He had besides two beautiful still-life paintings by Manet, one of a single pear, and one of a ham. He had thought him overworldly. '*Mais tu es aussi connu que Garibaldi; que veux-tu de plus?*'[3] Degas chaffed him once. Manet's answer came pat, '*Mon vieux, alors tu es au dessus du niveau de la mer.*'[4] He spoke with particular admiration of Manet, regretting that he had not appreciated him enough during his lifetime. Whistler habitually belittled Manet's work, disliking to hear us praise it. Like Whistler, Degas had no great opinion of Cézanne as an artist.

Degas was a confirmed bachelor of simple habits. He occupied two apartments, one above the other, in the rue Victor Massé, over which a devoted old servant ruled and guarded the painter against intruders. The walls of the lower flat were adorned with his beloved French masters, while upstairs he kept his own works. With those whom he admitted to his friendship he threw off most of his reserve, and showed and discussed his treasures. I eagerly listened to his affectionate tributes; he never tired of lingering over the beauties of his Ingres drawings. He pressed me to look out for unknown originals which he believed were in England; for Ingres had employed a tout in Rome and in this way got many commissions from English tourists before he became famous . . . .

Degas in appearance had something of Henley and something of Meredith, but too finely featured for Henley. His raised brows and heavily lidded eyes gave him an aspect of aloofness, and in spite of his baggy

---

[1]known.

[2]Now that's interesting, and by a powerful hand.

[3]But you're as famous as Garibaldi; what more do you want?
[4]In that case, old boy, you're well above sea level.

DEGAS *The Dancing Lesson c.*1874

DEGAS *Study for Portrait of Jules Perrot* 1875

clothes, he looked the aristocrat he was.

One or two things I saw at the rue Victor Massé remain in my memory; a beautiful pastel of a woman lying on a settee in a bright blue dress, a work which I have not seen again, nor seen reproduced; a small wax model of a horse leaping to one side, which he made use of in a well-known composition of jockeys riding. This was the most highly finished of Degas' *maquettes* which I saw at the rue Victor Massé. Until now I was unaware that Degas modelled. He owned some casts of an Indian dancing figure, a *nataraja* or an *apsara*, the first examples of Indian sculpture I had seen.

Degas was then making studies of laundresses ironing, and of women tubbing or at their toilets. Some of these were redrawn again and again on tracing paper pinned over drawings already made; this practice

allowed for correction and simplification, and was common with artists in France. Degas rarely painted from nature. He spoke once of Monet's dependence in this respect; *'Je n'éprouve pas le besoin de perdre connaissance devant la nature,'*[5] he mocked.

Degas complained much of his eyesight. Young people today who prefer the later work of Degas and of Renoir hardly realize how much of its looser character was due to their failing sight. Degas in the 'nineties was still able to see fairly clearly; but towards the end of his life he was obliged to use the broadest materials, working on a large scale, hesitating, awkward, hardly able to find his way over the canvas or paper.

He was by nature drawn to subtleties of character and to intricate forms and movements. He had the Parisian curiosity for life in its most objective forms. At one with the

[5]I feel no need to lose consciousness in the presence of nature.

[6]Opera girls.

[7]Dancing master.

Impressionists in rejecting the artificial subject-matter of the Salon painters, he looked to everyday life for his subjects, but he differed from Manet and his other contemporaries in the rhythmical poise of his figures and the perfecting of detail. He found in the life of the stage and in the intricate steps of the ballet, with its background of phantasy, an inexhaustible subject-matter which allowed for the colour and movement of romantic art, and yet provided the clear form dear to the classical spirit. He delighted in the strange plumage of the *filles de l'Opéra*[6] as they moved into the circle of the limelight or stood, their skirts standing out above their pink legs, chattering together in the wings. The starling-like flock of young girls, obedient to the baton of the *maître de danse*,[7] Degas rendered with astonishing delicacy of observation. He never forgot that he was a pupil of Ingres. Indeed he described, on one of my first visits, his early relations with Ingres; how fearfully he approached him, showing his drawings, and asking whether he might, in all modesty look forward some day to being an artist; Ingres replying that it was too grave a thing, too serious a responsibility to be thought of; better to devote himself to some other pursuit. And how, going again and yet again, pleading that he had reconsidered from every point of view, his idea of equipping himself to become a painter, that he realized his temerity, but could not bring himself to abandon all his hopes. Ingres finally relented, saying *'C'est très grave, ce que vous pensez faire, très grave; mais si enfin vous tenez quand même à etre un artiste, un bon artiste, eh bien monsieur, faites des lignes, rien que des lignes.'*[8] One of Ingres' sayings which came back to Degas was *'Celui qui ne vit que dans la contemplation de soi-même est un misérable.'*[9] . . .

Degas liked Forain and his work; he was interested too in Lautrec's. To my surprise he greatly disliked Rodin, who, in our eyes was one of the Olympians. Among English

artists he rated Charles Keene highly. He was curious about Brangwyn's work, which he had noticed somewhere, perhaps at Bing's. Bing was the well-known dealer who had spent many years in Japan. Through him collectors acquired their Japanese prints, paintings and lacquer. Sargent and Helleu Degas held in little esteem.

Monet's solitary obsession   1895

In 1895 Monet spent two months at Sandviken in Norway. On 6 April the Bergens Tiede *published an account of his stay there by a young poet, Henri Bang.*

One evening, after tea, when Claude Monet was sitting in the corner of the sofa, looking rather like a peasant smoking his pipe after a long day's work, the conversation turned to interviews, writers and reporters, and this led Monet to say; 'Anyway what do you want? What can be said about me? What indeed, I ask you, can be said about a man who is interested in nothing but his painting? His garden as well, of course, and his flowers, simple ones – they are so beautiful, so calm.' From that evening onwards, for a whole month I lived under the same roof as Claude Monet, and I came to realize that he had been right in what he said. There is nothing more to be said about him beyond what was contained in those words. His life is what he paints; and what he paints is his life.

He feels a young man when his painting is going well, an old one when things go wrong with it. One can hear it in his voice, in his first remarks, in the furrows on his brow. Is the work going well? The whole day reflects what he is doing, and how it is getting along; if his will and ability are clouded, his face is clouded. He can only see things from one point of view, but were there ever geniuses who could see things except from one point of view? He wants only one thing, to immerse himself in colour.

---

[8] It's a grave decision you have in mind; but if you still insist on being an artist, a good artist, well then, sir, make lines, nothing but lines.

[9]He who lives only in the contemplation of himself is a poor wretch.

'It is a pity,' he once said, 'that a man can only interest himself in one thing. But I can't do anything else. I only have one interest; work is nearly always a torture. If I could find some other interest I would be much happier, because I could use this other interest as a form of relaxation.

'Now I cannot relax; colours pursue me like a constant worry. They even trouble me in my sleep.'

One evening when he came back after ten hours of work in the bitterly cold Norwegian air, watching the sun and the colours of the landscape, this sixty-year-old said:

'No, it was no real hardship. And anyway, what else could I have expected? I am chasing a dream, I want the unattainable. Other artists paint a bridge, a house, a boat; and that's the end. They've finished.

'*I want to paint the air which surrounds the bridge, the house, the boat: the beauty of the air in which these objects are located, and that is nothing short of impossible.*

'If only I could satisfy myself with what is possible!'

Is not the whole life of a painter contained in these words? They are the words of a real artist who endures the dream of the impossible which is the same and the only one for all painters to entrap the beauty of things, that beauty which his eye has seen and his soul has adored.

The existence of Monet is elevated by this desire. He adores the whole beauty of nature, which he sees around him, and which tortures him, for that is what he is so anxious to translate into paint – the innumerable, ever-changing beauties of nature. That is just it; nature changes constantly; each minute an ever-changing light transforms the atmosphere, and the beauty of things.

But how then can one understand and fix something which we only see when it is finished? Whilst we are admiring, the object of our admiration is itself changing. How can we seize hold of something that we cannot understand until we have discovered

how to express it? If the photographer's film had a soul, or the artist had an incredibly skilful hand, it might be achieved. Now the artist has to get the utmost out of the few seconds that nature allows him. Monet has twelve or thirteen canvases which he is working on at different times, and each moment of the day has its own canvas. At each time of the day he goes to work on the canvas connected with it, so as to find, as closely as possible the same light which has the same beauty, and perhaps only to work on that particular part of each which his eye sees and his spirit understands at that particular moment. But nature mocks his art, and his dream fades as his hands cannot express what he wants them to. There are days when, in a blind rage, furious with himself and with the ineffectiveness of his colours, he tears his canvas in pieces and treads it into the snow. 'Ah,' he says, 'how often, when I was working at Le Havre, have I thrown my colour-box into the sea, and been forced the next morning to telegraph to Paris for a new one, because you always have to start again.' Claude Monet always starts again, something stronger than himself forces him to – the need to reproduce what he sees. But in actual fact there are no happy artists; those who seem to be happy because they produce masterpieces, still suffer because their dreams are always superior to their works. What we see in works of art is quite small; things which are infinitely greater always continue to be the dream which it is impossible to realize in the works which are actually produced.

At least, the effort to reproduce on canvas what he would like to fills the life of Monet, and the days when his eyes cannot express light, he dedicates to his garden, 'because they are so lovely and so calm, these ordinary flowers'.

His daily life is reflected in his conversation. What he loves in life and demands from it consists of one thing; to be in peace, to be left alone, to live peacefully within the bosom of his family, to be able to stay in his garden and tend his flowers without being disturbed. Life is a frenzied fairground, where breathless people buy and sell things which aren't worth a brass farthing, where jugglers show off to other jugglers. Claude Monet does not get involved in all this sound and fury. He stays at home; the swings and the roundabouts do not interest him. An ironic comment, which he might utter in a moment of relaxation, proves that he does in fact know the world and the people who inhabit it, but his main desire is always to escape from it. He lives at Giverny, an hour away from Paris, which despite its proximity he hardly ever visits. He knows nobody, and nobody knows him. If you ask him if he knows this or that famous person, he will reply twenty times out of a hundred, 'No, I live in the country, I know very few people, and those I do know are mostly friends of my youth.' It is not perhaps just antipathy, but a certain fear which makes Monet avoid the world. He has seen success play such havoc with people's lives. This is probably the reason that alone in his solitude and remoteness he maintains the integrity of his personality. We were speaking one evening about one of the famous personalities of our time, a French novelist, whose name is internationally famous, and who is one of Monet's contemporaries, and this led him to say 'He used to be so proud when he was young; proud and honest.' He fell silent for a moment and then went on, 'but life destroys that; it ruins everything.'

Is that his philosophy? Does he mean to say that it is only outside life that one can remain 'high-minded and honest'? Does he mean to say that one cannot live without lies? He despises pleasantries, he can't stand polite smiles. Or does he mean to say that the world is not worthy of his art? It is probably that, for the only thing in life which attracts him is art, and it is useless to live without that art.

He offers no excuses, and stays in his garden.

Of all that the world offers in the way of riches, he will accept nothing. A garden with flowers; that is all he desires. A wall. This wall is the judgment of Claude Monet on that world from which it separates him.

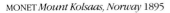

MONET *Mount Kolsaas, Norway* 1895

PISSARRO PAINTING IN THE ORCHARD AT ERAGNY,
WITH JULIE, PAUL-EMILE AND JEANNE

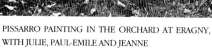

Patriarchs

*Indomitably, the Impressionists continued to
work, and to develop, as long as they lived; and
the open air retained its fascination.*

PHOTOGRAPH OF DEGAS IN THE BOULEVARD DE
CLICHY, c.1910

PHOTOGRAPH OF CÉZANNE PAINTING NEAR AIX, 1906

PHOTOGRAPH OF RENOIR PAINTING AT CAGNES, 1908

183

Cézanne's reputation among his colleagues 1895

Although Cézanne had been involved with the Impressionists from the beginning of his career, his connection with the movement was always erratic. In November 1895 he had an exhibition in Paris, and Pissarro wrote to his son about reactions to it, and other painters.

Yesterday at Portier's I made the acquaintance of an English painter, O'Kean, I don't know whether I am spelling his name correctly. He is very intelligent and greatly admires the Impressionists, especially my work. He didn't know me by sight, and he was praising my *Sunset in Knocke*, a canvas of 25 x 21 inches, so highly that I was abashed. He wanted to show me a canvas of his, so that I could advise him, which I did scrupulously. His painting, like that of many English artists, is literature, which is not a defect in itself, but does result from a lack of painting content; his work is thin and hard and lacks values. It is however intelligent, a little like Chavannes, sentimental and feminine, but, as I told him, it is not really painting. Speaking of England, I asked him how it was that we were so little understood in a country that had such fine painters. England is always late and moves in leaps. This is pretty much our opinion. On leaving Portier's I had this thought; How rarely do you come across true painters, who know how to balance two tones. I was thinking of Hayet, who looks for noon at midnight, of Gauguin, who however has a good eye, of Signac, who also has something, all of them more or less paralysed by theories. I also thought of Cézanne's show, in which there were exquisite things, still lifes of irreproachable perfection, *others much worked on*, and yet unfinished, of even greater beauty, landscapes, nudes and heads that are unfinished, but yet grandiose and so *painted*, so supple. Why? Sensation is there.

On the way to Durand-Ruel's, I saw two paintings by Puvis de Chavannes. No, no! that sort of thing is cold and tiresome! A representation of natives of Picardy, and very well composed. But all the same, the whole thing is at bottom an anomaly, it can't be seen as a painting, no, a thousand times no! On a great stone wall it is admirable, but it is not painting. I am simply noting my immediate impressions.

Curiously enough while I was admiring this strange, disconcerting aspect of Cézanne, familiar to me for many years, Renoir arrived. But my enthusiasm was nothing compared to Renoir's. Degas himself is seduced by the charm of this refined savage, Monet, all of us.... Are we mistaken? I don't think so. The only ones who are not subject to the charm of Cézanne are those artists or collectors, who have shown by their errors that their sensibilities are defective. They properly point out the faults which we all see, but the charm, that they do not see. As Renoir said so well, these paintings have an indefinable quality, like the things of Pompeii, so crude and so admirable. Nothing of the Académie Julian! Degas and Monet have bought some marvellous Cézannes. I exchanged a small sketch of Louveciennes for an admirable small canvas of bathers and one of his self-portraits.

Founded on nervous debility 1895

The appearance of any new art form is often attributed by its critics to moral, political or even physical 'degeneracy'. Max Nordau's Degeneracy, *first published in 1895 in Germany, was immensely popular, and eventually found a place in the dubious pantheon of Nazi literature. He was preoccupied with the notion that writers and artists were, in his sense of the word, 'degenerate' and applied this to the Impressionists in general and Manet in particular.*

The curious style of certain modern painters, 'Impressionists', 'Stipplers' or 'Mosaicists', 'Papilloteurs' or shakers; violent colourists, or those who deal only in gray or muted tints, becomes immediately intelligible to us if we keep in view the researches of the Charcot school into the visual derangements which occur in degeneracy and hysteria. The painters who assure us that they are sincere, and reproduce nature as they see it, speak the truth. The degenerate artist, who suffers from *nystagmus*, or trembling of the eyeball, will in fact perceive the phenomena of nature trembling, restless, lacking any firm outline, and if he is a conscientious painter, will give us pictures reminding us of the style practised by cartoonists of *Fliegende Blätter* when they represent a wet dog vigorously shaking itself. If his pictures fail to produce a comic effect, it is only because the spectator who is viewing them sees in them the desperate attempt to reproduce completely an impression which is actually incapable of being reproduced by the expedients of the painter's art, as devised by men of normal vision.

There is hardly a hysterical subject whose retina is not partly insensitive . . . . If the sensitiveness is completely lost (*achromatopsy*) he then sees everything in a uniform gray, but perceives differences in the degrees of brightness. Hence the spectacle of nature which is presented to him is that of an etching or a drawing, where the effect of absent colours is replaced by differences in the intensity of light, by greater or less depth and power of the white and black portions. Painters who are insensitive to colour will naturally have a predilection for neutral-toned painting, and a public suffering from the same malady will find nothing objectionable in falsely-coloured pictures, such as those of Puvis de Chavannes . . . .

Red has a peculiarity which explains the predilection shown for it by the hysterical. As a feeling of pleasure is always connected with dynamogeny, or the production of

force, every living being instinctively seeks for dynamogenous sense-impressions, and avoids enervating and inhibitive ones. Hence it is intelligible that hysterical painters revel in red, and that hysterical spectators take special pleasure in pictures operating dynamogenously and producing feelings of pleasure.

If red is dynamogenous, violet is correspondingly enervating and inhibitive. It was not by accident that violet was chosen by many nations as a mourning colour, and by us also for half-mourning. The sight of this colour has a depressing effect, and the unpleasant feeling awakened by it induces dejection in a mind of a melancholy disposition. This suggests that painters suffering from hysteria and neuraesthenia will be inclined to cover their canvases uniformly with the colour which corresponds most closely with their condition of lassitude and exhaustion. Thus originate the violet pictures of Manet and his school, which spring from no actually observable aspect of nature, but from a subjective view due to the condition of the nerves. When the entire surface of the walls in salons and art exhibitions of the day appears veiled in uniform half-mourning, this passion for violet is simply an expression of the nervous debility of the painter.

Clemenceau on Mutability and Monet   1896

Although he is mainly known as a politician, Georges Clemenceau was a gifted writer, a sensitive critic, and a close friend of Monet and other Impressionists. In Pan, *a volume of essays published in 1896, he commented on the idea of the constantly changing nature of vision, especially in relation to Monet's recent series of paintings of Rouen cathedral which had been extremely successful.*

185

The one thing that should give us pleasure in a constantly changing world is the awareness of that vital sense of life which powers the earth, the sea and the whole of nature. It is this constant sense of movement, to be found in every part of our planet, this ever-changing miracle, which itself engenders others, and which is to be found not only in men and animals, but in grass, trees and rocks, which provides for us a spectacle of which we can never tire. Wherever I go I analyse what I see; I try to grasp the fleeting, to understand the inexpressible mystery of things, and to savour the endlessly changing spectacle of life with a heightened awareness. Life takes place within the setting of a miracle, and man can derive endless joy from contemplating it. The only trouble is that man does not always perceive this miracle, or to be more precise, he has hardly started to formulate it to himself. For thousands of years the human eye has looked at that image of the world which has been conveyed to it by the rays of the sun. Everything which has come to us through the art of the past, from the first primitive axe, with its beautiful proportions and powerful colours, through the outlined shapes of bears and mammoths which some Leonardo of the stone-age has carved on those bones which are on view in the Musée de Cluny, right up to Monet's cathedral, allows us to appreciate in an encapsulated form those phases of visual understanding through which our race has passed.

Rouen Cathedral is an unchanging and unchangeable object, yet it is one which provokes a constant movement of light in the most complex way. At every moment of every day, the changing light creates a new view of the cathedral, which seems as though it were constantly altering. In front of Monet's twenty views of the building, one begins to realize that art, in setting out to express nature with ever growing accuracy, teaches us to look, to perceive, to feel. The stone itself becomes an organic substance,

MONET *Rouen Cathedral in Morning Light* 1894

and one can feel it being transformed as one moment in its life succeeds another. The twenty chapters of evolving light patterns of the paintings have been skilfully selected to create an ordered pattern of evolution. The great church itself, a testament to the vivifying light of the sun, hurls its mass against the brightness of the sky.

Pissarro addresses a young painter   1896-97

In 1896 or 1897 a young painter, Louis le Bail, wrote to Pissarro asking for general advice. He received the following answer.

Look for the kind of nature that suits your temperament. The motif should be observed more for shape and colour than for drawing. There is no need to tighten the form which can be obtained without that. Precise drawing is dry and hampers the impression of the whole; it destroys all sensations. Do not define too closely the outline of things; it is the brushstroke of the right value and colour which should produce the drawings. In a mass the greatest difficulty is not to give the contour in detail, but to paint what is within. Paint the essential quality, try to convey it by any means whatsoever, without bothering about technique. When painting, make a choice of subject, see what is lying at the right and the left, then work on everything simultaneously. Don't work bit by bit, but paint everything at once by placing tones everywhere, with brushstrokes of the right colour and value, while noticing what is alongside. Use small brushstrokes and try to put down your perceptions immediately. The eye should not be fixed on one spot, but should take in everything, while observing the reflections which the colours produce on their surroundings. Work at the same time on sky, water, branches, ground, keeping everything going on an equal basis and work unceasingly until you have got it. Cover the canvas at the first go, and then work on till you see nothing more to add. Observe the aerial perspective well, from the foreground to the horizon, the reflections of sky, of foliage. Don't be afraid of putting on colour, refine the work little by little. Don't proceed according to rules and principles, but paint what you observe and feel. Paint generously and unhesitatingly, for it is best not to lose the first impression. Don't be timid in the presence of nature; one must be bold at the risk of being deceived and making mistakes. One must have only one teacher – nature; she is the one always to be consulted.

Staying with the Renoirs   1899

In the summer of 1899 Julie Manet stayed for a while with the Renoirs in a house they had rented at Saint-Cloud, and spent much time listening to the master's views on art and society, which she recorded in her delightful Journal.

28 July. M. Renoir said that one learns more about a thing from looking at it in a painting than from looking at it in nature. Speaking of socialism, which is doing so much evil, he said 'It has completely deprived people, and especially workers, of religion, which was such a consolation to them, and has replaced it by an increase of 25 per cent in their wages. A working man isn't made happier by having to work fewer hours, for a man who has no work to do gets up to no good, and workmen at leisure spend that leisure in a bar. What is necessary is that his work should become less arduous. Today there is nothing interesting for the workman, who in the old days, for instance, could make a chair according to his own design, and get real pleasure out of it. Today one makes the legs, another the seat, a third the back, and somebody else puts them together. Everything has to be done as quickly as possible to get the money in quickly. In the old days an artist painted a picture of the Virgin with care, because it was a way of securing entry into heaven; now he bangs out a picture of her as quickly as he can so as to get his fee as quickly as possible.'

30 July. M. Renoir is very amusing and bright. He talked a lot with us; this evening he explained what was going on in the Dreyfus affair. He then went on to describe [President] Carnot's visit to the picture galleries at the opening of the '89 International Exhibition; the warders heading the procession, the sudden stopping of the procession in the middle of the galleries, Carnot's rigid

stance as he turned his neck to survey what was around him, and then the provincial, who finding himself suddenly face to face with the president shouted out in a strangled voice, 'Vive Le Président!' before collapsing, overcome with emotion, on a chair. Then he spoke equally amusingly about his dinner with his friend Lauth on the same day as the opening of the exhibition. He described the crowds hurling themselves on the buffet, and himself finding a huge mortadella under his arm.

1 August. 'One must understand', said M. Renoir, 'that that which is hidden, but which can be sensed, is what makes the charm of things. For instance Arab women, who only allow their eyes to be seen, and look so attractive, would seem much less so were they to lift their veils.'

4 August. M. Renoir's health varies from day to day, then either his feet or his hands swell; this malady is very tormenting, and he, although so highly strung, bears it with immense patience. He is cheerful, very gentle with us, and speaks in the most interesting way. What an intelligence he has! He sees clearly and correctly in everything, just as in his art. 'Education', he says, 'is the damnation of the people, that is why there are those who do not believe in God, and substitute science for Him.' This is exactly what Edgar Poe said – that science is mankind's loss. M. Renoir laughs at people who believe that one should paint differently from the great masters of the past. 'Geffroy concluded an article on the Corot centenary exhibition by saying: Finally this is the art of the past; now we are going to see the art of the future – alluding to the Impressionists. So I said to Alexandre, write in your article that the painting of Corot is the art of the future.'

M. Renoir spoke to us of the beauty of women, especially that of Judith Gauthier. 'She was the goddess; her sister was more gentle, more intimate.' He had a great admiration for Judith, I even think that he rather paid court to her.

6 August. The whole evening was spent listening to M. Renoir. He said that Renan had done a lot of harm; it was he and his followers who had deprived people of their simple faith. Then, as the conversation turned to arduous jobs such as those of stokers, in connection with the horrible accident which occurred yesterday evening at Juvisy, and miners, etc., he continued: 'It is necessary to make sacrifices to avoid misfortunes, and the socialists do not understand that they should begin by being less concerned about keeping themselves warm if they wish for equality, and so not have so many miners, just as we would have fewer stokers on trains if they were not so anxious to make the journey from Paris to Marseilles in 14 hours.'

Really one shouldn't complain about things which take a toll in life.

M. Renoir was very illuminating about the walks he used to take in Paris on Sundays with his mother.

7 August. This evening M. Renoir was talking about music, the violin and the piano. He said 'It must be very difficult with the violin, just as it is in painting, to find the right tone straight off.' Then, the conversation continuing, 'I think that any form of art which depends on some secret is inferior; in the paintings of Rubens, as in those of Velázquez, there is nothing hidden, nothing beneath the surface; it is just painting. Those who speak about finishes do not know what they're talking about, these colours painted transparently on a background do nothing but make the painting look heavy. You keep on looking for an undercoating which does not really exist, as in this copy which Degas made for young Rouart. Degas is very nervous and unsure of himself as a teacher. I once heard him say to an amateur artist, "When you start a landscape first of all find out if its tonality is green, violet or whatever, and make a sketch with the background in one of these tones." But I find that I have to brush in quickly when I start a painting, to try and get down as quickly as possible the

overall tone for which one is looking, and then once that has been achieved to paint the whole picture bit by bit as they used to in the old days with painters like old man Ingres. Pissarro has written to Georges Lecomte in connection with his book about Impressionism that you must banish black from your palette, as a useless colour. But I have found that it is only with black that you can infuse a certain lightness into your painting. Titian said that a great painter is one who can use black, and I would rather take Titian's advice than Pissarro's. There is nothing more difficult in painting than black and white. Manet's blacks are so beautiful, and always done with one brushstroke.'

Then Mr. Renoir went on to talk about Velázquez, of his light shadings, made up of black and white, and about paintings in the Madrid museums etc.

10 August. As we were arriving home this afternoon we met M. Renoir setting off on a steam-tricycle to have dinner with Durand-Ruel and Degas. He didn't look very confident.

11 August. It is impossible to find anybody with an intelligence as acute as M. Renoir's, and one which brings such precision to everything it considers. He sees life with the same clarity with which he sees it in his paintings. He is concerned about so many things; he thinks about everybody, especially the unfortunate, and in comparing himself with all who are in pain or distress, finds that he has nothing to complain about in his own illness. He teaches you to think of everything, and cultivates a warm heart. He drew a picture of the lives of steel-workers which was heartbreaking, and said that some live a life of mere subsistence, and that people do not always think about those human beings who live a life devoid of every kind of pleasure. Is this not proof of the fact that another world exists in which they will find happiness? Does one not realize what a debt one owes, and should one not therefore render thanks to God for all the benefits one has had in life, by prayer, righteous living and charity to the afflicted? Can one be happy without sharing this happiness with others? How wonderful it would be to work to put an end to the sufferings of these unhappy working men.

Truly it would be quite wrong to complain about anything when one does not lead such a horrible existence. Should one not, as M. Renoir says, deprive oneself of those many indulgences which nowadays the love of luxury seems to make indispensable, and yet which create these atrocious sufferings? People are upset about the fate of Dreyfus, but do not commiserate with the thousands of men who have done nothing, and are condemned to suffer as much as he. Ideas of combating this keep occurring to me, but what can I do? And yet I find that it is wrong not to be able to do something for the unfortunate. Doing good is really a difficult task.

More wisdom from Renoir   c. *1900*

Jean Renoir's Renoir *(Paris 1962) cannot be regarded as containing absolutely accurate transcripts of his father's sayings, but in varying degrees these give a convincing impression.*

Go and look at what others have produced, but copy only nature itself. If you copy you are assuming a creative personality which is not your own. Nothing that you did would ever be your own.

Young people should be trained to see things for themselves and not always seek guidance.

To be an artist you must learn to know the laws of nature.

Painters on porcelain only copy the work of others. Not one of them would think of looking at a canary in a cage to see how its claws are made.

RENOIR *The Artist's Son, Jean, Drawing* 1901

It's all very well to be sentimental about the past. Of course I regret the passing of hand-coloured plates, of furniture made by the village carpenter, of the days when every craftsman could use his imagination, and put something of himself into every object he made, however small. Today the only way you can get that pleasure is by being an artist, and signing your work, something I detest. On the other hand, in the days of Louis XV I would have been able to paint only commissioned subjects. What seems to me to be one of the most important things about our movement is that we have freed painting from the tyranny of subject-matter. I am free to paint flowers and call them flowers, without have to weave a story around them.

There isn't a single person, or landscape or subject which doesn't possess some interest, although it may not be immediately apparent. When a painter discovers this hidden treasure, other people are immediately struck by its beauty. Old Corot opened our eyes to the beauty of the Loing, which is just a river, like any other, and I am sure that the landscape of Japan is no more beautiful than that of any other country, but Japanese artists knew how to reveal their hidden treasures.

I like lovely materials, rich brocades, diamonds glittering in the light, though I would hate to wear such things myself. I am thankful, however, to those who do wear them, as long as they allow me to paint them. On the other hand I would just as soon paint cheap glass trinkets, and cheap cotton textiles.

It is the eye of the sensualist that I wish to open. Not everyone is a sensualist just because he wants to be. There are those who never become sensualists, no matter how hard they try. Someone gave a painting by a famous artist to one of my friends, who was delighted to have so precious an object in his salon, and showed it off to everybody. Then one day he suddenly came rushing in to see me. He told me that never until that morning had he realized why the painting was so beautiful. Until then he had only liked it because of the fact that the signature impressed everybody. My friend had just become a sensualist.

I have a horror of the word 'flesh' which

has become so over-used. Why not 'meat' while they are about it? What I love is skin; a young girl's skin that is pink, and shows that she has a good circulation. But above all else I love serenity.

I've spent my life making blunders. The advantage of growing old is that you become aware of your mistakes more quickly.

textures, and Manet for the extraordinary vitality of some of his portraits, such as the wonderful full-length of the engraver Marcellin Desboutin. But that the world, even the cultivated world, will ever see beauty in *Le Déjeuner sur l'Herbe* – the picture made famous by a well-known novel by Zola, is not to be believed.

No future for Impressionism 1900

Despite the enthusiasm of the Americans, and that of some critics and painters in Britain, the main body of artistic opinion in England was implacably hostile to Impressionism. On 5 June 1900 the art critic of The Times *unburdened himself when reviewing the painting section of the International Exhibition held in Paris in that year.*

Though the French artists have never abandoned their rightful belief in draughtsmanship and method, the most notable achievements for the last fifty years have been in directions opposed to Ingres. With what despair he would have looked upon the works of the great realist Edouard Manet, here assembled in one of the galleries, may only be imagined, nor would he have been much better pleased with the roomful of impressionist landscape painters, Claude Monet, Sisley, Pissarro, and the paintings of Degas and Renoir, here grouped together. It is not quite easy to decide how far the admiration for these things, which is now generally expressed in France, and among advanced collectors elsewhere, is genuine, and how far it is the result of a desire to appear 'in the movement', carefully forced by one or two clever dealers. We ourselves are inclined to think that the craze for the impressionists' landscapes will not last, but that people will continue to admire Degas for his unique gift of rendering certain movements and certain

Renoir on production difficulties 1901

Once a painter had become successful, his dealer expected an endless supply of pictures. But there were always complications, and painters were often not as loyal to their own dealers as perhaps they ought to have been. In 1901 Renoir had got himself into a tricky position. Durand-Ruel was demanding more pictures for an exhibition, but Renoir, as he confessed in this letter, dated 15 April, had been selling direct to the Abbé Gaugain, an inspired collector of Impressionist works, who bought both from Durand-Ruel and directly from his artists. Renoir had discovered that some of the paintings he had sold to the Abbé were coming up for sale on 6 May, so thought that he had better make a clean breast of it. What he did not realize was that the dealer had always been aware of the situation, and had in fact bought up the whole of the Gaugain collection before the sale for 101,000 francs.

Your talk of an exhibition makes me tremble. It seems to me that during the past year I have paid enough to be able to take a year off. I am not doing well with figure-painting, and I cannot supply you with 60 canvases a month. I'm sorry, but that's all I can do. I don't want to send you any unfinished canvases. I have sent off [the portrait of] our servant, and the notorious torso has gone to Essoyes with my wife. I am hoping to get in contact with the model again, and finish it, for this appalling thing isn't finished yet. I

CASSATT *Feeding the Ducks*

have been really ill; so bad indeed that I haven't been able to go up to my studio. Forgive me therefore for a little longer this year, and allow me, if not to get completely well, at least to get less confused. Apart from this things aren't so bad. The next time you write to me I shall be at Aix-les-Bains. I think that I shall be there by Monday or Tuesday. I am hoping that the weather will be better, and that the baths will be open.

I have been weak enough to commit a few infidelities to you with the Abbé though what I have given him would have been refused, and indeed thought horrible by you, which in fact is true enough. But if I only sold good paintings, I would die of hunger, and I thought that he would keep these horrors longer. For four years he has been begging me to sell him a view of the

Midi. It was a commission which for a long time I refused to accept. I ended up by running up for him a *View of the Palais des Papes* (at Avignon), and that's it. But I have lots of collectors, and I cannot live on hope.

So, my dear Durand-Ruel, let me get better, at least partially so, and let us get together a really fabulous exhibition, with new things, next year. I am going to spend two or three days in Lyons for my painting, and then I go on to Aix. My wife is staying at Essoyes, in her own part of the country, with Jean.

To repeat myself, please forgive my weaknesses. Hang, if you so wish, the large painting which I am giving you, when it is touched up, if you want to, and indeed if you still want the picture itself, and let us wait for next year.

Mary Cassatt on her prints   1903

Perhaps more than any of her fellow-Impressionists, Mary Cassatt paid especial attention to prints and the various processes they involved. On 9 January 1903 she wrote about them to Samuel P. Avery, President of the Board of Trustees of the Metropolitan Museum, New York.

I thank you very much for your kind letter. It is delightful to think that you take an interest in my work. I have sent with the set of my coloured etchings all the 'states' I had. I wish I could have had more, but I had to hurry on and be ready for my printer (M. Leroy) when I could get him. The printing is a great work; sometimes we worked all day (eight hours) both as hard as we could work, and only printed eight or ten proofs in a day. My method is very simple. I drew an outline in drypoint and transferred this to two other plates, making in all three plates, never more, for each proof. Then I put an aquatint wherever the colour was to be printed; the colour was painted on the plate as it was to appear in the proof. I tell you, this because Mr Lucas [George A. Lucas, a collector and friend of Whistler] thought it might interest you, and if any of the etchers in New York care to try the method, you can tell them how it is done. I am very anxious to know what you think of these new etchings. It amused me very much to do them, though it was hard work.

Mr Durand-Ruel is going to have an exhibition of my work pictures, pastels and etchings in the fall in New York. Will you be so kind as to lend him some of my early etchings? You are the only person who has everything I have done in that line.

I received the Annual Report of the Metropolitan Museum you were so kind as to send me. I should very much like to give something to the Museum, but I don't feel as though I were well enough known at home to make it worthwhile. After my exhibition, if I have any success with the artists and amateurs I will certainly present something to the Museum, if you think they would care to have it.

Again, thanking you, my dear Mr Amery for your kind sympathy.

Impressionism and the English   1904

Though criticized by Pissarro (cf. p. 194), Wynford Dewhurst's Impressionist Painting, its Genesis and Development *(1904) did more to make the movement popular in England than any other publication, and this, in part at least, because he paid such emphasis – to the point of exaggeration – on the movement's English ancestry.*

Those Englishmen who are taunted with following the methods of the French Impressionists, sneered at for following a foreign style, are in reality but practising their own, for the French artists simply developed a style which was English in its conception. Many things had assisted this development, some accidental, some natural. All the Englishmen had worked to a large extent in the open. Now the atmosphere of France lends itself admirably to Impressionist painting 'en plein air'. All landscapists notice that the light is purer, stronger, and less variable in France than in England.

By thus working in the open both Constable and Turner, together with their French followers, were able to realize upon canvas a closer verisimilitude to the varying moods of nature than had ever been attempted before. By avoiding artificially darkened studios, they were able to study the problems of light with an actuality impossible under a glass roof. They were, in fact, children of the sun, and through its worship they evolved an entirely new school of picture-making. The Modern Impressionist, too, is a worshipper of light, and is never happier than when attempting to fix upon his canvas some beautiful effect of sunshine, some exquisite gradation of atmosphere. Who better than Turner can teach the use and practice of value and tone? In triumph he fixed those fleeting mists upon his immortal canvases, immortal, unhappily, only so long as bitumen, mummy and other pigment abominations will allow.

The technical methods of the French Impressionists and of the early English group vary but little. The modern method of placing side by side upon the canvas spots, streaks or dabs of more or less pure colour, following certain defined scientific principles, was made habitual use of by Turner. Both Constable and Turner worked pure white in impasto through their canvases, high light and shadow, long before the advent of the Frenchmen. . . .

The Impressionists, therefore, continued the methods of the English masters. But they added a strange and exotic ingredient. To the art of Corot and Constable they added the art of Japan, an art which had profoundly influenced French design one hundred years before the opening of the Treaty Ports flooded Europe with craftwork from the islands. From Japanese colour-prints, and the gossamer sketches on silk and rice-paper, the Impressionists learnt the manner of painting scenes as observed from an altitude, with the curious perspective which results. They awoke to the multiplied gradation of values and to the use of pure colour in flat masses. This art was the source of the evolution to a system of simpler lines.

In colour they ultimately departed from the practice of the English and Barbizon schools, discarding blacks, browns, ochres and muddy colours generally, together with all bitumens and siccatives. These they replaced by new and brilliant combinations, the result of modern chemical research,

which enabled them to attain a higher degree of luminosity than was before possible. Special care was given to the rendering of colour, and also to the reflections to be found in shadows.

Pissarro disagrees   1903

In the course of preparing his book Wynford Dewhurst had spoken with Pissarro, and quoted one of his letters. The painter wrote to his son Lucien on 8 May 1903.

This Mr Dewhurst understands nothing of the Impressionist movement, he sees only a mode of execution, and he confuses the names of artists, he considers Jongkind inferior to Boudin. So much the worse for him! He says that before going to London we [Monet and Pissarro in 1870] had no conceptions of light. The fact is we have sketches which prove the contrary. He omits the influence which Claude Lorraine, Corot, the whole eighteenth century and Chardin especially exerted on us. But what he has no suspicion of, is that Turner and Constable, while they taught us something, showed us in their works that they had no understanding of *the analysis of shadow*, which in Turner's painting is simply used as an effect, a mere absence of light. As far as tone division is concerned, Turner proved the value of this as a method, among methods, although he did not apply it correctly and naturally. Besides, we derived from the eighteenth century. It seems to me that Turner, too, looked at the works of Claude Lorraine, and if I am not mistaken one of Turner's paintings, *Sunset*, hangs next to one of Claude's. [It does; in the National Gallery, London.] Symbolic, isn't it? Mr Dewhurst has his nerve.

Degas the collector   1904

Degas was an assiduous collector of paintings and drawings from the past, especially those of Ingres. In 1904 he drew up an inventory of his collection, remarkable for its grasp of detail. Typical of the entries is that on Ingres' portraits of M. and Mme Leblanc, which he contemplated bequeathing to the Louvre.

Ingres. *Portrait of M. and Mme Leblanc*, painted in Florence in 1823. Bought at the Hôtel [Drouot], the man for 3,500, the woman for 7,500, total with the charges 11,500, 23 January 1896, in a sale after the death of Mme Place, their daughter.

I remember having seen these portraits in 1854, in the home of M. Leblanc, their son, in the rue de la Vieille Estrapade, a house with an iron fence that still exists, on the ground floor. M. Poisson-Seguin, a lawyer and friend of father's, took us there with his wife. The younger M. Leblanc was an assistant teacher at the Ecole Polytechnique. I saw these portraits again at the World's Fair, on the Avenue Montaigne. Mme Place obtained them from her brother, a bachelor, who came to live with her after the death of her husband, and died before her.

There were also portraits in pencil; Mme and M. Leblanc standing, which entered Bonnat's collection; the young Leblanc, which was once owned by Albert Goupil, and which Gérôme, his heir, sold to Mme de Scey-Montbeliard; two others, a young man and a young woman with headbands and leg-of-mutton sleeves, who could well have been the young Mme Place. The two drawings were sold together at the same sale to Morgand of the Passage des Panoramas, and sold by him to Bonnat (at the sale sold for 2,160 francs). I also have two photographic reproductions of the two full-length portraits in pencil that Bonnat gave to the family.

The family, which had never shown the paintings, had had the background of the man repainted to match that of the woman. I was able to have it removed in my presence, easily enough to prove that this revision must not have been more than ten years old. The original red background was found intact. There are fools among the aristocrats as everywhere else.

Vulgar but splendid: a verdict   1904

In 1904 Camille Mauclair (1872-1945) published his L'Impressionnisme, son histoire, son esthetique, ses maîtres, *which was in effect a virtual canonization of the movement, as he was art critic of the* Mercure de France *and notorious for his artistic conformism (and his anti-Semitism, which found its most repellent expression in a book on Jews in art which he published during the Vichy régime).*

Not that the movement is without its faults. In an attempt to belittle it some people have said that it only has the value of an interesting experiment, having only been able to point where perfection lay, without achieving it. This is not true. It is absolutely evident that Manet, Monet, Renoir and Degas have created masterpieces which can rank with those in the Louvre, and the same might be said of some of their less famous colleagues. But it is also clear that the time spent on research as well as on agitation and the debilitating controversies which it has provoked over the past twenty-five years have wasted much of their time and effort. There has been a fundamental divergence between Realism and the actual techniques of Impressionism. Its realistic origins have inclined it to vulgarity. Often it has treated indifferent subjects in the grand side, and too frequently it has beheld life from the anecdotal aspect. It has lacked psychological insight (if we except Degas).

All too willingly it has refused to accept all that lies hidden under the appearance of things, and has presumed to separate painting from those ideological considerations which influence all art. Hatred of academic allegory, defiance of symbolism, abstraction and romantic subjects, have led it to reject a whole category of ideas and influences, and has made the painter no more than a craftsman. This was necessary when the movement was new, but it is no longer necessary, and the Impressionists now understand this themselves. Finally it has often been too superficial even in obtaining effects; it has surrendered to the mere wish to satisfy the eye, of playing with tonal values merely for the love of sophistication. It often makes one sad to see symphonies of magnificent colour being wasted sometimes in pictures of people in boats or of café corners, and we have arrived at a degree of complex intellectuality which is no longer satisfied even with these rudimentary themes. Impressionism has come to indulge in useless exaggerations, faults of composition, and of harmony. This fact is undeniable.

But Impressionism still remains splendid and fascinating for its gifts, which will always arouse enthusiasm – freedom, impetuosity, youth, brilliancy, fervour, the sheer joy of painting, and a passion for beautiful light. It is, on the whole, the greatest movement in painting that France has known since Delacroix; it brings the nineteenth century to a glorious finish and presages well for the next. It has accomplished the great feat of having brought us once again into the tradition of our great national heritage, far more so than Romanticism did, for this was diluted by foreign elements. In Impressionism we have painting of a sort which could only have been conceived in France, and we have to go right back to Watteau in order to receive again the same feeling about an art form. Impressionism has brought us an almost unhoped-for renaissance, and this consti-

tutes its most irrefutable claim on the gratitude of our race.

Impressionism has exercised a marked influence on foreign painting. Among the foreign painters attracted by its ideas we must mention the Germans Max Liebermann and Kuehl; the Norwegian, Thalow; the Dane Kroer; the Belgians Théo van Rysselberghe, Emile Claus, Verheyden, Heymanns, Verstraete and Baertson; the Spandiards Zuloaga, Sorolla y Bastida, Dario de Regoyos; the Italians Boldini, Segantini and Michetti; the Americans Alexander, Harrison and Sargent, and in the British Isles the painters of the Glasgow School, Lavery, Guthrie and the late John Lewis Brown. All these men come within the influence of this French movement, and one may say that the honour of having first recognized the truly national character of this art must be given to those foreign countries which have enriched their museums and galleries with works which were despised in the land which had witnessed their birth. At the present moment the effects of this new vision are felt all over the world, right into the bosom of the Academies themselves, and at the Salons, from which the Impressionists are still excluded, can be seen an invasion of paintings inspired by them, which even the most retrogressive juries cannot refuse to accept. To whatever degree modern artists accept Impressionism, they still remain deeply preoccupied with it, and even those who hate it have to take it into account.

The Impressionist movement today, therefore, whatever the attacks on it, whatever the exaggerated praise it may receive, must be seen as an artistic phenomenon which has entered into the domain of history, and it can be studied with the impartial application of those methods of critical analysis which are usually applied to the art of the past.

A militant school   1905

Poet, playwright, painter, socialist, pacifist, feminist, Laurence Housman (1865-1959) was almost predestined to become art critic of The Manchester Guardian, *a post he occupied from 1905 till 1911. Typical of his spirited defence of Impressionism are these extracts from a review which appeared in the paper on 17 January 1905, on the occasion of an exhibition which included 19 works by Manet, 55 by Monet, 35 by Degas, 59 by Renoir, 40 by Pissarro, 36 by Sisley, 10 by Cézanne, 13 by Berthe Morisot and 38 by Boudin.*

The exhibition at the Grafton Galleries, London, of Messrs Durand-Ruel's collection of pictures by the great French Impressionists does something more than supplement where it was weak the French section at the International [Gallery]. Within its limits this is perhaps the most important collection of French art that has been seen in London for a generation. Of the nine painters here represented five are now dead, but their work, already classic in its reputation, still wears the note of championship of a but partially understood cause. Between Boudin, Manet, Madame Morisot, Sisley and Pissarro – names now of the past, – and Cézanne, Degas, Monet and Renoir, whom we may yet claim as contemporaries, there is no dividing line to be drawn; their tenets are still the tenets of a militant school, out of which we may expect further developments and fresh reputations to arise.

But of the artists here named, Boudin and Manet are the two whose influence we see resting with the weight of authority rather than as a mere contemporary stimulus upon the work of the remainder. And it is after them that the point of development arises in the history of the school which has brought about so wide a difference between English and French Impressionism in the present day. It is the emphasis of this difference, which, for an understanding of all that Impressionism means, gives its special value to the present show. Deriving from Boudin and Manet through Whistler, English Impressionism may be said to deal with tone-values far more than with problems of colour; the scrupulous avoidance of too penetrating a search after form, the discovery of a scientific rather than an imaginative basis for the uniformity of outlook which it predicates as necessary to pictorial harmony – these broadly speaking, are the marks of the English school; and as its concern is mainly with tone, much that it seeks to convey can be reduced to monochrome. But from the Impressionism of Claude Monet, Sisley and Pissarro, monochrome is at the furthest remove of all; reproduced in black and white their work becomes absolutely lost; and in the reason for this lies the true departure of the Impressionists of colour from the Impressionists of tone. The distinguishing mark of the former is their lyrical note; a quality like music pervades their work, and while it conveys an impression of truth – as all things which give an emotion with completeness are bound to do – it is an imaginative rather than a literal truth, a perfect expression, but as far removed from a mere visual record as song and music are from ordinary speech and sound.

That so vast a departure in the character of the results should have come about from the consistent workings of the school is but another proof of the transcendent part which personality in art plays. At a first glance it would be difficult to find work more fundamentally opposed than is that of Manet, with its sombre, emphatic breadth and jaundiced colouring, to the vibrating, emotional, sun-steeped art of Claude Monet, yet in each case Impressionsim is the root principle, and it is easy to see in the work of Degas and Renoir close links between these two, who, when viewed alone, seem worlds apart.

THREE PHOTOGRAPHS OF THE EXHIBITION AT THE
GRAFTON GALLERIES, LONDON 1905

The great unsold

*The 'greatest Impressionist exhibition ever to have
been organized' (John Rewald) was mounted by
Paul Durand-Ruel at the Grafton Galleries in
London in 1905. As the photographs show, it was
full of masterpieces, all of which had long been
on Durand-Ruel's hands, and all of which were
for sale. None was sold. The London critics were
dismissive, and the masterpieces, from Renoir's*
On the Terrace *(centre of lower picture) to
Monet's* Monsieur Pertuiset *(through the door-
way), went back into Durand-Ruel's stock. A sub-
scription was mounted, after the show, to buy one
Boudin for the National Gallery.*

Signac pays tribute to Monet   1912

In June 1912 Monet exhibited his recent paintings of Venice, some twenty-nine in all, at the Bernheim Gallery in Paris. After seeing the exhibition, Signac wrote him a letter.

I am sorry that the state of my health has kept me away from Paris at the time of your exhibition, an event which gives me the greatest of pleasure.

But before I left Paris I was able to see quite a number of your new paintings. Looking at your Venice paintings I felt deeply aware of your admirable interpretation of those scenes which I know so well, and also of an emotion as strong and comprehensive as that which I experienced about 1879 in the exhibition galleries of *La Vie Moderne*

in front of your *Railway Stations*, your *Beflagged Streets* and your *Trees in Blossom*, an experience which determined my choice of career.

Always a Monet has moved me profoundly. Always I have found something to learn from, and in my days of doubt and discouragement a Monet has always been for me a friend and a guide.

And these paintings of Venice, more beautiful, more robust than ever, painting in which everything conforms to the expression of your will, where no detail runs contrary to the emotion, and in which you have carried out that happy act of self-denial which Delacroix recommends: I admire these paintings as the highest possible expression of your art.

I hope that you will accept, dear Master, the most sincere and deeply felt expression of my admiration and respectful friendship.

MONET *Grand Canal, Venice* 1908

MONET *Palazzo da Mula* 1908

PHOTOGRAPH OF RENOIR, ALINE AND COCO 1912

Renoir at seventy   c. *1911*

Most of those who saw Renoir during the period of the Great War and just before were struck by his frailty. His son Jean described him as he was at this time.

What struck outsiders coming into his presence for the first time were his eyes and hands. His eyes were light brown, verging on yellow. Often he would point out to us on the horizon a bird of prey flying over the valley of the Cagne, or a ladybug climbing up a blade of grass, lost amongst other blades of grass. So much for the physical quality of his eyes. As for their expression, imagine a mixture of irony and tenderness, of joking and sensuality; they always looked as though they were laughing, as though perceiving the ridiculous side first. But this laugh was a tender laugh, a loving laugh. Perhaps it was also a mask. For Renoir was extremely modest, and did not like to reveal the emotion which overwhelmed him

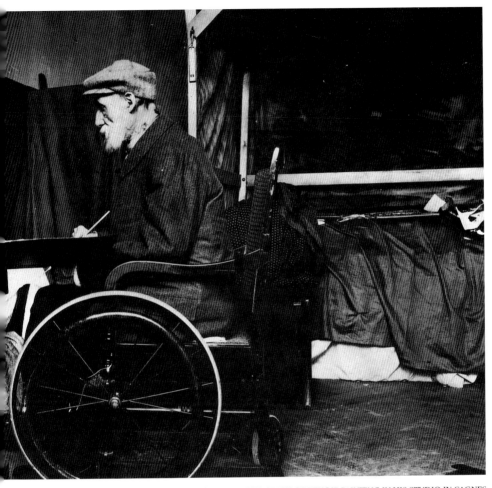

while he was looking at flowers, women or clouds in the sky, the way other men touch and caress.

His hands were terribly deformed. Rheumatism had cracked the joints, bending the thumb towards the palm, and the other fingers towards the wrist. Visitors who were not used to this mutilation could not take their eyes off it. Their reaction, which they did not dare express, was 'It's not possible. With those hands he can't paint these pictures. There's a mystery.' The mystery was Renoir himself. . . . His hands with the fingers curved inwards could no longer pick up anything. It has been said and written that his brush was fastened to his hand. The truth is that Renoir's skin had become so tender that contact with the wooden handle of the brush injured it. To avoid this difficulty he had a little piece of cloth inserted in the hollow of his hand. His twisted fingers gripped rather than held the brush. But until his death his arm remained as steady as that of a young man.

Monet in his studio

Monet in old age can be seen showing a visitor the central surviving fragment of his huge unfinished Déjeuner sur l'herbe *intended for the Salon of 1866. He left it with his landlord at Argenteuil in lieu of rent in 1878 and did not redeem it until 1884, when it was much the worse for wear. Then he seems to have cut it up. Behind him is an early portrait of his first wife Camille. Always a* plein-air *painter, he nevertheless used the studio for final touches.*

PHOTOGRAPH OF MONET RETOUCHING A PAINTING IN HIS STUDIO, 1920

PHOTOGRAPH OF MONET IN HIS STUDIO WITH THE
DUC DE TRÉVISE, 1920

The effects of age on Monet
c. *1920*

In 1914 Clemenceau, a close friend and frequent visitor to Giverny, encouraged Monet to commence the last series of water-lily panels, now in the Orangerie, which provide justification for those who see in him the progenitor of Abstract Expressionism. In the early 1920s he wrote to Clemenceau about the process of their composition.

Colours no longer looked as brilliant to me as they used to; I no longer painted shades of light so correctly. Reds looked muddy to me, pinks insipid and the intermediate or lower notes in the colour scale escaped me completely. As for forms, I could see them as clearly as ever, and render them as decisively. At first I tried pertinacity. How many times have I remained for hours by the little bridge, exactly where we are now, in the full glare of the sun, sitting on my camp-stool, under my sunshade, forcing myself to resume my interrupted task, and to recapture the freshness my palette had lost. A waste of effort! What I painted was more and more mellow; more and more like an 'old picture', and when the attempt was over, and when I compared it with what I used to do in the old days, I would fall into a rage, and I slashed all my pictures with a penknife.

Though I remained insensitive to the subtleties and delicate gradations of colour seen at close quarters, my eyes at least did not deceive me when I drew back and looked at the subject in its broad lines, and this was the start of a new composition. A very modest starting point, to tell the truth. I distrusted myself; I was resolved to leave nothing to chance. Slowly I tried my strength in innumerable rough sketches which convinced me in the first place, that the study of bright light was now, once and for all, impossible for me – but also reassured me by showing that while I could no longer go on playing about with shades or for landscape in delicate colours, I could see as well as ever when it came to vivid colours, isolated in a mass of dark tones.

How was I to put this to good use?

My intentions gradually became clearer. Ever since I entered my sixties I had had the idea of setting about a kind of 'synthesis' in each of the successive categories of themes that held my attention – of summing up in one canvas, sometimes in two, my earlier impressions and sensations. I had given up the notion. It would have meant travelling a good deal, and for a long time revisiting one by one all the places through which my life as a painter had taken me, and verifying my former emotions. I said to myself, as I made sketches, that a series of general impressions captured at the times of day when I had the best chances of seeing correctly would not be without interest. I waited for the idea to consolidate, for the grouping and composition of the themes to settle in my brain, little by little, of their own accord, and the day when I felt I had enough cards to try my luck with a real hope of success, I determined to pass to action and did so.

PHOTOGRAPH OF CLEMENCEAU, MONET AND ALICE
BUTLER ON THE JAPANESE BRIDGE AT GIVERNY, JUNE
1921

Biographies

Agnew, William (1825–1910). The Agnews had been art dealers in Manchester since the eighteenth century, and William, to whom Degas must have been referring, belonged to the third generation. In 1860 they opened a London branch, which is still in existence.

Astruc, Zacharie (1835–1907). Poet, painter, sculptor and critic, who was intimately connected with the Impressionists, especially Manet, and whose sonnet *Olympia* may have suggested to the painter the title for his work of that name. He features in *Music in the Tuileries* (1862), and Manet painted his portrait two years later.

Bartholomé, Albert (1848–1928). Commencing his artistic career as a painter, in the style of Manet, Bartholomé was moved by the death of his young wife to turn to sculpture to create a monument for her, and it was in this medium that he achieved his greatest success. A close friend of Degas, he gave him constant advice about the techniques of sculpture.

Bastien-Lepage, Jules (1848–84). A successful portrait painter, who also made a reputation for peasant paintings in the style of Millet.

Baudelaire, Charles (1821–67). His aesthetic writings are centred around *L'Art romantique* (1899) and *Curiosités esthétiques* (1923), both posthumous collections of writings originally scattered through a large number of periodicals. In 1863 he also wrote a long appreciation of Constantin Guys, entitled *Le Peintre de la vie moderne*. He appears in Manet's *Music in the Tuileries* and Courbet's *The Painter's Studio*.

Bazille, Frédéric (1841–70). One of the early Impressionists before the movement was known by that name, he had met Monet, Renoir and Sisley in the studio of Gleyre. He was killed in the Franco-Prussian war, before he had time adequately to realize his potential as a painter.

Bellio, Georges de (died 1894). A doctor of Romanian origin, he was a great supporter of the Impressionists, whose social gatherings he frequented throughout his life. He made it a principle to buy those works which seemed less likely to sell.

Blanche, Jacques-Émile (1861–1942). Painter of portraits, writer and man-about-town. A friend of Renoir, and a great admirer of Manet and Degas.

Blémont, Émile (Léon Petitdidier, (1839–1927). A successful journalist and man of letters, he was a strong defender of the Impressionists.

Bonnat, Léon (1834–1923). A native of Bayonne, he studied painting in Spain before moving to Paris, where he built up a considerable reputation both as a portrait and an 'historical' painter. He met Degas in Italy and became his friend. He had a fine collection of Old Master drawings.

Bonvin, François (1817–87). A self-educated artist, who achieved a considerable reputation as a genre painter. He became almost completely blind at the age of sixty.

Boudin, Eugène-Louis (1824–98). Born in Honfleur, he did not take up painting till he was in his mid-twenties, when he moved for a time to Paris and became a friend of Baudelaire. A forerunner of Impressionism, and a kind of honorary member of the movement, he greatly influenced Monet, and later Dufy and Braque.

Bracquemond, Félix (1833–1914). Painter and engraver, who taught Manet the techniques of etching. Independent in style, his work was greatly admired not only by Manet, but by Baudelaire, Fantin-Latour, Gavarni and the Goncourt brothers. He participated in the Impressionist exhibitions of 1879, 1880 and 1886. His wife Marie was also an artist.

Brangwyn, Sir Frank William (1867–1956). Painter, etcher and muralist, whose reputation in Continental Europe was probably higher than it was in Britain.

Burty, Philippe (1830–90). Critic and defender of the Impressionists, he was the author of a novel in which he recounts the origins of the movement in fictional form.

Cabanel, Alexandre (1823–89). The favourite painter of the Emperor Napoleon III, he was overwhelmed with official commissions, and was a successful society portraitist. The Impressionists saw him as the archetype of the officially approved academic artist.

Caillebotte, Gustave (1848–94). A naval engineer and amateur painter, who studied under Bonnat, he inherited a considerable fortune and was an inspired collector of works by the Impressionists. The works he acquired now form the nucleus of the Impressionist collection of the Musée d'Orsay in Paris.

Carnot, Sadi (1837–94). Politician and President of the Republic. He was assassinated at Lyon.

Carolus-Duran, Charles-Émile (1838–1917). Painter and sculptor, director of the French School at Rome, his style, which owed a lot to Velázquez, earned him a great reputation as a society portrait painter.

Cassatt, Mary (1845–1926). Born in Pittsburgh,

daughter of a rich banker, she came to Europe to study art in 1868, and became a close friend of Degas. She helped many of the Impressionists financially, and came to the rescue of Durand-Ruel when he was having problems. She was a talented painter, and an exceptional engraver.

Castagnary, Jules (1830–88). Critic and politician, a friend of Baudelaire, a defender of Courbet, naturalism and the Impressionists. In 1887 he became Directeur des Beaux-Arts. His critical writings were published in collected form in 1864, *Les Artistes au XIXe Siècle*, and 1892, *Salons*.

Cézanne, Paul (1839–1906). A banker's son from Aix-en-Provence, forced at first to study law, he arrived at the Académie Suisse in Paris in 1861, and soon met Guillaumin, Bazille and the future Impressionists. In the early 1870s, he worked with Pissarro at Pontoise north of Paris and adopted the Impressionist 'divided' brushstroke. Mocked by critics and public, he kept out of the second Impressionist exhibition in 1876 and gradually turned away from Impressionism as such, concentrating more and more on form and geometric space. Always a difficult character, he withdrew to Provence for good in 1882. He broke with Zola over the character of Claude Lantier in *L'Oeuvre* (1886), which was based on him. Reconciled with his father only in the 1880s, he inherited his fortune.

Charpentier, Georges (1846–1905). Publisher of the works of Zola and Daudet, in 1879 he founded the magazine *La Vie Moderne*, which not only espoused the causes of the Impressionists but provided accommodation for their exhibitions. It was there that Monet's first one-man exhibition was held in 1880. Renoir's famous portrait of Charpentier's wife Marguerite, her children and Pyrenean mountain dog, was painted in 1878; it was the artist's first great Salon success.

Chocquet, Victor (1821–1898). A highly placed civil servant, who was a gifted and inspired collector of works by the Impressionists. His original liking for the works of Delacroix led him to an appreciation of Renoir, who introduced him to Cézanne. His collection was sold at the Hôtel Drouot in July 1899, and included 32 Cézannes, 11 Monets, 5 Manets, 11 Renoirs and works by Courbet, Corot and Manet.

Clemenceau, Georges (1841–1929). One of the leading politicians of his time, Clemenceau was deeply interested in art and literature. A friend of Manet, who painted two portraits of him, he became especially intimate with Monet, at

whose house he met Cézanne, Rodin and others. He was responsible for the acquisition by the State of Monet's *Nymphéas* (*Waterlilies*).

Corot, Camille (1796–1875). He brought into French painting a new note of natural realism, tinctured with a lyricism which greatly attracted most of the Impressionists, many of whom looked upon him as a kind of father figure. He had contacts with Berthe Morisot, Sisley and Pissarro, to whom he gave useful advice.

Daubigny, Charles-François (1817–79). One of the earliest exponents of *plein-air* painting. His works are marked by their clear simplicity and exerted a considerable influence on both Boudin and Monet, whose works he tried to get into the Salon.

Degas, Edgar (1843–1917). A banker's son, like Cézanne, and a pupil of Ingres, he began as a history painter before embarking on a long career of audacious experimentation in colour, in technique and in composition. He did not like to be categorized as an Impressionist, although he showed with them. A sharp-tongued solitary, he sacrificed much of his private fortune in 1876 when his brother René became insolvent. He died nearly blind.

Delaroche, Hippolyte, called Paul (1797–1856). The most successful history painter of the nineteenth century, whose style was imitated throughout Europe. He painted many works for major public buildings.

Desboutin, Marcellin (1823–1902). Painter, engraver and critic, Desboutin was one of Manet's closest friends, and an habitué of the Café Guerbois. Degas painted him in the company of the actress Ellen Andrée in *L'Absinthe*, and Manet used him for *L'Artiste*.

Dewhurst, Wynford (1864–1941). An English painter, born in Manchester, whose own works were greatly influenced by Monet. He was a frequent contributor to *The Studio*, in whose pages his writings on Impressionism first appeared.

Diaz de la Peña, Narcisse Virgile (1807–76). Commenced his artistic career as a painter on porcelain, and at the age of thirty went to Barbizon, working incessantly in the forest of Fontainebleau. There he met the young Renoir, whom he influenced.

Dreyfus, Alfred (1859–1935). The central figure in the famous spy trial of 1894, the question of whose guilt or innocence divided French opinion for the best part of ten years. His final acquittal was largely due to Zola's memorable pamphlet *J'Accuse*.

Durand-Ruel, Paul (1831–1922). His father had dealt in the works of Delacroix and other 'advanced' artists, and Paul took over the business in 1865. His first real contact with the Impressionists occured when he was in London during the Franco-Prussian war. Henceforward he became their main dealer, and despite a great financial setback in 1885 he was able to recover thanks to being introduced to the American market by Mary Cassatt. His selling techniques, and the exclusive contracts he arranged with his artists, created new precedents in the art-gallery world.

Duranty, Louis-Émile-Edmond (1833–80). Writer and art critic, who with the Goncourt brothers did much to promote the concept of realism in France. He wrote extensively about art, always championing and explaining the attitudes of the avant-garde. His most important writings were contained in *La Nouvelle Peinture* (1876) and *Le Pays des arts* (1881). He wrote several novels dealing with the art life of his time.

Duret, Théodore (1838–1927). Commencing his career as a political journalist, he soon turned to art criticism, and in establishing the links between the Impressionists and traditional European painting in his *Histoire des peintres impressionistes* (1906) he probably did more than anyone else to establish their reputation. He also wrote studies of Manet (1902) and Renoir (1924).

Fantin-Latour, Théodore (1836–1904). Painter and engraver, who from 1857 onwards was a friend of Manet. One of a group, including Whistler, who showed their paintings at Bonvin's studio, he was an habitué of the Café Guerbois, and his painting of the group connected with that place, *A Studio in Les Batignolles*, was shown at the Salon of 1870. He had a liking for group portraits, and was very popular – especially in Britain – on account of his exquisite flower paintings.

Faure, Jean-Baptiste (1830–1914). Singer and composer who was one of Durand-Ruel's most assiduous clients, buying works by Manet, Degas, Sisley, and Pissarro. The fact that he often sold them suggests that, in part at least, his interests were speculative. He participated in the social life of the Impressionists.

Forain, Jean-Louis (1852–1931). Painter and draughtsman who concentrated on lively drawings of contemporary life which appeared in the pages of journals such as *La Vie Parisienne*. The successor to Constantin Guys, his work was close to that of Degas, and he exhibited at the

4th, 5th, 6th and 8th Impressionist exhibitions.

Forbes, James Staats (1823–1904). General Manager of the London, Chatham and Dover Railway, and later of the London District Railway, he was an enlightened collector of paintings by contemporary artists.

Frith, William Powell (1819–1909). One of the most successful Victorian artists, whose paintings of scenes from everday life, such as *Derby Day*, *The Railway Station* and *Ramsgate Sands* earned him great popularity. His *Autobiography* (1877/8) is a mine of information about the art life of his time.

Fromentin, Eugène (1820–76). A painter who specialized in Oriental scenes, but who is best known for his book on Flemish painting, *Les Maîtres d'autrefois* (1876), and for his novel *Dominique* (1862).

Gautier, Théophile (1811–72). Poet and writer, who had a considerable influence on the orientation of French art and literature, propounding, with considerable verve, the notion of Art for Art's Sake. He wrote a considerable body of art criticism and was one of the first to appreciate Manet and Renoir (as well as Wagner!). Baudelaire dedicated *Les Fleurs du Mal* to him.

Gavarni (Sulpice Guillaume Chevalier, 1804–66). French caricaturist with strong social preoccupations, who strongly criticized bourgeois life, and commented on the miseries of the poor in savage drawings which appeared in magazines such as *L'Artiste* and *La Mode*.

Geffroy, Gustave (1855–1926). Originally a political journalist working for Clemenceau's *Justice*, his increasing acquaintance with the Impressionists led him to become an art critic, his collected works in this vein being published in eight volumes. Author of the first complete history of Impressionism (1894), he was especially close to Monet.

Gérôme, Jean-Léon (1824–1904). Painter, sculptor and engraver, who became a sought-after teacher. He was violently opposed to Impressionism and was mainly responsible for the initial rejection of the Caillebotte collection bequeathed to the State in 1893.

Gleyre, Charles (1808–74). A successful painter of Swiss origin in whose teaching studio Monet, Renoir, Bazille and Sisley were trained. Renoir once said of him: 'He was not very much help to his students, but at least he deserves credit for leaving them alone.'

Goncourt, Edmond (1822–96) and Jules (1830–70) de. Two brothers who made a lasting impact on the French culture of their time, partly by their realistic novels, partly by their art criticism which rehabilitated the painting of the eighteenth century. Their *Journal* is a rich source of information about the period, and they were always at the hub of Parisian life.

Guillaumin, Jean-Baptiste-Armand (1841–1927). A minor civil servant and a veteran of the Salon des Refusés (1863) and the Café Guerbois, he made it his rule to paint only landscape, and only in the open air. He was a friend of Van Gogh. Guillaumin owed his ultimate financial independence not to painting but to fortune: he won 100,000 francs in a lottery in 1891.

Guillemet, Antoine (1843–1918). A pupil of Corot, who introduced Manet to Zola, and was a close friend of Pissarro. He encouraged Cézanne, one of whose paintings he got admitted to the Salon of 1862 on the grounds that he was his pupil. Although he was supportive of the Impressionists, his own art was basically academic, the more so as he got older.

Guthrie, Sir James (1859–1930). Largely self-trained, and one of the original Glasgow School. The vitality and charm of his early works was later supplanted by a modified academicism, which won him official recognition on an extensive scale.

Guichard, Joseph-Benoît (1806–80). After working in Delacroix's studio, he spent some time in Italy and became famous for his romantic and religious paintings. He had a good reputation as a teacher, and both Bracquemond and Berthe Morisot worked in his studio.

Halévy, Ludovic (1834–1908). A prolific writer of novels and the *libretti* for operas, including Offenbach's *La Belle Hélène*. He was much involved in the artistic life of his time.

Hamerton, Philip Gilbert (1834–94). Artist and critic who was responsible for founding and editing the influential *Portfolio* magazine. He was also art critic to the *Saturday Review*.

Helleu, Paul César (1859–1927). A graphic artist, who specialized in drypoint etchings of French social life. Proust based his character Elstir on a combination of him and Monet. He also painted Impressionistic landscapes.

Hook, James Clarke (1819–1907). Originally an historical painter until 1854, when he visited Clovelly and began to paint landscapes, mostly of coastal scenes. He became a Royal Academician in 1860.

Horsley, John Calcott (1817–1903). A painter rigorously opposed to the study of the nude, who became an R.A. in 1856, and organized the important exhibitions of Old Masters at the Royal Academy in the years 1875–90. He was a friend of the composer Mendelssohn.

Hoschedé, Ernest (1838–90). Director of a large Parisian store (until his business failed in 1877) and an enthusiastic collector of Impressionist paintings. He allowed Monet to use his country property at Montgéron, where he painted several of the canvases he exhibited in 1877. Hoschedé's widow Alice married Monet.

Housman, Laurence (1865–1959). An art critic of force and wit, who worked for the *Manchester Guardian* from 1895 to 1911. He wrote plays, novels and an autobiography. 'A pioneer feminist, pacifist and socialist, he was too impetuous, insensitive and muddled to be altogether effective.' *Dictionary of National Biography*.)

Huysmans, Joris-Karl (1848–1917). A novelist and critic who after beginning as a realist, turned to a kind of exoticism which first found expression in the 'decadent' novel *A Rebours*, but later took on more mystical tendencies. His writing was visual, and he was deeply interested in art.

Innes, James Dickson (1887–1914). A painter mainly of mountain subjects, but occasionally of figures, he painted in an Impressionist manner, following Philip Wilson Steer (1860–1942), though later he was influenced by John Sell Cotman and Post-Impressionism. He spent much time in France.

Ionides, Constantine Alexander (1833–1900). A London stockbroker of Greek origin, with a good eye for painting, who built up a collection including works by Degas, Fantin-Latour and others, the bulk of which he left to the nation. It is now in the Victoria and Albert Museum.

Isabey, Jean-Baptiste (1767–1855). A miniature painter, who was a great favourite of Napoleon I, for whom he organized fêtes and the like. His success continued under subsequent régimes.

James, Henry (1843–1916). American-born, he spent most of his life in Europe, predominantly in England and France. He was much in the company of artists, writing about painting in prose of considerable sinuosity.

Jongkind, Johan Barthold (1819–91). A Dutch landscape painter, who spent most of his working life in France, where he was in close contact with Corot, Monet, Boudin and others, exhibiting with them at the Salon des Refusés in 1863. His personal life was tormented, almost in the style of Van Gogh.

Keene (sometimes spelt Keen), **Charles Samuel**

211

(1823–91). Illustrator and painter, who worked extensively for *Punch* and *The Illustrated London News*. He was awarded a gold medal at the Paris Exhibition of 1890.

Lavery, Sir John (1856–1941). Born in Belfast, apprenticed to a painter-photographer in Glasgow, where he studied at the School of Art before going to the Académie Julian in Paris. There he came under the influence of Whistler and his circle. He later became a very successful portrait painter.

Lecomte, Georges (1867–1958). A writer of plays and novels, who in 1892 wrote *L'Art impressionniste d'après la collection privée de M.Durand-Ruel avec 36 eaux-fortes*. He also produced studies of various artists, including an important one on Pissarro in 1922.

Lecoq de Boisbaudran, Horace (1802–97). After studying at the École des Beaux-Arts he specialized in drawing and became director of the school of drawing, where he taught a method which involved development of the memory and 'penetration' of the subject, and wrote three standard text-books. Amongst his many pupils were Legros, Fantin-Latour and Rodin.

Legros, Alphonse (1837–1911). Painter, sculptor and engraver. Unable to read till the age of eleven, he became a house painter and then a stage decorator. Eventually he became a pupil of Lecoq de Boisbaudran and an associate of the Impressionists, exhibiting at the Salon des Refusés and the second Impressionist exhibition. On the invitation of Whistler he came to London, and as Slade Professor at University College had a great influence on English art.

Leighton, Frederic, Baron Leighton of Stretton (1830–96). Probably the most influential painter in England in the nineteenth century, holding high office, and being pre-eminently successful in a neoclassical style of painting. A man of many interests and wide tolerance, he was buried in St Paul's Cathedral.

Lépine, Stanislas-Victor-Edouard (1835–92). A pupil of Corot, whose work had some affinities with that of Jongkind, and who was especially interested in the effects of light and movement in clouds and water.

Mallarmé, Stéphane (1842–98). A poet who taught English for a living, he wielded great personal influence on a whole group of writers ranging from Henri de Régnier to Gide and Claudel. He was preoccupied with matching visual and verbal effects, and was an impassioned defender of the Impressionists, writing

a brilliant article on Manet and persuading the State to buy some of Berthe Morisot's paintings.

Manet, Edouard (1832–83). A judge's son, he began his career auspiciously by signing on as a cabin-boy on a ship bound for Brazil. Overcoming some parental opposition, he spent six years in Thomas Couture's studio. Rejected at the Salon in 1859, he mounted a show of his own, and his works caused a great scandal. The pattern was to repeat itself with variations throughout his life. There was nothing provocative or even unconventional about Manet the man, but his works constantly caught the critics on the raw. He was more classical in technique than Impressionists such as Pissarro and Monet, but the influences were reciprocal and manifold. He died early.

Manet, Julie, *see* Morisot.

Mauclair, Camille (1872–1945). Poet, novelist and art critic, who in 1903 published an important book on Impressionism, though his later career was devoted to the theatre.

Maximilian, Emperor of Mexico (1832–76). An Austrian archduke who was persuaded by Napoleon III to lead a French invasion of Mexico. He became Emperor of that country, but the French abandoned him and he was shot.

Meissonier, Ernest (1815–91). A highly successful painter of small, detailed battle scenes, mostly connected with the campaigns of Napoleon. He was also a gifted sculptor. His reputation has recently been rehabilitated by Salvador Dalí.

Meredith, George (1828–1909). Novelist and poet, who was connected with the Pre-Raphaelites and other groups of artists.

Meyerbeer, Giacomo (1791–1864). A German-born composer of highly successful operas, the *bête noire* of Wagner (who nevertheless owed him some favours).

Millais, Sir John Everett (1829–96). Painter who, after beginning his career as a Pre-Raphaelite, became a sought-after portrait painter, President of the Royal Academy, and producer of pretty genre paintings.

Millet, Jean-François (1814–75). Son of a Norman peasant, he did not achieve success until he was in his fifties. Working in the Barbizon tradition, he painted pictures of slightly sentimentalized realism, achieving enormous popularity with his *Angelus* of 1868. He had a considerable influence on Pissarro, Van Gogh and others.

Mirbeau, Octave (1848–1917). Novelist and art critic, who wrote a good deal in defence of the Impressionists. He was a close friend of Pissarro, contributing to a short-lived magazine published by Durand-Ruel, and writing elsewhere on Monet and Renoir. At the suggestion of Mal-larmé, he also defended Gauguin.

Monet, Claude (1840–1926). His petit-bourgeois family in Le Havre tried to dissuade him from becoming an artist. Encouraged in his youth by Boudin, he studied with Renoir and others in Gleyre's studio. In London in 1870-1, he there-after lived at Argenteuil and Vétheuil, north of Paris, before settling for good at Giverny-sur-Epte, in his native Normandy, in 1883. He was often in dire financial straits, and only in the 1880s, through Durand-Ruel, did he begin to earn appreciable sums. Fame came after his joint exhibition with Rodin at Petit's in 1889. His increasingly mystical communion with land-scape (he abandoned the figure for good in his thirties) led him to the frontiers of abstraction at the end of his career.

Moore, George (1853–1933). An Irish writer who went to Paris at the age of twenty to study paint-ing. Manet took to him and did three portraits of him, and he moved a great deal in Impress-ionist circles. A realist novelist and one of the creators of the Irish literary renaissance, he wrote extensively about the Impressionists and was largely responsible for popularizing their works in England.

Morisot, Berthe (1841–95). Daughter of a highly placed but royalist Prefect, she studied under Guichard, and showed great and precocious ability. In 1874 she married Manet's brother Eugène. She contributed to all the Impression-ist exhibitions, being mainly responsible for mounting the last one in 1886. Her daughter Julie married Ernest Rouart, son of Henri.

Murer, Eugène (1845–1906). *Restaurateur* and *pâtissier*, he came into contact with the Im-pressionists through Guillaumin, who had been a childhood friend. They held dinners on Wednesdays in his restaurant on the Boulevard Voltaire. He built up a most important collec-tion of works by the leading Impressionists, and, when he took over an hotel in Rouen, acted as host to Pissarro for a lengthy period. On retiring to the Auvergne, he himself took up painting and held two exhibitions of his works.

Nadar (Félix Tournachon, 1820–1910). One of the most famous photographers of the nineteenth century, he began his career as an artist, and always continued producing carica-tures. He amassed a great collection of works by Constantin Guys, and knew many of the Im-pressionists whom he met in the Café Guer-bois. It was in his former studio that the first Impressionist exhibition was held in 1874.

Napoleon III (1808–73). Son of Louis Bonaparte, he became President of France in 1848 and Emperor four years later. Defeated by the Ger-mans, he was deposed in 1870 and went into exile in England. Whatever his faults, he was strongly supportive of the arts, made consider-able reforms in art education, replanned Paris, and was responsible for a considerable public expenditure on the arts generally.

Nieuwerkerke, Emilien, Comte de (1811–92). Dutch by origin, he became the most important cultural functionary in the Second Empire, and was himself a practising sculptor. In 1849 he was nominated Director-General of the Musées Nationaux, and in 1863 Surintendant des Beaux-Arts. His apartments in the Louvre were for long the centre of the cultural life of Paris.

Nordau, Max (1849–1923). An ardent Zionist, and indeed one of the founders of the modern Zionist moverment, he was born in Germany but spent most of his life in Paris, where he produced an endless flow of semi-philosophical books of the most deplorable kind, lambasting the evils of contemporary society. One of the most popular was *Degen-eration*, which appeared in 1895, was trans-lated into several languages, sold millions of copies, and influenced much Nazi thinking – if that word can be used in this context – on cultu-ral matters.

Pissarro, Camille (1830–1903). Born in the Virgin Isles of Creole and French-Jewish parentage, he went to school in France and moved there for good in 1855. He became a proclaimed realist, showed landscapes at the Salon in the 1860s as well as the Salon des Refusés of 1863, and evolved an Impressionist technique alongside Monet, Renoir and Sisley. At Pontoise, north-east of Paris, in the 1870s, he became a painter of peasant life and worked with Cézanne who lived at nearby Auvers. He became famous only in his sixties, dividing his time between Eragny-sur-Epte and Paris.

Pissarro, Lucien (1863–1944). The eldest son of Camille, he established himself in England, be-coming a member of the New English Art Club, founder of the Eragny Press and an intimate of Sickert's circle. There was a large-scale centen-ary exhibition of his works in England in 1963.

Poe, Edgar Allen (1804–49). An American poet and novelist who had a considerable influence in Europe. His writing has a great visual impact which appealed to Baudelaire, who saw in him the poetic equivalent of Delacroix.

Proust, Antonin (1832–1905). A childhood friend

of Manet's, with whom he remained in friendly contact throughout his life, often writing about him, and in 1880 obtaining the Legion of Honour for him. Proust started as a journalist, and then became secretary to the statesman Gambetta. Between 1881 and 1882 he was minister of Fine Arts, and in 1889 became Commissioner of Fine Arts at the Exposition Universelle.

Puvis de Chavannes, Pierre (1824–98). Painter of vaguely mystical, often large-scale works, who was considered the foremost decorative painter of his time. The freshness of his colour, which probably owed more to fresco than anything else, and the simplicity of his outlines, appealed to most of the Impressionists and influenced artists such as Gauguin.

Renoir, Auguste (1841–1919). An apprentice china-painter, he found his way to Gleyre's studio but was influenced by Courbet, by Diaz and Corot, and by his fellow-students Monet, Bazille and Sisley, and became a pioneer Impressionist. In the 1880s the emphasis in his work shifted in the direction of form, permanence and solidity, and contemporary subject-matter began to recede. In his old age, progressively crippled by gout, he lived in Provence.

Rigault, Raoul (1846–71). A republican journalist who was sought by Napoleon III's police for the publication of a vicious attack on the government, *Le Grand Complot*, he rose to power under the Commune, first as Prefect of Police and then as public prosecutor. He was notorious for his intransigence and violence. He ordered the execution of the hostages held by the Commune and the destruction of many monuments. He was executed by government forces.

Rodin, Auguste (1840–1917). Often, though with little justification, described as an 'Impressionist sculptor', Rodin really belonged to the basic romantic tradition, though his concern with the realization of three-dimensional effects put him in touch with contemporary artistic thinking, and he was friendly with many of the Impressionists, especially Monet.

Rothenstein, Sir William (1872–1945). Bradford-born painter and illustrator, who studied at the Slade School of Art and later at the Académie Julian where he became friendly with many of the Parisian artists of the time, about whom he wrote entertainingly in his *Men and Memories* (1931).

Rouart, Henri (1845–1902). A great friend of Degas and a passionate collector, whose paintings included works by El Greco, Corot, Daumier and most of the Impressionists. His son Ernest married Julie Manet.

Rousseau, Théodore (1812–87). The principal figure of the Barbizon group, which worked in the forest of Fontainebleau, painting and drawing directly from nature in a rather romantic way. After years of penury he achieved recognition at the Exposition Universelle of 1855. He was admired by most of the Impressionists.

Saint-Victor, Paul de (1827–81). Journalist and man of letters, who, though mostly interested in music and the theatre, contributed art criticism to the periodical press.

Sargent, John Singer (1856–1925). A gifted American-born painter who studied in Paris under Carolus-Duran and achieved his greatest successes in a style which owed a great deal to the early Manet. In his later life he did much landscape painting, in which his Impressionist allegiances are clearly discernible.

Seurat, Georges (1859–91). After studying at the École des Beaux-Arts, he became interested in the colour theories of Eugène Chevreul, and in 1882 started producing paintings in which colour effects were produced by the juxtaposition of small spots of pure colour, and in which the monumentality of the figures was accented.

Signac, Paul (1863–1935). He decided to become a painter as a result of seeing an exhibition of works by Monet, who gave him a good deal of advice, but in the middle 1880s he abandoned this on meeting Seurat, whose disciple he became. He was the propagandist of Divisionism, otherwise known as Pointillism and Neo-Impressionism.

Silvestre, Armand (1837–1901). Man of letters, playwright and librettist, who moved in Impressionist circles and defended their works with clarity and percipience. His autobiographical writings are a rich source of information about the cultural life of the later nineteenth century in Paris.

Sisley, Alfred (1839–99). Paris-born, the son of an English merchant, he soon gave up business for art. After meeting Renoir and Monet at Gleyre's studio he became a pure Impressionist landscapist, mostly working in the Ile de France, around Paris. His father died in 1870, leaving him a poor man. Not very communicative about his art, he clearly felt some bitterness at his lack of material success. He never succeeded in becoming a French citizen. Hardly had he died, however, when his prices rose steeply and his work represented France at the 1900 Exposition Universelle.

Stevens, Alfred (1823–1906). A Belgian painter who was an intimate friend of Manet, whom he introduced to Bazille. Although basically a socialite painter, and a successful one, he moved freely in Impressionist circles, and in 1886 produced a book *Impressions sur la peinture* which became very popular.

Tissot, James (1836–1902). Painter and etcher, specializing, like Alfred Stevens, in depicting high society. During the Commune he fled to England, where he established a considerable reputation in the years between 1871 and 1882. He ended as an illustrator of the Bible on a megalomaniac scale. He was influenced by Manet and Degas, with both of whom he had close connections.

Troyon, Constant (1810–65). A landscape and animal painter who, like Renoir, started in the Sèvres porcelain factory. He was connected with the Barbizon school and much admired by the younger generation, especially Pissarro.

Valéry, Paul (1871–1945). Mathematician, poet, writer and art critic, Valéry applied Cartesian principles of analysis to the investigation of human feelings. He has written extensively and constructively about Degas, Monet, Manet, Renoir and others, having become an intimate of the social circles of Berthe Morisot and Henri Rouart.

Vizetelly, Henry (1820–94). Artist and writer, correspondent of the *Illustrated London News* in Paris 1865-72. Became a publisher specializing in English translations of French novels; fined in 1888 for publishing Zola's *The Land*, and imprisoned in the following year for repeating the offence. Published an autobiography in 1893.

Vollard, Ambroise (1865–1939). An art dealer who had a gallery in the rue Lafitte, and who in 1895 devoted a large exhibition to the works of Cézanne. He was a friend of most of the Impressionists, and Pissarro, Renoir, Degas as well as Rodin were amongst those whose works he showed. Later he became an enthusiastic supporter of artists such as Matisse, Picasso, Rouault and Chagall. In 1937 he published *Recollections of a Picture-dealer*.

Wallis, Henry (1805–90). Artist and book-illustrator who became a highly respected London picture-dealer. Despite going bankrupt selling Old Masters he made a come-back and opened the French Gallery at 120 Pall Mall, which was so successful that he died leaving nearly £60,000.

Whistler, James Abbott MacNeill (1834–1903). American-born painter, writer and engraver, who came to Paris, entered Gleyre's studio, met Degas, Legros, Bracquemond and Fantin-Latour, and kept in contact with the whole Impressionist circle. Settled in London and led a life of some notoriety and real, though not popular, artistic success.

Wolff, Albert (1835–91). Born in Germany, he moved to Paris and became the secretary of Alexandre Dumas *père*. He was a prolific writer of plays and memoirs and became art critic of *Le Figaro*, in which position he waged a relentless campaign against the Impressionists.

Zola, Emile (1840–1902). Novelist, critic and pamphleteer, who wrote a brilliant series of novels about contemporary life. He had been a schoolfellow of Cézanne's at Aix, and waged a constant campaign in the pages of *L'Evénement*, of which he was art critic, in favour of the Impressionists.

Chronology

Births:

1830 Pissarro; 1832 Manet; 1834 Degas; 1839 Cézanne and Sisley; 1840 Monet; 1841 Renoir and Morisot; 1845 Cassatt.

1855 Pissarro arrives in Paris from the Virgin Isles; Universal Exhibition in Paris.
1856 Duranty publishes magazine *Le Réalisme*. Renoir attends evening classes in drawing.

1858 Manet rejected at Salon.
1862 Manet meets Degas; praised by Baudelaire. Monet meets Jongkind; Renoir enters Gleyre's studio at the same time as Sisley and Bazille.
1863 Salon des Refusés; death of Delacroix.
1865 Manet's *Olympia* criticized at Salon; he goes to Spain. Monet, Pissarro, Degas and Morisot exhibit at Salon.
1866 Zola writes *Mon Salon*; Degas, Monet, Sisley, Bazille exhibit at Salon.
1867 Paris World Fair; Manet and Courbet hold own exhibitions. Pissarro, Monet, Cézanne,

and Renoir rejected at Salon.

1868 Manet paints Zola; makes trip to England; Morisot meets him.

1869 Café Guerbois becomes meeting place for group. Manet exhibits *Le déjeuner sur l'herbe* at Salon.

1870 Franco-Prussian war; Monet and Pissarro go to England; Bazille killed.

1871 Commune takes power in Paris; defeated by Government forces after two months. Monet rejected by Royal Academy.

1872 Durand-Ruel buys 29 paintings from Manet; meets Degas and Sisley.

1873 Degas in the USA; Renoir meets Durand-Ruel; Manet's *Le Bon Bock* successful at Salon.

1874 First Impressionist exhibition of 30 painters at Nadar's old studio.

1875 Deaths of Corot and Millet. Auction of pictures by Impressionists.

1876 Second Impressionist exhibition in rue Le Peletier. Degas loses a lot of money in family business.

1877 Death of Courbet. Third Impressionist exhibition at rue Le Peletier. Second auction sale (average price 169 francs).

1878 Death of Daubigny. Duret publishes *Les Impressionnistes*. World's Fair in Paris; Renoir and Sisley exhibit at Salon.

1879 Fourth Impressionist exhibition at 28 avenue de l'Opéra; 15 participants. Renoir has big success at Salon.

1880 Fifth Impressionist exhibition, 10 rue des Pyramides; 118 participants; Manet's *Execution of Maximilian* shown in Boston; Monet has one-man show at *La Vie Moderne* and a work accepted at the Salon.

1881 Sixth Impressionist exhibition, 35 boule-

vard des Capucines; 13 participants. Manet gets medal at Salon. Antonin Proust becomes Minister of Fine Arts; State control of Salon abandoned.

1882 Seventh Impressionist exhibition at 251 rue Saint-Honoré. Durand-Ruel involved. Manet gets Légion d'Honneur; exhibits *Bar at the Folies-Bergère* at Salon. Renoir exhibits 35 works at group show.

1883 Death of Manet. Impressionist exhibition in Berlin. Huysmans publishes *L'Art Moderne*. One-man exhibitions of Monet, Renoir, Pissarro and Sisley at Durand-Ruel gallery.

1884 Société des Artistes Indépendants founded; no juries or prizes. Memorial exhibition to Manet at Ecole des Beaux-Arts.

1886 Last Impressionist exhibition, 1 rue Lafitte; 17 participants. Durand-Ruel has success in the USA. Georges Petit begins to sell Impressionist works.

1889 Monet and Rodin exhibit at Petit's.

1890 Death of Van Gogh.

1891 Death of Jongkind and Seurat.

1892 Pissarro retrospective at Durand-Ruel's.

1895 Death of Berthe Morisot.

1898 Death of Boudin.

1899 Death of Sisley.

1902 Death of Zola.

1903 Death of Pissarro

1906 Death of Cézanne.

1907 Death of Huysmans.

1908 Cézanne retrospective exhibition.

1910 Death of Nadar.

1917 Death of Degas.

1919 Death of Renoir.

1922 Death of Durand-Ruel.

1926 Deaths of Monet and Cassatt.

Bibliographical note

Most of the major books containing documentary information about the Impressionists are recorded below under '*Sources*'. Additional references will be found in the most recent edition of John Rewald's essential *The History of Impressionism* (New York and London 1973), the bibliography of which contains, under the name of each artist, sections devoted to both 'The Artist's Own Writings' and 'Witness Accounts'. Subsequent to Rewald's study, however, there have been a number of publications which throw light on various aspects of Impressionism and its participants. These include Rewald's own *Studies in*

Impressionism (London and New York 1985) and three major exhibition catalogues: *Manet,* the exhaustive catalogue of the exhibition held first in Paris and then at the Metropolitan in New York (Paris, London and New York 1983); *The New Painting, Impressionism 1874-1886* (Seattle and Oxford 1986) which documents with extensive comments the eight Impressionist exhibitions, and is also the catalogue of an exhibition held in San Francisco; and *A Day in the Country: Impressionism and the French Landscape* (Los Angeles 1984), the well-documented catalogue of an exhibition held at the Los Angeles County Museum of Art. *Renoir* by Barbara Ehrlich White (New York 1985) is the most complete study of that artist ever published, and can be supplemented by the catalogue of the Renoir exhibition held in London, Paris and Boston 1985-6. An outstanding contribution to understanding the social and historical context has been made by T. J. Clark in his *The Painting of Modern Life* (New York and London 1985). There are significant essays in *French Nineteenth Century Painting and Literature,* ed. Ulrich Finke (Manchester 1972), which is not in Rewald's bibliography.

Source acknowledgments

Periodical sources are given in the text.

20 'Monet in Paris', G. Geffroy, *Claude Monet, sa vie, son temps, son oeuvre,* Crès, Paris 1922, pp. 20-21.

22 'An Art School', Zola, *L'Oeuvre,* Charpentier, Paris 1886, pp.78-9.

28 'Monet on the morality of observation', G. Poulain, *Bazille et ses amis,* La Renaissance du livre, Paris 1932, p. 39.

28 'Manet's Spanish connection' Moreau-Nelaton, E. *Manet raconté par lui-même,* Laurens, Paris 1926, vol. I, p. 98.

30 'Zola addresses Cézanne', E. Zola, *Mes Haines,* Faure, Paris 1866, preface.

32 'Renoir is turned down by the Salon', quoted from *Cahiers d'Aujourdhui* in B. E. White, *Renoir, his Life, Art and Letters,* Abrams, New York 1984, p. 21.

34 'Cézanne appeals for a chance to exhibit', *Cézanne, Letters,* Cassirer, London 1941, pp. 70-1.

34 'Manet: Sincerity not protest', E. Bazire, *Manet,* Quantin, Paris 1884, p. 54.

35 'Bazille at the birth of an idea', G. Poulain (as 28), p. 65.

35 'Being painted by Manet', E. Zola, *L'Evénement illustré,* 10 May 1868, reprinted in *Salons,* Minard, Paris 1959, p. 54.

37 'An election at the Salon', E. Zola, *L'Oeuvre,* Charpentier, Paris 1886, pp. 132-3.

38 'Boudin on a proper subject for painting', G. Jean-Aubry, *Eugène Boudin d'après les documents inédits,* Bernheim-Jeune, Paris 1922, p. 93.

39 'Monet in Le Havre', G. Poulain (as 28), p. 130.

40 'Manet and the Maximilian Affair', *Manet* (catalogue), The Metropolitan Museum of Art, New York, 1983, pp. 530-2.

42 'Berthe Morisot at the Salon', D. Rouart, ed., *Correspondance de Berthe Morisot,* Quatre Chemins/Editart, Paris 1950, p. 47.

44 'Monet in penury', G. Poulain (as 28), p. 160.

45 'Durand-Ruel in London', L. Venturi, *Les Archives de l'Impressionnisme,* Durand-Ruel, Paris 1939, vol. II, pp. 176-80.

67 'Degas in America', Marcel Guérin, ed., *Lettres de Degas,* Grasset, Paris 1945, p. 78.

68 'Degas on the View from New Orleans', *Lettres de Degas* (as 67), pp. 85-6.

78 'Manet and Degas Contrasted', G. Moore, *Confessions of a Young Man,* Sonnenschein & Lowry, London 1888, p. 102.

78 'The New Painting: an analysis', A. Silvestre, *Galerie Durand-Ruel: recueil des estampes,* Durand-Ruel, Paris 1873, vol. I (introduction).

84 'The merits of the Salon', L. R. Pissarro and L. Venturi, *Camille Pissarro, son art, son oeuvre,* Durand-Ruel, Paris 1939, vol. I, pp. 33-4.

85 'The first group exhibition: "appalling"', *Correspondance de Berthe Morisot* (as 42), p. 80.

88 'Manet in Venice', A. Vollard, *Recollections of a Picture-dealer,* Constable, London 1936, pp. 151-3.

89 'Carolus-Duran Teaches Portraiture', R. A. M. Stevenson, *Velasquez,* Bell, London 1900, pp. 107-8.

91 'Berthe Morisot in the open air', *Correspondance de Berthe Morisot* (as 42), pp. 81-3.

92 'A generous gesture from Manet', L. Venturi (as 45), vol. II, p. 54.

92 'The meditative and the decorative', G. Moore, *Modern Painting,* Scott, London 1893, pp. 143-7.

103 'Duranty hails the New Painting', P. Duranty, *La Nouvelle Peinture,* Dentu, Paris 1876, pp. 87-90.

110 'Impressionists in competition', B. E. White (as 32), p. 79.

110 'Manet receives an academician', A. Proust, *Edouard M[anet], souvenirs,* Laurens, Paris 1895, p. 102.

111 'Japanese Influences', T. Duret, *Les Peintres impressionnistes,* Heymann & Perois, Paris 1878, pp. 12-15.

115 'Degas makes an embarrassing confession', *Lettres de Degas* (as 67), p. 160.

115 'Degas, the horse and the camera', P. Valéry, *Degas, danse, dessins,* Vollard, Paris 1936, p. 54.

118 'Zola on the Philistine public', E. Zola (as 30), p. 671.

122 'Sisley on the "life-giving factor"', R. Goldwater and M. Treves, eds., *Artists on Art,* Pantheon, New York, and Kegan Paul, London 1947, p. 194.

124 'Manet paints a single figure', A. Proust (as 110), p. 76.

126 'Conflicts at the fifth exhibition', *Lettres de Degas* (as 67), p. 160.

127 'Signac seeks advice', G. Geffroy (as 20), p. 105.

127 'Degas on the technique of aquatint', *Lettres de Degas* (as 67), p. 180.

130 'Mary Cassatt at the sixth exhibition', J. K. Huysmans, *L'Art moderne,* Plon, Paris 1883, pp. 67-8.

131 'Renoir paints Wagner', reproduced in *L'Amateur de l'Autographe,* Paris 1913, pp. 231-3.

134 'Renoir on art and politics', L. Venturi (as 45), vol. I, p. 122.

139 'Sisley argues for group shows', L. Venturi (as 45), vol. II, p. 56-7.

140 'Impressionists and Aesthetes', C. Pissarro, *Letters to his Son Lucien,* ed. J. Rewald, translated by Lionel Abel. Routledge & Kegan Paul, London 1980, p. 362. In USA copyright 1943 by Pantheon Books Inc. Reprinted by permission.

140 'Degas in need of money', L. Venturi (as 45), vol. II, p. 73.

141 'Advice from Degas', C. Pissarro (as 140), p. 35.

142 'And from Pissarro', C. Pissarro (as 140), pp. 38-9. 'Pissarro contemplates his own work', C. Pissarro (as 140), p. 46-7.

145 'Pissarro on the bourgeois', C. Pissarro (as 140), p. 67.

145 'Impressionist Humbug', George Inness Jr., *The Life and Times of George Inness,* Century, New York 1918, pp. 168-73.

146 'Caillebotte on art and letters', G. Geffroy (as 20), Paris 1922, pp. 180-1.

146 'Renoir unfolds a plan', L. Venturi (as 45), vol. I, pp. 126-9.

148 'The Manet auction', *Correspondance de Berthe Morisot* (as 42), pp. 121-3.

149 'Monet as a gardener', J. P. Hoschedé, *Claude Monet ce mal connu,* Cailler, Geneva 1960, vol. I, pp. 61-3.

154 'Pissarro on elections', R. E. Shikes and P. Harper, *Pissarro, his Life and Works,* Horizon Press, New York 1980, p. 231.

156 'Renoir on the nude', B. E. White(as 32), p. 130.

160 'Rifts', C. Pissarro (as 140), pp. 72-5.

162 'A final fiasco', *Correspondance de Berthe Morisot* (as 32), p. 138.

163 'George Moore at the last Impressionist group show', G. Moore (as 78), pp. 49-57.

165 'Degas, his models and his pastels', G. Vollard (as 88), pp. 177-9.

167 'Dinners at the Café Riche', G. Geffroy (as 20), pp. 155-6.

169 'Degas writes to his landlord', *Lettres de Degas* (as 67), p. 280.

170 'Mary Cassatt in an unaccustomed role', F. A. Sweet, *Miss Mary Cassatt,* University of Oklahoma Press, Norman 1966, pp. 132-3.

170 'The Duret sale', J. Manet, *Journal 1895-1899,* Klincksieck, Paris 1979, p. 30.

174 'Degas and Renoir', A. Vollard (as 88), pp. 17-20.

175 'Bloodshot Cézanne', F. A. Sweet (as 170), pp. 146-7.

176 'Degas intercedes for a model', *Lettres de Degas* (as 67), p. 150.

177 'Degas at sixty', W. Rothenstein, *Men and Memories, 1872-1900,* Faber & Faber, London, and Coward-McCann, New York 1931, vol. I, p. 102. By courtesy of Sir John Rothenstein and Mr Michael Rothenstein.

179 'Monet's Solitary Obsession', J. P. Hoschedé (as 149), vol. II, pp. 112-16.

184 'Cézanne's reputation among his colleagues', C. Pissarro (as 140), pp. 275-6.

184 'Founded on nervous debility', M. Nordau, *Degeneracy,* Heinemann, London, and Appleton, New York 1897, p. 209.

185 'Clemenceau on Mutability and Monet', G. Clemenceau, *Le Grand Pan,* Charpentier, Paris 1896, pp. 87-8.

186 'Pissarro addresses a young painter', J. Rewald, *The History of Impressionism,* The Museum of Modern Art, New York, and George Allen & Unwin, London 1973, p. 458.

187 'Staying with the Renoirs', J. Manet (as 170), p. 209.

189 'More wisdom from Renoir', J. Renoir, *Renoir,* Hachette, Paris 1962.

191 'Renoir on production difficulties', L. Venturi (as 134), vol. II, pp. 74-5.

193 'Mary Cassatt on her prints', F. A. Sweet (as 170), pp. 120-1.

193 'Impressionism and the English', W. Dewhurst, *Impressionist Painting,* Newnes, London 1904, p. 47.

194 'Pissarro disagrees', C. Pissarro (as 140), pp. 355-6.

195 'Degas the collector', T. Reff, *Degas: the Artist's Mind,* The Metropolitan Museum of Art, New York, and Thames and Hudson, London 1976, pp. 88-9.

195 'Vulgar but splendid: a verdict', C. Mauclair, *L'Impressionnisme, son histoire, son esthétique,* Librairie de l'art ancien et moderne, Paris 1906, pp. 112-15.

200 'Signac pays tribute to Monet', G. Geffroy (as 20), p. 248.

202 'Renoir at seventy', J. Renoir (as 189), pp. 22-3.

206 'The effects of age on Monet', R. Friedenthal, ed., *Letters of the Great Artists,* Thames and Hudson, London, and Random House, New York 1963, pp. 131-2.

List of Illustrations

Dimensions are given in centimetres and inches, height before width. References are to the pages on which works are reproduced.

Bazille, Frédéric (1841-70) 42 *View of a Village* 1868. Oil on canvas 132.4×90.5 (52⅛×35⅝). Musée Fabre, Montpellier. 96 *The Studio in the Rue de La Condamine* , 1869. Oil on canvas 98.7×119.4 (38⅞×47). Musée d' Orsay, Paris. Photo Giraudon. 97 *The Artist's Studio, Rue Furstenberg* 1866. Oil on canvas 80×65 (31½×25⅝). Musée Fabre, Montpellier.

Bertall 27 *see Documents, below.*

Boudin, Eugène (1824-98) 17 *Jetty and Wharf at Trouville* 1863. Oil on panel 34.6×57.8 (13⅝×22¾). Paul Mellon Collection, Upperville, Virginia.

Caillebotte, Gustave (1848-94) 121 *Rower in Top Hat* 1879. Oil on canvas 90×117 (35⅜×46). Private Collection. Photo Wildenstein. 121 *Diver* 1877. Oil on canvas 72×92 (28⅜×36¼). Musée Municipal d'Agen. Photo Giraudon.

Cassatt, Mary (1845-1926) 60 *The Cup of Tea* 1879. Oil on canvas 92.4×65.4 (36⅜×25¾). The Metropolitan Museum of Art, New York (Gift of Dr Ernest Stillman). 192 *Feeding the Ducks* undated. Colour etching. The Metropolitan Museum of Art, New York (Bequest of Mrs H.O. Havemeyer).

Cézanne, Paul (1839-1906) 13 *La Maison du Pendu* 1872-73. Oil on canvas 56.5×67.9 (22¼×26¾). Musée d' Orsay, Paris. Photo Giraudon. 31 *The Artist's Father* 1866. Oil on canvas 198.4×119.4 (78⅛×47). National Gallery of Art, Washington D.C., Collection of Mr and Mrs Paul Mellon. 55 *Le Château de Médan c.* 1880. Oil on canvas 59.1×72.4 (23¼×28½). The Burrell Collection, Glasgow Art Gallery and Museum. 56 *Still-life with Soup Tureen* undated. Oil on canvas 65×81.5 (25½×32). Musée d'Orsay, Paris. Photo Réunion des musées nationaux. 87 *Self-portrait* 1876. Oil on canvas 63.8×53 (25⅛×20⅞). Musée d'Orsay, Paris. Photo Réunion des musées nationaux. 88 *Ambroise Vollard* 1899. Oil on canvas 100×81 (39⅜×31⅞). Petit Palais, Paris. Photo Bulloz. 168 *Gustave Geffroy* 1895. Oil on canvas 116×89 (45⅝×35). Private Collection. Photo Réunion des musées nationaux.

Courbet, Gustave (1819-77) 17 *The Artist on the Seashore at Palavas-les-Flots* 1858. Oil on canvas 38.1×46 (15×18⅛). Musée Fabre, Montpellier. Photo Giraudon.

Degas, Edgar (1834-1917) 62 *After the Bath* 1895-98. Pastel 94.5×80.5 (37¼×31¾). Kunstmuseum, Solothurn, Dübi-Müller Stiftung. Photo Swiss Institute for Art Research, Zürich. 64 *At the Milliner's* 1882. Pastel 75.9×84.8 (29⅞×33⅜). Thyssen-Bornemisza Collection, Lugano, Switzerland. 69 *Cotton Buyer's Office* 1873. Oil on canvas 74×92.1 (29⅛×36¼). Musée des Beaux-Arts, Pau. 74 *Absinthe* 1876. Oil on canvas 92×68 (36¼×26¾). Musée d'Orsay, Paris. Photo Réunion des musées nationaux. 75 *The Nouvelle-Athènes* 1878. Pencil. Private Collection. 76 *Women on a Café Terrace* 1877. Pastel over monotype 40.6×59.7 (16×23½). Musée du Louvre, Paris, Cabinet des Dessins. Photo Réunion des musées nationaux. 77 *Concert at the Ambassadeurs c.* 1875-7. Pastel over monotype 36.8×26.7 (14½×10½). Musée des Beaux-Arts, Lyons. Photo Giraudon. 104 *Edmond Duranty* 1879. Distemper, watercolour and pastel on linen 101×100.3 (39¾×39½). The Burrell Collection, Glasgow Art Gallery and Museum. 116 *The False Start c.* 1870. Oil on canvas 32.1×40 (12⅝×15¾). Collection of Mrs John Hay Whitney, New York. 117 *Two Trotting Horses c.* 1882. Charcoal 24.2×26.7 (9½×10½). Private Collection, Hamburg. 117 *Jockey Leaning Back in the Saddle c.* 1884-8. Charcoal 30.5×23 (12×9). Private Collection, Switzerland. 121 *Singer with Glove* 1878. Pastel and liquid medium on canvas 53×41 (20⅞×16⅛). Harvard University Art Museums, The Fogg Art Museum. Bequest – Collection of Maurice Wertheim, Class of 1906 129 *Mary Cassatt in the Louvre* 1879-80. Etching, aquatint and crayon 26.7×23.2 (10½×9⅛). Kupferstichkabinett, Berlin. 130 *Mary Cassatt c.* 1884. Oil on canvas 71.5×58.7 (28⅛×23⅛). National Portrait Gallery, Smithsonian Institution, Washington D.C., Gift of the Morris and Gwendolyn Cafrits Foundation and the Regents' Major Acquisition Fund 175 *The Dancing Lesson c.* 1878 Pastel 64.6×56.3 (25½×22⅛). The Metropolitan Museum of Art, New York, Anonymous Gift. The H.O. Havemeyer Collection. 178 *The Dancing Lesson c.* 1874. Oil on canvas 82.9×75.9 (32⅝×29⅞). Private Collection, New York. 178 *Study for Jules Perrot* 1875. Essence on grey-green paper 47.6×29.8 (18¾×11¾). Philadelphia Museum of Art, the Henry P. McIlhenny Collection.

Diaz de la Peña, Narcisse Virgile (1808-76) 17 *Jean de Paris Hill, Fontainebleau* 1867. Oil on canvas 84.1×106 (33⅛×41¾), Musée du Louvre, Paris. Photo Giraudon.

Draner *121, 137 see Documents, below.*

Fantin-Latour, Henri (1836-1904) 29 *Edouard Manet* 1867. Oil on canvas 116.8×90.2 (46×35½). Art Institute of Chicago, the Stickney Fund. 97 *Manet's Studio in Les Batignolles* 1870. Conté crayon 29.2×39.4 (11½×15½). The Metropolitan Museum of Art, New York. Gift of Mrs Helena M. Loewel, 1919, in memory of her brother Charles W. Kraushaar.

Leloir 120 *see Documents, below.*

Manet, Edouard (1832-83) 24 *Lola de Valence* 1862-7. Oil on canvas 123.1×92.1 (48½×36¼). Musée d'Orsay, Paris. Photo Réunion des musées nationaux. 24 *Le déjeuner sur l'herbe* 1863. Oil on canvas 208.3×264.2 (82×104). Musée d'Orsay, Paris. Photo Réunion des musées nationaux. 24 *Christ Mocked* 1865. Oil on canvas 190.8×148.3 (75⅛×58⅜). Art Institute of Chicago,

Gift of James Deiring. 26 *Olympia* 1865. Oil on canvas 130.5×189.9 (51⅜×74¾). Musée d'Orsay, Paris. Photo Giraudon. 41 *Execution of Maximilian* 1868. Lithograph 33.3×43.3 (13⅛×17). Bibliothèque Nationale, Paris. 42 *The Balcony* 1868-9. Oil on canvas 168.9×125.1 (66½×49¼).Musée d'Orsay, Paris. Photo Réunion des musées nationaux. 49 *Emile Zola* 1868. Oil on canvas 146×114.3 (57½×45). Musée d'Orsay, Paris. Photo Réunion des musées nationaux. 57 *Waitress Serving Bocks* 1879. Oil on canvas 97.1×77.5 (38¼×30½). National Gallery, London. 71 *The Dead Toreador* c. 1864. Oil on canvas 75.9×153.3 (29⅞×60⅜). National Gallery of Art, Washington D.C., Widener Collection. 73 *The Café Guerbois* 1869. Pen and ink on paper 29.5×39.5 (11⅝×15½). Harvard University Art Museum, The Fogg Art Museum, Meta and Paul J. Sachs Bequest. 73 *Le Bon Bock – the Engraver Bellot at the Café Guerbois* 1873. Oil on canvas 94×82.9 (37×32⅝). Philadelphia Museum of Art, Mr and Mrs Carroll S. Tyson Collection. 75 *George Moore (George Moore in the Café)* c. 1879. Oil on canvas 65.4×81.3 (25¾×32). The Metropolitan Museum of Art, New York, Gift of Mrs Ralph J. Hines. 76 *At the Café* c. 1878. Oil on canvas 47.5×30.2 (18⅝×15⅜). The Walters Art Gallery, Baltimore. 76 *At the Café* c. 1880. Watercolour 18.5×11.9 (7¼×4⅝). Musée du Louvre, Cabinet des Dessins. Photo Réunion des musées nationaux. 77 *Café du Théâtre-Français* 1881. Pastel on canvas 32.4×45.7 (12¾×18). The Burrell Collection, Glasgow Art Gallery and Museum. 81 *Monet Working on his Boat at Argenteuil* 1874. Oil on canvas 81.3×99.7 (32×39¼). Bayerische Staatsgemäldesammlungen, Munich. 96 *An Exhibition of Paintings* 1876. Watercolour 14.6×9.9 (5¾×3⅞). Musée du Louvre, Paris, Cabinet des Dessins. Photo Réunion des musées nationaux. 101 *Albert Wolff* 1877. Oil on canvas 87.6×71.1 (34½×28). Private Collection. 104 Detail of 124. 105 *Stéphane Mallarmé* 1876. Oil on canvas 26.9×35.9 (10⅝×14⅛). Musée d'Orsay, Paris. Photo Giraudon. 105 *George Moore* 1879. Pastel on canvas 55.2×35.2 (21¾×13⅞). The Metropolitan Museum of Art, the H.O. Havemeyer Collection, Bequest of Mrs H.O. Havemeyer. 112 *Music at the Tuileries* 1862. Oil on canvas 76.2×118.1 (30×46½). National Gallery, London. 124 *Self-portrait* 1878-9. Oil on canvas 95.6×63.6 (37⅝×25). Bridgestone Museum of Art, Ishibashi Foundation, Tokyo. 124 *Théodore Duret* 1868. Oil on canvas 43.2×34.9 (17×13¾). Musée du Petit Palais, Paris. Photo Bulloz. 125 *Antonin Proust* 1880. Oil on canvas 129.5×95.9 (51×37¾). Toledo Museum of Art. 138 *A Bar at the Folies-Bergère* 1882. Oil on canvas 96×130 (37¾×51¼). Courtauld Institute Galleries, Home House Trustees, London. 148 *The Folkestone Boat* 1869. Oil on canvas 62×100 (24⅜×39⅜). Oskar Reinhart Collection, Winterthur. 172 *Repose (Berthe Morisot)* 1870. Oil on canvas 148×111.1 (58¼×43¾). Museum of Art, Rhode Island School of Design, Providence, Bequest of Edith Stuyvesant Vanderbilt Gerry.

Monet, Claude (1840-1926) 6 *Corner of a Studio* 1861. Oil on canvas 182×127 (71⅝×50). Musée d'Orsay, Paris. Photo Giraudon. 12 *The Luncheon* 1868. Oil on canvas 230×150 (90½×59). Städelsches Kunstinstitut, Frankfurt. 13 *Impression, Sunrise* 1872. Oil on canvas 48×63 (18⅞×24¾). Musée Marmottan, Paris (stolen in 1985). Photo Giraudon. 15 *Boulevard des Capucines* 1873-4. Oil on canvas 79.4×59 (31¼×23¼). The Nelson Atkins Museum, Kansas City. Acquired through the Kenneth A. and Helen F. Spencer Foundation Acquisition Fund. 16 *A Man* c. 1856. Pencil. The Art Institute of Chicago, Mr and Mrs Martin A. Ryerson Collection. 33 *Camille*, or *The Lady in a Green Dress* 1866. Oil on canvas 231×151 (91×59½). Kunsthalle, Bremen. 39 *The Sea at Le Havre* 1868. Oil on canvas 59×80 (23¼×31½). Museum of Art, Carnegie Institute, Pittsburgh. 47 *View of Green Park* 1871. Oil on canvas 34×72 (13⅜×28⅜). Philadelphia Museum of Art, The Wilstach Collection. 47 *The Thames Below Westminster* 1871. Oil on canvas 47×72.5 (18½×28½). National Gallery, London. 50, 51 *La Grenouillère* 1869. Oil on canvas 73×92 (28¾×36¼). National Gallery, London 52 *Red Boats at Argenteuil* c. 1875. Oil on canvas 55×65 (21⅝×25⅝). Musée de l'Orangerie, Paris, Walter-Guillaume Collection. 53 *Waterlilies, Sunset, Left-hand section* undated. Oil on canvas. Musée de l'Orangerie, Paris. 54, 55 *The Turkeys* 1877. Oil on canvas 170×170 (66⅞×66⅞). Musée d'Orsay, Paris. Photo Giraudon. 80 *The Studio Boat* 1876. Oil on canvas 72×60 (28⅜×23⅝). The Barnes Foundation, Merion, Pennsylvania. 81 *Red Boats at Argenteuil* c. 1875. Oil on canvas 60×81 (23⅝×31⅞). Harvard University Art Museums, The Fogg Art Museum, Bequest – Collection of Maurice Wertheim, Class of 1906. 99 *Mme Monet in Japanese Costume* 1875-6. Oil on canvas 231.8×142.2 (91¼×56). Courtesy Museum of Fine Arts, Boston (1951 Purchase Fund). 136 *Grainval near Fécamp* 1881. Oil on canvas 61×80 (24×31½). Private Collection. 153 *The Waterlily Pond* 1899. Oil on canvas 88.3×92.1 (34¾×36¼). National Gallery, London. 171 Detail of 54. 181 *Mount Kolsaas, Norway* 1895. Oil on canvas 65×100 (25⅝×39⅜). Musée d'Orsay, Paris. Photo Réunion des musées nationaux. 186 *Rouen Cathedral in Morning Light* 1894. Oil on canvas 107×73 (42⅛×28¾). Musée d'Orsay, Paris. Photo Giraudon. 200 *Ducal Palace, Venice* 1908. Oil on canvas 81×100.3 (31⅞×39½). Courtesy Brooklyn Museum. 201 *Grand Canal, Venice* 1908. Oil on canvas 73.7×92.4 (29×36⅜). Courtesy Museum of Fine Arts, Boston. 201 *Palazzo da Mula* 1908. Oil on canvas 62.2×93 (24½×36⅝). National Gallery of Art, Washington D.C., Chester Dale Collection.

Morisot, Berthe (1841-95) 12 *Hide and Seek* 1873. Oil on canvas 45.1×54.9 (17¾×21⅝). Collection of Mrs John Hay Witney, New York. 58 *In the Dining-room* 1886. Oil on canvas 61.3×50.2 (24⅛×19¾). National Gallery of Art, Washington D.C., Chester Dale Collection.

Piette, Ludovic (1826-78) 82 *Pissarro at Work* c. 1870. Gouache. Present whereabouts unknown.

Pissarro, Camille (1830-1903) 46 *Lower Norwood Under Snow* 1870. Oil on canvas 35.3×45.7 (14×18). National Gallery, London. 46 *The Crystal Palace* 1871.

Oil on canvas 48.3×73.7 (19×29). Art Institute of Chicago, Collection of Mr and Mrs B.E. Bensinger. 50 *Factory near Pontoise* 1873. Oil on canvas 45.7×54.6 (18×21½). Springfield Museum of Fine Arts, the James Philip Gray Collection. 128 *Effect of Rain* (2nd state) 1879. Aquatint 16×21.4 (6¼×8⅜). Ashmolean Museum, Oxford. 128 *Effect of Rain* (6th State) 1879. Aquatint 16×21.4 (6¼×8⅜). New York Public Library, Avery Collection. 136 *La Mère Larchevêque* 1880. Oil on canvas 73×59.1 (28¾×23¼). Metropolitan Museum of Art, New York, Gift of Mr and Mrs Nate B. Spingold. 142 *Lucien Pissarro* 1883. Pastel 55.2×37.6 (21¾×14¾). Ashmolean Museum, Oxford. 143 *Peasant Girl Drinking Coffee (Young Peasant Woman Drinking her Coffee)*, 1881. Oil on canvas 63.8×54.3 (25⅛×21⅜). Art Institute of Chicago, Potter Palmer Collection. 144 *Peasant Girl with a Branch* 1881. Oil on canvas 81×64.8 (31⅞×25½). Musée d'Orsay, Paris. Photo Réunion des musées nationaux. 154 *Capital* 1889. Pen and ink 31.5×24.5 (12⅜×9⅝). Private Collection. 155 *Social Iniquities* 1889. Pen and ink 31.5×24.5 (12⅜×9⅝). Private Collection.

Pissarro, Georges Manzana (1871-1961) 82 *Impressionist Picnic 1881* undated. Pen and ink. Private Collection, Philadelphia.

Renoir, Pierre-Auguste (1841-1919) 13 *Ballet Dancer* 1874. Oil on canvas 142.5×94.5 (56⅛×37¼). National Gallery of Art, Washington D.C., Widener Collection. 14 *Les Grands Boulevards* 1875. Oil on canvas 50×60.5 (19¾×23¾). Philadelphia Museum of Art, the Henry P. McIlhenny Collection. 58, 59 *Nude in Sunlight* 1876. Oil on canvas 81×65 (31⅞×25⅝)., Musée d'Orsay, Paris. Photo Réunion des musées nationaux. 61 *Luncheon of the Boating Party* 1880-1. Oil on canvas 130×173 (51⅛×68⅛). Phillips Collection, Washington D.C. 63 *The Large Bathers* 1917. Oil on canvas 110×160 (43⅜×63). Musée d'Orsay, Paris. Photo Réunion des musées nationaux. 83 *Monet Painting in his Garden* 1873. Oil on canvas 50.2×106.7 (19¾×42). Courtesy Wadsworth Atheneum, Hartford. 87 *Self-portrait* c.1875. Oil on canvas 39.1×31.7 (15⅜×12½). Sterling and Francine Clark Art Institute, Williamstown. 87 *Portrait of Monet* 1875. Oil on canvas 85×60.5 (33½×23¾). Musée d'Orsay, Paris. Photo Réunion des musées nationaux. 100 *Bazille at Work* 1867. Oil on canvas 106.3×74.3 (41⅞×29¼). Musée d'Orsay, Paris. Photo Giraudon. 105 *Victor Chocquet* 1876. Oil on canvas 46×36 (18⅛×14⅛). Oskar Reinhart Collection, Winterthur. 106 *Mme Charpentier and her Children* 1878. Oil on canvas 154×190 (60⅝×74¾). Metropolitan Museum of Art, New York, Wolfe Fund, 1907, Catherine Lorillard Wolfe Collection. 113 *Moulin de la Galette* 1876. Oil on canvas 131×175 (51⅝×68⅞). Musée d'Orsay, Paris. Photo Bulloz. 123 *Alfred Sisley* 1879. Oil on canvas 65.1×54 (25⅝×21¼). Art Institute of Chicago, Mr and Mrs L.L. Coburn Memorial Collection. 133 *Richard Wagner* 1882. Oil on canvas 44.5×38.7 (17½×15¼). Musée d'Orsay, Paris. Photo Réunion des musées nationaux. 135 *Paul Durand-Ruel* 1910. Oil on canvas 65.4×57.2 (25¾×22½). Durand-Ruel Collection. 136 *On the Terrace* 1881. Oil on canvas 100.3×81 (39½×31⅞). Art Institute of Chicago, Mr and Mrs L.L. Coburn Memorial Collection. 136 *Woman with a Fan* 1881. Oil on canvas 64.8×50.2 (25½×19¾). State Hermitage Museum, Leningrad. 136 *Sleeping Girl with Cat* 1880. Oil on canvas 120.7×89.9 (47½×35⅜). Sterling and Francine Clark Art Institute, Williamstown. 136 *Young Girl Sleeping* 1880. Oil on canvas 48.9×60 (19¼×23⅝). Private Collection. 156 *Bathers* 1887. Oil on canvas 117.8×170.8 (46⅜×67¼). Philadelphia Museum of Art, Mr and Mrs Carroll S. Tyson Collection. 157 *Study of Two Nudes* 1886-7. Red chalk 125.1×140 (49¼×55⅛). Harvard University Art Museums, The Fogg Art Museum, Bequest of Maurice Wertheim. 157 *Study of Three Nudes* c. 1886-7. Red and black chalk 87.6×52.1 (34½×20½). Private Collection. 190 *The Artist's Son, Jean, Drawing* 1901. Oil on canvas 45.1×54.6 (17¾×21½). Virginia Museum of Fine Arts, Gift of Mr and Mrs Paul Mellon.

Seurat, Georges (1859-91) 161 *The Lighthouse at Honfleur* 1886. Oil on canvas 66.7×81.9 (26¼×32¼). National Gallery of Art, Washington D.C., Collection of Mr and Mrs Paul Mellon.

Signac, Paul (1863-1935) 161 *The Railway Junction at Bois-Colombes* 1886. Oil on canvas 33×47 (13×18½). Leeds City Art Gallery.

Sisley, Alfred (1839-1899) 50 *The Seine at Port Marly, the Sand Heaps* 1875. Oil on canvas 54×73.3 (21¼×28⅞). Art Institute of Chicago, Mr and Mrs Martin A. Ryerson Collection. 93 *Fog* 1874. Oil on canvas 49.8×61 (19⅝×24). Musée d'Orsay, Paris. Photo Réunion des musées nationaux. 93 *Bougival Lock* 1873. Oil on canvas 47×65 (18½×25⅝). Musée d'Orsay, Paris. Photo Réunion des musées nationaux. 122 *Snow at Veneux-Nadoux* 1879-82. Oil on canvas 54×73 (21¼×28¾). Musée d'Orsay, Paris. Photo Bulloz.

Stop 138 *see Documents, below.*

Documents. 12 Catalogue of the first Impressionist exhibition, 1874. 12 Nadar's studio at 35 boulevard des Capucines. Bibliothèque Nationale, Paris. 14 Boulevard des Capucines, *c.* 1890. Photo Roger Viollet. 21 Monet at twenty photographed by Carjat. 26 State purchases from the Salon of 1865. Bibliothèque Nationale, Paris. 27 Bertall, *Manette, ou la Femme de l'ébéniste par Manet*, published in *Le Journal Amusant*, 27 May 1865. 27 Frontispiece and title-page of *Edouard Manet* by Zola with an engraving by Bracquemond. Bilbiothèque Nationale, Paris. 74 The Nouvelle-Athènes. Bibliothèque Nationale, Paris. 86 Degas *c.* 1862. Bibliothèque Nationale, Paris. 86 Manet photographed by Nadar. Bibliothèque Nationale, Paris. 87 Monet *c.* 1877. Photo Roger Viollet. 95 Renoir's list of painting materials, *c.* 1879. Photo Durand-Ruel. 106 Georgette and Paul Charpentier, *c.* 1878. 106 Mme Charpentier, *c.* 1876. 109 Manet, Mallarmé and Méry Laurent, 1872. Bibliothèque Nationale, Paris. 112 Couples dancing in Paris on 14 July *c.* 1900. Photo Roger Viollet. 114 Renoir and Mallarmé photographed by

Index

Page numbers in italic refer to works illustrated.